MASTERI...

MACMILLAN MASTER SERIES

Astronomy
Australian History
Background to Business
Banking
Basic English Law
Basic Management
Biology
British Politics
Business Communication
Business Law
Business Microcomputing
Catering Science
Catering Theory
Chemistry
COBOL Programming
Commerce
Computer Programming
Computers
Data Processing
Economic and Social History
Economics
Electrical Engineering
Electronics
English Grammar
English Language
English Literature
Financial Accounting
French
French 2
German

Hairdressing
Italian
Italian 2
Japanese
Keyboarding
Marketing
Mathematics
Modern British History
Modern European History
Modern World History
Nutrition
Office Practice
Pascal Programming
Physics
Practical Writing
Principles of Accounts
Restaurant Service
Social Welfare
Sociology
Spanish
Spanish 2
Spreadsheets
Statistics
Statistics with your Microcomputer
Study Skills
Typewriting Skills
Word Processing

MASTERING
COMPUTERS

THIRD EDITION

GRAHAM WRIGHT

MACMILLAN

First edition 1982
Reprinted 1982 (3times), 1983 (twice)
Second edition 1984
Third edition 1988
Reprinted 1989

001-64
WRI

Published by
MACMILLAN EDUCATION LTD
Houndmills, Basingstoke, Hampshire RG21 2XS
and London
Companies and representatives
throughout the world

Typeset by
TecSet Ltd, Wallington, Surrey

Printed in Hong Kong

ISBN 0–333–45640–8 Pbk
ISBN 0–333–45641–6 Pbk export

CONTENTS

CONTENTS

vii

FIGURES

FIGURES

ACKNOWLEDGEMENTS

My thanks are due to the following companies for the use of illustrations, which are individually acknowledged in the text:

Hewlett-Packard Computers Ltd
The Open University
Digital Equipment Corporation Ltd
The National Computing Centre
Acornsoft Ltd
Epson (UK) Ltd
The Welsh Joint Education Committee
Technology For Business (TFB)
Motorola Ltd
ICL
Psion Ltd
WH Smith Ltd
Sony UK Ltd
BOS Software Ltd
Intasun Holidays Ltd
ABTA
Research Machines Ltd

This third edition, like the first two, is dedicated to my wife, Jane, in gratitude for her continued support through thick and thin.

GRAHAM WRIGHT

PREFACE TO THE THIRD EDITION

The third edition of this book has two objectives; firstly, a general updating of material in a subject in which the pace of progress continues to accelerate, and secondly to accommodate significant changes of emphasis in both the practice and the teaching of the subject. In a dynamic society one might hope that these changes would occur at about the same time in both teaching and practice; in fact the long lead time in both publishing and producing syllabuses means that in both cases it is necessary to look ahead. In fact, the need for a general updating also coincides with a major and rare occurrence of forward planning in education, in the shape of a new 16+ examination structure, the GCSE which in form integrates the GCE and GCSE examination structures, and in content introduces the principle of graded teaching objectives and of a practical coursework contribution to a final examination mark.

Most Computer Studies syllabuses have contained such a coursework element for many years, and it has always been high on the list of reasons why students have chosen the subject. That element has nearly always consisted of writing computer programs, which is a fundamental part of the subject, but sometimes dominates it to the detriment of other aspects. In practical computing, however, writing your own programs is often an expensive and otherwise undesirable exercise, one that shows no sign of coming down in cost and growing in availability as has happened to computer equipment of all types and particularly to microcomputers. The specific guidelines for the GCSE examination now reflect such a change, away from writing computer programs and towards the evaluation and use of standard or 'packaged' software – which is going to pose a problem, since teaching programming is direct and popular, with a good supply of textbooks, while good application software is often hard to find out about and acquire.

The main difference, therefore, immediately perceivable from the contents list of this edition is a treatment of one general application area that follows the general treatment of computers and computing throughout the book, to emphasise this difference of approach. After much thought, I chose the travel trade as the application area, mainly because it is relatively open to study – by looking in at travel agents, picking up holiday brochures, 'browsing' through the Prestel or Ceefax pages, and by looking at the documents which come the way of the very many people who travel abroad, for business or pleasure, each year. One, and perhaps the main, reason why this number is so high is the way that computer systems have contributed to keeping costs as low as they are, and it is therefore valuable to be able to identify a fruitful application of computers that does not have the overtones of restriction, whether of employment or of access. It is, finally, an area of direct and happy experience as a producer and consumer, which I hope to pass on to the reader and student.

GRAHAM WRIGHT

INTRODUCTION

The ascent of man into twentieth-century civilisation has been intricately bound up with the development of machines, from the five basic devices of the ancient Greeks — the lever, wheel, pulley, wedge and screw — to today's highly complex and interlinked technology. This development has not always occurred at a steady pace or with acceptable social consequences — the first Industrial Revolution, for instance, in the space of fifty years transformed Great Britain from an agricultural and village-based economy into an industrial town-based economy. And just over a hundred years ago a spate of inventions occurred of particular significance to our subject — the first telephone in 1876, the first typewriter in 1879, the first commercial electricity service in 1882. We are now in the prelude of the second Industrial Revolution, one which is likely to have the same large-scale and not always desirable consequences as the first. At the heart of this revolution is a spate of invention and innovation associated with the computer, or the electronic digital computer to give it its formal title.

And yet, when the first computers were developed forty years ago, there were influential and informed opinions (including, it is alleged, that of the founder of IBM, now the world's largest computer manufacturer by a very wide margin) that no more than a handful of these machines would ever be needed.

So what is it about the computer that makes it so different and so powerful? What makes it so versatile that it can become an integral part of the work of scientists, engineers, accountants and many other professional people and yet at the same time can enrich the leisure time of adults and children at home? Why is it that the computer, which has helped to take man to the Moon, is now being blamed as a threat to millions of jobs? This book sets out to answer such global questions. At the end of most chapters in the book the reader will also find a list of specimen questions which indicate the type of detailed questions asked of students in first-level public examinations in Computer Studies — GCSE, A level and National Diploma. This book is therefore intended to provide the answers both to questions of fact and interpretation that will enable the interested reader to start mastering the computer.

INTRODUCING
THE COMPUTER

1.1 WHAT IS A COMPUTER?

Mastering computers calls for an understanding of computers as machines in the service of man, and how they have come to be the characteristic machines of our age to such an extent that this part of the twentieth century is often called 'The Computer Age'. The popular image of a computer as an electronic brain, or the professional jargon which attributes 'intelligence' and 'memory' to computers, serves only to confuse a proper understanding of computers as machines designed and built by people, for use by people. Although it is not easy to describe a computer in a few words, in principle the computer is a simple machine, or rather a group or system of simple machines, co-ordinated by a novel form of automatic control. Its full name is the electronic digital computer:

- *electronic* because it consists of electronic components: transistors, capacitors, resistors and now of course the ubiquitous integrated circuit or microchip. These components are activated by electrical impulses;
- *digital* because these electronic components are designed to represent and perform operations on digital as opposed to analog signals. The best way to explain the difference between the words *analog* and *digital* is to consider the two types of clocks and watches now currently available. They both measure time, but the digital watch divides time up into a series of separate or 'discrete' packets: seconds or some fraction of a second. The analog watch, on the other hand, exactly copies the 'flow' of time (like an 'ever-rolling stream') by the continuous movement of hands over a dial;
- *computer* because originally (but not necessarily now) these operations were concerned with numerical computation.

1.2 THE COMPUTER AS AN INFORMATION PROCESSOR

These digital values, coded into an appropriate electrical form, can be made to represent information of any and every sort, and a computer can therefore best be described as an *information-processing machine*. Information is provided to the computer from the real world — people or other machines — in the form of messages, signals, numbers, instrument readings, letters, business transactions, enquiries, etc. It has to be encoded in such a manner that the computer can understand and respond correctly to it. As an electronic device a computer can only comprehend electronic signals — electrical impulses — and so, if the information has been originally encoded on paper tape, magnetic discs or any other medium, the codes retained on these have to be converted by an appropriate device into the electrical impulses which the computer can understand.

Once processing of information has taken place the electrical signals which constitute the output from the computer have to be converted by the electronics attached to a screen or a printer, or even a voice 'output unit', into a form understandable by human beings. This means that the computer is *interfaced* with the outside world by devices which convert data understandable to humans into data comprehensible to the computer, and vice versa. If required, the output signals from the computer can be fed directly to machines in order to control their operation. This constitutes automatic control or *automation*.

We talk of these stages as *input*, *processing* and *output* (see Fig. 1.1), and the equipment which feeds information to the processing unit and relays the results of processing from it as *input/output* (I/O) *devices* or *peripherals*. Computer *terminals*, or just terminals, are a particularly important class of I/O device because they are designed for use by people at their normal place of work, like any other piece of domestic or office equipment (see Chapter 4). Our ability to connect a computer to so many different types of I/O device is part of the general-purpose power of a computer. I/O devices are described in more detail later. The functional components of a computer are shown in Fig. 1.2.

Fig 1.1 *the computer as an information processing system*

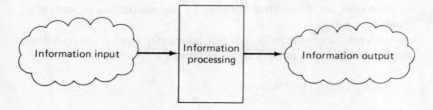

Fig 1.2 *the five functional components of a computer*

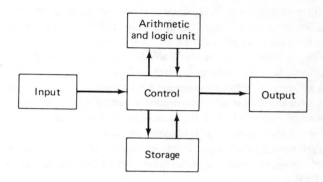

These five functional components may be packaged in a variety of forms, separately or integrally, but must all be present somewhere in the computer.

(a) The processor
The heart of the computer is called the central processing unit (CPU), or *processor*. All computers contain a CPU but some larger machines can contain several of these, hence the term *multiprocessor*. The actual definition of what is contained in a CPU is not entirely consistent. Certainly they all contain what is termed an arithmetic and logic unit (ALU) and a control unit. Opinion is divided as to whether the CPU contains the internal storage of the computer. Whether it does or does not need not really concern the reader at this time since the term *internal storage* or *main memory* will always be used in an unambiguous way. The function of the CPU is to perform a series of clearly defined operations consisting of the following:

(i) arithmetic operations (for example, ADD, SUBTRACT);
(ii) logical operations (logical choices resulting from a comparison of two pieces of data);
(iii) I/O operations (from READ, WRITE to various parts of the computer system);
(iv) internal data movements (moving data between parts of storage);
(v) data manipulations (changing the structure of pieces of data);
(vi) jump instructions (for example, JUMP, GOTO instructions whose particular and unique contribution will be discussed later in this chapter).

The actual list of instructions which any computer can execute is known as its *basic instruction set*.

Data is stored and manipulated inside the processor in the form that is most efficient for the electronic implementation of these operations – the *binary* form (see Section 3.1). Binary means taking only one of two possible values at a time – on/off, up/down, 1/0 – and the basic unit of binary information is called the *bit* or *bi*nary dig*it*.

It is beyond the scope of this book to enter into a deep discussion of the electronic workings of a computer; suffice it to say that by the conversion of all data into bit format, even, say, the continuous temperature readings of a thermometer, the computer can process it using very simple techniques of arithmetic and Boolean logic (Boolean logic deals only with true/false values – another good reason for using a binary system.) There are in fact very many simple electronic kits which demonstrate the elements of computer logic for those who wish to investigate this fascinating subject further.

(b) A computer program

It is the *control unit* which gives the computer its ability to decode and then execute a stored program. It acts rather like a very complex switching centre sending instructions to various parts of the computer and causing the millions of electronic switches or *gates* to be opened and closed. A computer operates under the control of instructions selected from its basic instruction set in order to perform a specific task. This list of instructions is known as a computer *program*. A program is fed, via the CPU and its control unit, into its internal storage. The program is started off, usually (but not always) by a human operator, and it continues automatically, instruction by instruction, until it finishes. At that point the program can either be executed again using perhaps a different set of data, or can be replaced by another program and the sequence repeated. For this purpose the control unit contains:

- a program counter, to initiate and control the performance, or 'execution', of the instructions in a program in the required sequence, one at a time (or 'serially');
- a register to hold the instruction currrently being executed and the data currently being operated on (or 'operands');
- a decoder to activate the action required by an instruction, either through the ALU, if it is an arithmetic or logical operation, or by causing transfers of data within the processor or between the processor and I/O devices;
- a clock to control the timing of operations; and
- registers to hold the current result of processing (the 'accumulator') and other intermediate data.

(c) Internal storage (or 'main memory')

This is required to support the processor for two reasons; firstly to hold the stored program(s) currently being executed, and secondly to hold the data which is being processed by these programs, in one of three states: 'raw' data transferred in from an input device, partly processed data, and fully processed data ready for transfer to an output device. This second purpose is vital because a processor works at much higher speeds than input/output devices, and therefore it needs to work from data that has already been made ready and waiting for it. This use of internal storage is known as 'buffer' storage. The control unit and internal storage are linked by what is called a data *bus* or data *highway* and it is along this, which is merely a set of wires rather like an electricity ring main, that data flows both to and from internal storage.

The fundamental unit of storage within a computer is the bit (*bi*nary digi*t*) as has already been described. However, a single bit is not a conveniently sized unit of data. For most purposes, the smallest unit in which useful data can be stored is the *byte*, which consists of 8 bits. Larger units of data storage are called *words* which in general consist of 2 or more bytes, although some very large machines use a word consisting of 60 bits. It is by the size of its internal storage that the size of a computer is often judged. Storage sizes are usually quoted in multiples of 1024 (2^{10}) bytes. 1024 bytes is known as 1 K. (K is used as a close approximation of 1024 although the K prefix usually means 1000.) A computer which is said to be a 32 K machine has an internal storage of $32 \times 1024 = 32\,768$ bytes. Similarly, larger computers often have internal storage in the megabyte range. One megabyte (1 M) is $2^{20} = 1024 \times 1024 = 1\,048\,576$ bytes, or approximately 1 million.

Fig. 1.3 shows the way in which the various units of the processor work together, in a functional rather than operational form. Chapter 3 will describe the way in which a computer works in more detail.

(d) The self-modifying program

The concept of a program, as a list of instructions for performing a task, will be a familiar one: a recipe is a program for preparing food and a crochet pattern is a program for producing an item of clothing (see Fig. 1.4). Even a gramophone record is a form of program where the instructions, in analog form for the conventional vinyl disc, control the movement of the air carrying the music to your ears. A computer is as useless without a computer program as a record player without records. Operating under the control of an appropriate stored program, the computer can perform any of a wide range of tasks, to be investigated more fully in the next chapter, without human intervention and therefore at full electronic

Fig 1.3 *the working organisation of a computer*

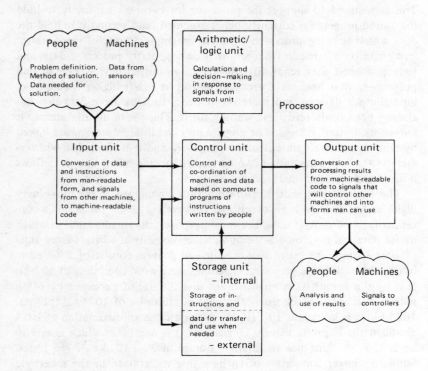

speeds, measured now in fractions of a second and ultimately limited only by the speed of light. Early computers took their program instructions from an external source which could have been punched paper tape, punched cards or even plug boards which actually connected certain memory locations together with wires. The big advance in computing technology was made when computers were built which could 'remember' a set of instructions and execute them whenever required.

Not every stored-program machine, however, qualifies as a computer; other machines can be equipped with automatic control to enable them to perform a sequence of operations automatically, such as an automatic washing machine (although upmarket 'electronic' washing machines may well have a small computer instead of electrical controls). The significant difference is that, in addition to those classes of instructions already described, a computer program can also include instructions that can cause a variation in the sequence in which other instructions are executed. Instead of instructions being performed in a fixed sequence, one by one from beginning to end of a program, the sequence can be varied, with *condi-*

Fig 1.4 *examples of 'programs': a computer program, a recipe and a crochet pattern*

```
>LIST
    10 REM THIS PROGRAM CALCULATES THE DAY OF THE WEEK
    20 REM ON WHICH ANY DATE FALLS
    30 REM BETWEEN 1ST MARCH 1900 AND 28TH FEBRUARY 2100
    40 DIM DAY$(7)
    50 DATA "SUNDAY","MONDAY","TUESDAY","WEDNESDAY"
    60 DATA "THURSDAY","FRIDAY","SATURDAY"
    70 FOR X=1 TO 7: READ DAY$(X): NEXT X '
    80 PRINT "ENTER DATE AS DAY,MONTH,YEAR IN NUMERICAL FORM"
    90 INPUT DAY,MONTH,YEAR
   100 IF MONTH>2 THEN N1=INT(365.25*(YEAR))
   110            ELSE N1=INT(365.25*(YEAR-1))
   120 IF MONTH>2 THEN N2=INT(30.6*(MONTH+1))
   130            ELSE N2=INT(30.6*(MONTH+13))
   140 N3=N1+N2+DAY-621049
   150 DAYN=(N3 MOD 7)+1
   160 PRINT DAY;"/";MONTH;"/";YEAR;" FALLS ON ";DAY$(DAYN)
   170 END
>
>
>RUN
ENTER DATE AS DAY,MONTH,YEAR IN NUMERICAL FORM
?17,10,1983
         17/10/1983 FALLS ON MONDAY
>
```

HOT CHICKEN SALAD

2 cupfuls cooked chicken; ½ head celery; 1 small green pepper; 1 medium onion; ½ can concentrated chicken soup; 2 tablespoons mayonnaise; juice of ½ lemon; 1 teaspoon salt; For the topping: 50 g grated Cheddar cheese; 1 cupful chrushed potato crisps.

The amounts of the ingredients are 'more or less'. Cut the chicken into neat pieces. Chop the celery and pepper coarsely and the onion finely. Combine the chicken, vegetables, soup, mayonnaise, lemon juice and salt in a large bowl and stir well. Put the mixture into a gratin dish and smooth over. Make the topping by combining the cheese and crisps and scatter over the dish to cover completely. Bake in a preheated oven at regulo 5, 190 °C (375 °F) for about 20 minutes. Serve hot. *[Serves 4 to 6]*

MOTIF (Make 64)

With L., work 5 ch.; join into ring with sl.st.

1st round—With L., 3 ch., 2 tr. into ring (1 ch., 3 tr. into ring) 3 times, 1 ch.. join to 3rd of 3 ch. with sl.st. Break off L.

2nd round—With M., join yarn in last 1 ch. sp. of previous round, 3 ch., 2 tr. in same sp., (1 ch., 3 tr., 2 ch., 3 tr. in next sp.) 3 times, 1 ch., 3 tr. in next sp. 2 ch., join to 3rd of 3 ch. with sl.st. Break off M.

3rd round—With D., join yarn in last 2 ch. sp. of previous round, 3 ch., 2 tr. in same sp., (1 ch., 3 tr. in next sp., 1 ch., 3 tr., 2 ch., 3 tr. in next sp.) 3 times, 1 ch., 3 tr. in next sp., 1 ch., 3 tr. in next sp., 2 ch., join to 3rd of 3 ch. with sl.st. Break off D.

Using D. join 48 motifs into strip 4 × 12, and rem. 16 into square 4 × 4. Join one edge of square to top edge of 1st. 4 motifs along strip, then opposite edge of square to top edge of last 4 motifs of strip.

tional and *unconditional jump* instructions. A computer can be programmed to make logical decisions so that it appears to have a glimmer of 'intelligence'. But because all its decisions are based on a set of simple arithmetical or logical comparisons no element of judgement is introduced. In other words the computer can decide the amount of someone's pay rise according to the amount of pay already earned, but it cannot decide if the person is worthy of a pay rise.

A conditional jump can be used to cause one of two alternative subsequences (or 'paths') to be followed, depending on the result of a calculation or test ('IF ... THEN ... ELSE ... '), or to repeat a sequence of instructions a fixed number of times or until a certain point has been reached ('DO ... UNTIL ... '). An unconditional jump takes the flow of control away from the next instruction to another instruction elsewhere in the program ('GOTO ... '). Chapter 7 deals with the construction of a program using these and the other classes of instructions in various forms known as 'programming languages'.

The self-modifying program, as this attribute is known, is the final distinguishing mark of a true computer, and makes it a general-purpose and flexible information-processing machine, because it can perform information-processing tasks as they really are (to be described in the next Chapter). Most tasks are not a single unvarying list of actions, but involve alternatives, such as income tax deductions at varying rates of tax depending on income and allowances, or mathematical work involving iterative calculations. It is also this feature of a computer which leads to descriptions of computers taking decisions, or solving problems – both peculiarly human attributes. In truth, the computer is merely obeying the rules and instructions programmed into it by a human programmer; it is the program which incorporates selection or decision-making, and the computer is a machine which executes such a computer program.

(e) Data storage and communication
The various types of computer programs that are needed for computers to handle a variety of tasks with efficiency and ease are known collectively as 'software', to distinguish them from the bare machine, known as 'hardware'. Most computers now need so much software (which will be discussed more fully in Chapter 7) that it cannot all be held in internal storage, and one of the two main functions of *external* or *backing storage*, or mass memory, is to store that part of a machine's software that is not currently required inside the processor for processing. The other, and usually predominant, use of external storage is as a repository for information of all types which is required permanently for processing, such as mathematical and business tables, library indexes, and all the 'files' of information that every business needs on employees, customers, products, shareholders,

accounts, stocks, machines, etc. Information processing has come to rely heavily on large volumes of stored information which can be retrieved ('accessed') speedily, brought into the processor, and then either returned to external storage if it has been changed ('updated') during processing, or merely transmitted to an output device.

Most forms of external storage hold data in binary form on some form of magnetic medium, either tape or disc. Disc storage has the advantage of providing access directly to any part of the stored data, and is known as a *direct access storage device* or DASD. This works rather like a gramophone record: just as you can place the stylus at any position you wish on the record, the magnetic read/write head can be positioned easily over any part of the disc. If tape is used as a storage medium it is essential that any search begins at the start of the tape. This is called a *serial* search and is exactly the method which has to be used for finding a piece of music stored on a recording tape. A DASD can be functionally regarded as an extension of internal storage, as shown in Fig. 1.3, but usually operates as a fast I/O device.

The final element of a computer system is the link between its various components. These linkages can be very short, or 'local', that is, all the components are in one room or equally near.

Local communication links are sometimes known as 'buses' or 'channels', and it is usual for a computer to have at least an external storage device and one I/O device (for operator use, known as a 'console') connected locally by an I/O bus. Other I/O devices, however, can be connected 'remotely', such remoteness even extending to other continents. Remote connections can use most appropriate forms of telecommunication — cables, microwave radio links, satellite radio links. The combination of computers and telecommunications is generally thought to be the single most significant development in computing, and it enormously improves the power (and, for some people, increases the threat) of the computer to be able to process data physically input hundreds or thousands of miles away, or merely to output data at locations remote from a central storage unit.

1.3 COMPUTERS TODAY

At this point we can describe computers as machines, or systems of machines to denote their multi-machine organisation, with the following characteristics:

- an organised aggregate of mainly electronic units — processors, I/O devices, local storage, external storage devices — and communication links to make it operate as a single system;

- able to work on digital information coded in a binary format for processing at electronic speeds;
- under central processor control in the form of stored computer programs, composed of basic machine instructions including self-modifying features;
- and thus able to perform a wide variety of information-processing tasks in such diverse fields as business, engineering, education and finance.

(a) Computer performance

In Chapter 3 we shall be looking in more detail at computer hardware and how it works, but the main concern of this book is with what computers can be used for, and how they can be put to use. The first true electronic computer was invented around 1945 and, after four decades of rapid development, it has encompassed a wide range of performance, capability and cost. In fact, the range between the smallest computer and the largest is probably greater, proportionally, than any other class of machines in existence — certainly greater than the difference between the smallest and largest road or air transport vehicles, and perhaps on a par with electrical power generators. The tiny electronic computer installed as a controller in automatic washing machines and the largest supercomputers working in weather forecasting all share the same characteristics, but with vastly different performance capabilities.

The two dimensions of performance in computers are *speed* and *capacity*. The fractions of speed are very small, the complement of capacity very large, and the scale of measurement will be familiar only to those who have mastered SI units (see Table 1.1).

Table 1.1

Prefix	Description	Abbreviation	Application
Milli	1 thousandth	m	
Micro	1 millionth	μ	seconds
Nano	1 billionth (American) i.e. 10^{-9}	n	
Pico	1 billionth (British) i.e. 10^{-12}	p	
Kilo	1 thousand or 1024*	K	
Mega	1 million or 1024^2 *	M	bytes, words,
Giga	1 billion (American) or 1024^3 *	G	hertz, bauds
Tera	1 billion (British) or 1024^4 *	T	

*The reason for this alternative value will be given in chapter 3.

The principal features of a computer in which speed and capacity vary, and which are therefore commonly used in describing a particular computer and its component units, are given in Table 1.2.

Table 1.2

Component	Feature	Units of measurement
Processor	Instruction speed (time taken to execute one instruction – ADD, SUBTRACT, STORE, etc.); Sometimes quoted as the number of instructions carried out per second	Nanoseconds or microseconds Millions of instructions per second (MIPS)
Internal storage	Total storage capacity Access time* Cycle time*	$\begin{cases}\text{Kilobytes or megabytes}\\\text{Kilowords or megawords}\end{cases}$ Nanoseconds
External storage	Capacity Transfer rate (to/from processor) Access time (DASDs only) Density of storage	Megabytes or gigabytes Megabytes/second Milliseconds Bits/inch (b.p.i.)
I/O devices	Speeds (of input/ output) Capacity of I/O media (e.g. screen, card, paper)	Cards, lines or characters, etc., per second Characters
Communication links	Speeds – remote lines – data and I/O buses	Bits/second ($\approx$ bauds) $\begin{cases}\text{Bytes/second}\\\text{Words/second}\end{cases}$

*These two terms refer to the speed with which data is transferred between internal storage and the processor and will be defined in Chapter 3.

(b) Important types of computer
Within this wide range are some major types of computer (see Fig. 1.5) which either represent different starting or stage points in the evolution of computers, or form distinctive products for different markets – principally *mainframe computers, minicomputers, microcomputers, small business computers, word processors, personal computers, supercomputers*. They are the equivalents of the different types of road transport vehicles –

Fig 1.5 *cost and performance of different types of computer*

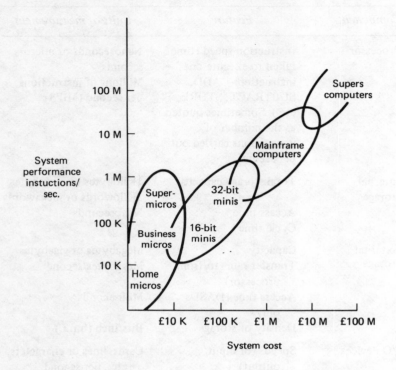

saloons, sports cars, HGVs, etc. An appropriate starting point for a knowledge of how to use a computer is to select the appropriate class of machine in the first place.

(i) Mainframe computers

Mainframes are the current descendants of the original computers, still built on the same structure (which we call the Von Neumann machine in honour of one of the significant contributors) but with vastly different technology. These significant shifts in technology we used to call 'generations' and we had reached the third generation by the late 1960s. Because of the rapid and continuous developments of the 1970s, this term has ceased to have any real meaning except as a sales blurb, but we are supposed (in 1987) to be selling fourth generation equipment and looking forward to the fifth. Mainframes are still large and expensive, costing from £250 000 upwards to about £10 000 000; their use is synonymous with single-processor, centralised computing, in which significant economies of scale are thought to exist (typified in Grosch's law: the power ratio of two computers varies as the square of the ratio of their costs; that is, if you buy a computer twice as expensive you should get four times the power). This indicates that along with their high costs they are used mostly by large companies for gainful reasons (cost-reduction or profit-improvement).

Other characteristics of mainframes are that they:

- are mainly American manufactured; ICL is the sole significant non-American manufacturer outside the protected Japanese market;
- require a large volume of software, partly because of multi-user requirements, and also because they need to run several programs simultaneously ('multi-programming') to keep a large processor busy, so they also require a large internal storage capacity;
- need environmental support in sealed rooms; this is because many of the moving parts on such devices as disc drives are affected by excess dust or wide variations of temperature or humidity;
- generally demand quite a large number of professional staff to run them;
- are available in a variety of versions of processor and storage capacity, but often with a limited range of I/O device types; this enables them to be tailored, or 'configured', to satisfy both storage-dominated and processor-dominated applications, and to meet a company's specific requirements.

Fig. 1.6 shows a typical mainframe computer system, with still relatively large separate units, connected by cables hidden in false floors.

Fig 1.6 *a typical mainframe computer system*

A - Central processing unit and internal storage
B - High-speed printer
C - Operator console
D - Card reader
E - Magnetic disc drives
F - Magnetic tape drives

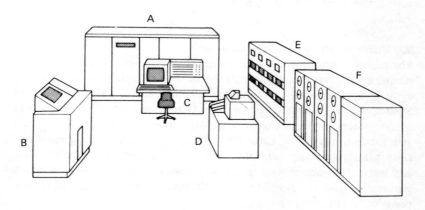

(ii) Minicomputers

Minicomputers ('minis') began to emerge in the 1960s, still recognisably based on the original computers but primarily designed for different uses. They were able to exploit some of the first moves towards miniaturisation in electronics, or integrated circuits, so that they gained in compactness and cheapness. They were designed primarily for various types of engineering and control work (particularly characterised now by industrial robots in the automotive industry), which led to some important demands and characteristics:

- high reliability;
- ease of use;
- limited number of uses, often dedicated to single use;
- relatively simple software;
- ease of device attachment;
- robustness for use in uncontrolled environment, and packaged in rack-mounted units (see Fig. 1.7).

This resulted in a significantly different internal organisation of hardware and software (or 'architecture'). Typical configurations (much less variety) cost from £15 000 to £500 000. Minis are manufactured by a different sector of manufacturers, still US-dominated but with some significant indigenous manufacturers. Their software and the ready availability of simple terminals made them a great step forward in approachability and usability, and their benefits have, in the process of time, moved them away from their original markets.

Minis are now often found in supporting roles to mainframes (for example, as 'front end processors' where the preparation and checking of data are performed by a separate minicomputer before the data is handed over to the mainframe for processing) and, as rivals to smaller mainframes, they have been promoting a trend away from centralised computing (known as 'distributed computing'). The latest 32-bit 'superminis' are among the most sophisticated and effective computers systems on the market.

(iii) Microprocessors and microcomputers

The process of making the basic electronic components of computers ever smaller (see Chapter 3, Section 2) led to the production of initially hundreds and subsequently thousands of circuits on one wafer, or 'chip', of a particular type of material, usually silicon. Examples of building blocks of computers made in this way (firstly Large Scale Integration or LSI and subsequently Very Large Scale Integration or VLSI) are microprocessors, interfaces to enable units such as printers and discs to be attached, and internal storage chips. Fig. 1.8 shows one of the most powerful microprocessors currently available, with 200 000 of the basic electronic components ('transistors') on one chip.

Fig 1.7 *a minicomputer (above) and supermicro computer (below)*

(courtesy of Digital Equipment Corporation Ltd)

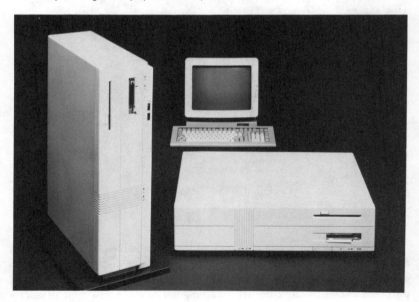

(courtesy TFB)

Fig 1.8 *a microprocessor (the Motorola 68020)*

(courtesy of Motorola Ltd)

A microprocessor contains a processor and some interface functions on a single chip. 'Single-chip' computers are limited-role microprocessors with a small amount of integral storage on the chip, and are used for such purposes as controlling automatic washing machines. A new type of microprocessor with its own storage has recently been developed, known as the Transputer; it will be used coupled together into large-scale multiprocessor arrangements, to build a new generation of computers, the so-called fifth generation of computers. One important characteristic of these computers is that they will be able to perform many operations at the same time, through parallel processing; all computers hitherto have been serial processors, able to perform only one operation at a time, based on the same principle of operation originally conceived by Von Neumann, the true father of the computer.

Microprocessors are principally used, along with storage and interface chips, and other commensurate I/O and storage devices, to build microcomputers. The smallest and cheapest microcomputers, with limited facilities and 'domestic' peripherals such as TV monitors and cassette recorder are sold as personal computers for use in the home and are now a familiar part of our home electronics, costing from about £100 upwards. The expected expansion of home computer usage has, however, petered out into an electronic games market of a degree of sophistication that far outshines the original Space Invaders.

More upmarket machines, with floppy disc drives and cheap printers, are sold in large quantities as personal computers in schools, colleges, in small businesses and as 'desktop' computers at work, with software scaled down from larger computers or specifically introduced for individual or small organisation use. This book was written with the aid of Word Processing software on such a machine, which can be obtained for as little as £400. Word or text processing represents a typical activity for machines of this size and availability. The Word Processor was in fact the first commercial exploitation of the microcomputer, derived from earlier intelligent typewriters and 'memory' keyboards in the process of helping typists achieve higher productivity. The stand-alone Word Processor was a microcomputer dedicated to this one activity, and its success was achieved primarily by making the hardware and software fit the application and suit the user – the very reverse of what the original mainframe computers often offered.

The continued development of the microprocessor has led to more powerful models appearing on the market, primarily from three companies, Intel, Motorola and Zilog. These models are described by the size of the unit of data that can be carried through the processor; thus the first widely available micros were 8-bit micros; most commercial microcomputers are based on 16-bit microprocessors, and the latest 32-bit microprocessors are now being used to produce single- or multi-user microsystems that rival in power and performance the current competition from smaller mainframe computers and minicomputers. These microprocessors also have the necessary power to control industrial robots – machines that are equipped with sensors to 'see' and 'feel' and attachments to grasp and move.

Meanwhile the original 8-bit micros are available at such a low cost that they can represent a potential monitoring and control component inside many other electronic or electro-mechanical systems, e.g. cookers, hi-fi, burglar alarms, car controls, heating systems; their use is restricted only by the ability of system designers and engineers to exploit them. Typically, microprocessors are now being used within the I/O and telecommunication devices attached to or used in conjunction with computers; they are used to control the air conditioning equipment necessary to keep mainframe computers running, and in the security systems with electronic keys that are used to protect computer rooms against unauthorised access.

(iv) Small business computers

Very small mainframes, minicomputers and larger microcomputers are now, to the user, virtually indistinguishable particularly when built up with extra software and more sophisticated attachments for the business market. Companies who operate in this way generally buy the basic computer from the original manufacturer (who is known as the 'original equipment manufacturer' or OEM in this context) and produce their own 'product' with their own packaging and brand name. Such companies are sometimes known as 'systems houses'.

Small business systems are usually sold as complete package of hardware and software. Customers will expect to find a full range of business software from which to select:

- business accounts
- wages and salaries
- sales and purchases
- word processing and other office functions
- business planning
- production planning.

They will also expect to be able to select the size of their initial system, and to be able to expand it as their business grows or as they wish to extend their computer provision. Finally they will expect it to be easy to set-up in their premises and to operate in a normal work environment. In the business field small computer systems of this type are taking a lot of the mystery and mystique out of computers, just as personal computers have done so in our homes.

The marketing success of word processors can be attributed to two features apart from their purposeful hardware and software and overall packaging: firstly a playing down of their computer applications, and secondly a close attention to making them as unobtrusive and sympathetic in an office environment as possible (see Fig. 1.9). In the business field small systems of this type are taking a lot of the mystery and mystique out

Fig 1.9 *typical microcomputers for (a) business and (b) personal use (courtesy of Acornsoft Ltd)*

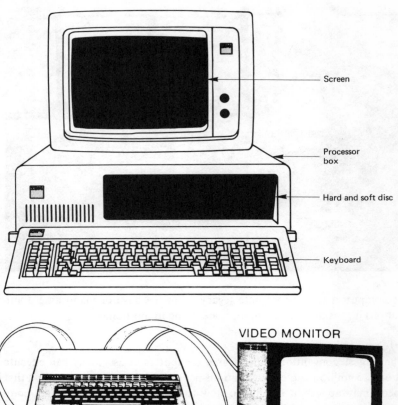

Screen

Processor box

Hard and soft disc

Keyboard

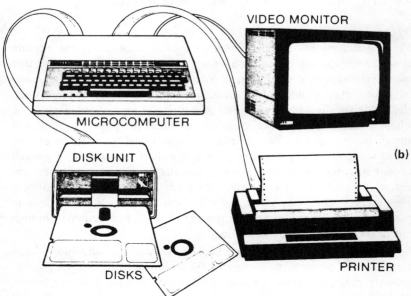

VIDEO MONITOR

MICROCOMPUTER

DISK UNIT

(b)

DISKS

PRINTER

Fig 1.10 *a small business in an office environment (courtesy of ICL)*

of computers (an unfortunate legacy from the days of mainframe domination) just as personal computers are doing in our homes.

(v) Supercomputers

The largest conventional mainframe computers in use today can execute about 25 million typical instructions per second. However astounding that speed may appear, it is still too slow to permit the solution by the computer of certain problems in science, such as instant weather forecasting, aircraft design simulations and flood or earthquake predictions. Such tasks, whose solution could make great contributions to personal safety and energy usage, can take days to run on conventional machines or are too big to work at all. So, while the growth elsewhere has been in very much smaller machines, scientists have required the development of *supercomputers*, some built on completely different designs from conventional computers in that they allow the execution of multiple instructions in parallel (rather than the serial processing of single instructions), through one of several alternative mechanisms.

Current supercomputers, which have been ordered in surprisingly large numbers, can perform up to about 100 million instructions per second, properly programmed for the appropriate tasks. Already, however, NASA (the US National Aeronautics and Space Administration) has called for designs for a supercomputer ten times faster than the current models, with a performance of about 1000 million instructions per second, for wind tunnel simulation. It seems that there will always be a place for bigger and faster computers — users will be continually finding bigger and bigger problems to tackle with them. One such problem is to be found in the US Government's Space Defense Initiative (better known as the Star Wars Program), an integral part of which would be a network of large space-borne computers that would need, on current estimates, to be able to process a very large program, of about 100 million instructions, in order to successfully detect enemy missiles and launch counter-missiles. It is only fair to report that many eminent computer scientists believe that computers could not and should not be trusted with such critical decisions.

(vi) Portable computers
At the same time our computers have been contracting in the reverse direction. For several years it has been possible to buy a true stored-program computer of the size of a pocket calculator, and many of the smallest home computers would fit into a shopping bag, but their lack of an external storage facility limits their usefulness. Now we have a wide range of portable, transportable and lap-held computers, with full keyboards, usually flat-bed displays, floppy disc drive and sometimes a narrow-width printer, in a ruggedised package with a carrying handle. The development of a high-power long-life electric battery will finally free us from the restrictions of the power point, (though some models can be powered from a conventional car battery), so that a computer may go wherever man may go.

1.4 COMPUTERS, TRAVEL AND LEISURE

The 'Leisure Industry' can be described as those organisations whose objective is the provision of organised facilities and activities for leisure, pleasure and recreation. A chart of the industry is shown in Fig. 1.12. The industry contains a mix of public, commercial and private enterprises, and a cross-section of size from the smallest private guest-house at one end to the largest hotel chain at the other. The leisure industry is an important part of Western economies, and perhaps, apart from the electronics sector and the crime business, the only growing industry in Britain today. It is also an important industry internationally, because increasingly people spend much of their leisure time and funds abroad, as tourists. Tourism is international, and providing for tourists is a major part of the economy of many countries in Europe, Africa and Asia. So, in 1984 (the last year for which full statistics are available) in Britain we spent about $2\frac{1}{2}$ per cent, or one-fortieth, of our income on holidays (£4.25 billion), most of that on foreign holidays, thus helping to sustain the economies of Spain, Greece, Italy and elsewhere. At the same time large numbers of foreign tourists

Fig 1.11 (a) a portable computor (courtesy of Hewlett-Packers Computers Ltd)

Fig 1.11   *(b) a hand-held computor (courtesy of Psion Ltd)*

Fig 1.12   *a diagram of the leisure industry*

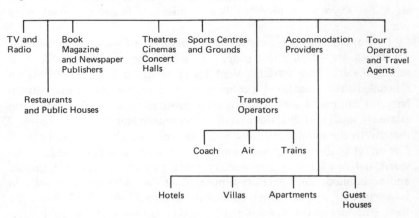

also came to Britain, about six million of them, sustaining our own tourist industry by spending about £5 billion. Most countries have a similar 'balance of payments' situation in tourism — their own nationals go abroad and foreigners come to them, all of them in search of something that their own country lacks (in our case, warmth and sunshine). People also travel abroad for other reasons – to work or study abroad, to export goods and services, to meet colleagues in international organisations, on military or diplomatic service – all of which contributes to the international business of Travel and Tourism.

Travelling abroad, at its very minimum, requires transport and accommodation, and unless you hitch-hike/drive your own car and use your own tent/villa, you will be a customer of a Transport Operator (coach/plane/ferry/rail) and an Accommodation Provider (campsite/hotel/villa/apartment/guest house) as a holiday-maker – on a cruise ship the two are combined. Most people, however, do not make their own travel or holiday arrangements, particularly for holidays abroad, partly because of the well-known fear of foreign languages and partly because they could not do it as cheaply or as efficiently as companies who specialise in so doing on their behalf.

For holidays, therefore, we mostly leave travel and accommodation arrangements in the hands of Tour Operators, as they are collectively known. (In fact, most people do not tour, they stay in one place on holiday, but the word has remained with us from the days of the Grand Tour of the previous centuries, when foreign travel was the privilege of the rich and the military.) They organise a season of 'packaged' holidays using, mostly, block allocations of seats in specially arranged 'charter' flights and block bookings in hotels and other accommodation. Some Tour Operators possess their own aircraft, and some airlines also operate their own holidays. The key word is 'block' – they organise in bulk and aim to sell every one.

To do this they are assisted by the retailers of packaged holidays – Travel Agents – high street shops – to whom they make available their selling material and services. Most travel agents also arrange flights on scheduled airlines and hotel accommodation on an individual basis, particularly for business travel, which is more profitable form of business but a relatively small part of travel overall. Some tour operators sell (exclusively) directly to the public, and some also run their own chain of travel agents. The travel business therefore consists of two types of basic facility providers and two types of intermediary. Finally some of the larger transport and accommodation operators support their own sales offices, mostly in large cities or at their other operational centres. Figure 1.13 shows the basic structure of the business and the main relationships between them; it is in fact a simple form of a diagram used in a part of computing concerned with analysing data and relationships in a problem area.

The operational objectives of companies in the travel and holiday sector are broadly those of most commercial companies – to sell the services

Fig 1.13 *the travel business*

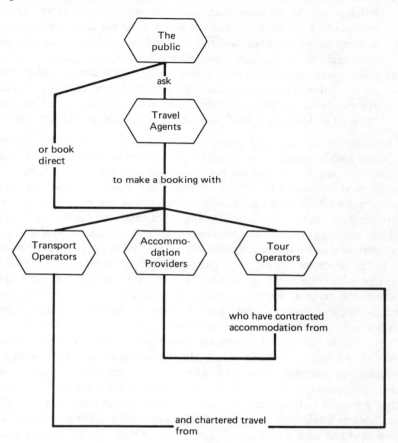

which they offer and thereby stay in existence and create profits. In fact, they face some particular problems which makes this harder than for other sectors of the economy and accounts for their characteristic use of computers:

(a) A highly seasonal market, partly a hangover from habits originally caused by the short-lived summer in northern climates, and reinforced by the school summer holidays;

(b) A highly competitive business with a lot of unused capacity except at a few peak periods, partly created by (a) above and partly because of national economics (tourism) and national pride in airlines;

(c) their product has a short shelf life — once the date has passed, or the plane taken off, it does not exist;

(d) As a result profits are low (a Tour Operator's net profit on a packaged holiday may be no more than a few pounds, and the Travel Agent takes only a small commission of about 7-10 per cent), or are non-existent for most airlines and railways; and for commercial companies the margin between success and failure is very slight;

(e) Commercial success depends partly on customer service and partly on low prices which are achieved by getting the maximum use out of the expensive facilities of planes, coaches and hotels — it is bottoms on seats and bodies in beds that count, or the load/occupancy factor.

Like other commercial and public organisations companies in the travel business have sought the appropriate assistance from computers in achieving these commercial and operational objectives. In some sectors computer usage is very advanced, and no Holiday Tour operator could consider operating without some assistance; indeed, some are organised almost around their computer system. On the other hand, the number of travel agents reserving, selling and accounting for their ticket sales with the use of their own computer is still relatively small. The larger companies, such as the international airlines, have been using computers for many years and currently operate large mainframe computers with universal terminal access; the smallest companies will be a typical market for commercial microcomputer salesmen; and the large hotels and theatres were one of the earlier users of software packages on minicomputers.

In most of the following chapters there will be a section at the conclusion of the technical theme of the chapter which examines the ways in which these companies have been realising their objectives, in the face of their particular problems. The success of the holiday business is the way that packaged holidays abroad, once reserved for the privileged few, are available at a relatively low cost to a large proportion of the population. If you have had such a holiday recently, you will have seen and experienced the use of computers by the tour operator and travel agent, and you will have the brochures and documents somewhere which are the external aspects of their computer systems; if you have not, it is worthwhile accompanying a serious study of this book by paying your local travel agent a visit and taking home a typical brochure.

SPECIMEN QUESTIONS

In this list of specimen examination questions, and in all the lists at the end of later chapters, those marked '*' have been based on or derived from questions set in examinations in Computer Studies of the Welsh Joint Education Committee.

1. Define a computer and describe its essential characteristics.

2. Describe the development of computers since the 1940s by referring to
   (i) the three generations of computers;
   (ii) minicomputers and microcomputers.
   In each case name one distinctive feature and name one typical application for each type of computer. *

3. Differentiate between a microprocessor and a microcomputer.

4. Outline the changes that have taken place in computing over the last thirty years, explaining how the reliability, power, and speed of hardware and software have developed. What effects do you think these changes have had on the use of computers? *

5. Explain how the recent rapid developments in computer technology have led to a situation in which a huge variety of different types and commercial sources are available on the market. *

6. Explain briefly the following terms and abbreviations:
   (a) bit, (b) byte, (c) k, (d) Mb, (e) ms, (f) CPU, (g) ALU.

7. Outline the distinguishing characteristics of micro, mini and mainframe computers in terms of costs, hardware and software capacities and types of application.

CHAPTER 2

THE WHO, WHAT, AND WHY OF COMPUTERS

Although reliable official statistics are not available, the best estimate is that computer hardware accounts for 15 per cent of the UK's annual investment in plant and equipment and that in the UK one home in five now contains a personal computer. More important, in the face of world-wide stagnancy and even decay in trade and production, expenditure by business and domestic users on computers is likely to grow at a rate of about 15 per cent per annum until the end of the decade.

The figures do not show, however, the wide ranges of uses which computers have found, nor do they reveal how deeply they have become embedded in some aspects of our life. Like many other features of modern life, we only realise their impact when they become unavailable for one reason or another, as for instance when computer operators come out on strike and make their machines inoperative. Such action brings most of the routine work of their companies to a halt, and trade unions have come to realise the strategic position which computers and their staff now occupy. In their forty years of use and development, computers have moved into many and different applications, any classification of which is merely arbitrary, but it is most meaningful to identify their uses in the following areas:

- numerical computation;
- data processing;
- automatic control;
- personal computing;
- information systems and information technology.

2.1 COMPUTERS IN NUMERICAL COMPUTATION

As their name suggests, computers were originally invented as computing machines (compute: 'determine by calculation' — *Shorter Oxford English Dictionary*). They succeeded and replaced mechanical calculating machines

or engines (a term which, incidentally, has returned to use for a type of microcomputer) which dated back 100 years and which can now be seen in museums such as the Science Museum in London. Much scientific work has always demanded numerical computation that was beyond human capabilities in terms of:
- volume (number of operations), and therefore speed of completion;
- accuracy (freedom from induced errors);
- precision (level of detail).

The calculation of paths of stars and comets in astronomy, and of tide tables in meteorology, are two long-standing examples and, more recently, military and space programmes have added a greater urgency to this demand.

The particular features of computers which made possible a transfer of this work were firstly their ability to perform arithmetical operations very fast, and secondly the use of a stored program to enable sequences and combinations of simple arithmetic to be performed automatically and repeated as required. These are common features of all true computers, with the result that numerical work features prominently in the use of most computers, from the highest flights of scientific experimentation (where there remain some problem areas unsolvable without a further step ahead in computer power), down to the domestic computer which can be programmed to keep a family's budget, or merely to perform some difficult or tedious piece of arithmetic. At this level, its use is not too far removed from that of an electronic calculator; the dividing line between programmable calculators and very small computers is a fine one, but significant difference include:
- calculators handle only numerical values;
- programmable calculators are still very difficult to program;
- programmable calculators have very limited storage.

This should do no more than emphasise that nowadays people use computers for different reasons — what is essential to a scientist is a convenience to a home computer fanatic. The middle ground is occupied by what most people experience from computers — the performance of simple but repetitive tasks such as calculating pay and printing a payslip or providing electricity or gas bills. This is the work generally classified as data processing. Such work is not impossible without computers, but vastly more superior results in terms of speed and accuracy accrue from the use of computers, and for a public gas supplier it is the speed with which a bill can be produced after a meter is read that makes all the difference. Fig. 2.1 shows a simplified procedure for calculating a gas bill as a sequence of arithmetical operations, in the form of a *flowchart*, which is widely used in computing and which will be examined in Chapters 5 and 6.

Fig 2.1 *arithmetical procedure for gas bill calculation*

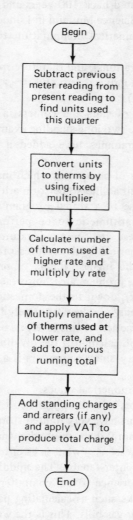

For highly demanding computational work (popularly known as 'number-crunching') the following features of a computer are of particular importance:
- the way that numbers are represented and held in the computer;
- the way that arithmetical operations are performed;
- the way that a computer can be programmed to perform mathematical functions other than add, subtract, multiply or divide, such as square roots, by a process known as 'numerical analysis';

– the sets of rules (or algorithm) through which a solution will be found for a mathematical problem if followed long enough.

2.2 COMPUTERS IN DATA PROCESSING

Despite their name and origin, and despite the prominence (but not pre-dominance) of numerical work on computers of all types, it would be wrong to think of computers just as giant calculating machines. The large majority of non-domestic computers today are used in the context of *business data processing*. Data processing (DP) was a term that pre-dated computers by about a generation (in human, not computer, terms!), and was used to describe a part of company work that dealt with the routine computational work that any company has to arrange, such as calculation of pay, production of accounts and keeping of ledgers and the mainten-ance of its information ('data') on employees, customers, suppliers, products, etc., kept in subject aggregates known as 'files', but now more generally described as the company's (corporate) data base.

Our inheritance from pre-computer data processing is widespread and includes:

– business machines now connected to the computer directly, or 'on-line', using a communications line and interface attachments in either device, so that the business machine becomes a peripheral device to the Com-puter. An 'off-line' device is one that is not directly connected to a computer, but both devices use a compatible medium to hold data to be transferred from one to the other, e.g. a magnetic tape, so that the output from the one device becomes the input to the other.
– media such as cards, tape, listing paper and forms;
– techniques and methods of handling data, particularly the delayed pro-cessing of transactions in accumulated batches, or 'batch processing'.

The first of these factors is particularly important because it changes the shape of computers.

The use of a computer as the heart of a data processing activity, now described as electronic data processing (EDP) or automatic data processing (ADP), turns what was originally a single machine into a multi-machine system. In such a computer system the value and importance of peripherals typically far exceed that of the processor itself. Fig. 1.6 shows a typical computer configuration from a mainframe data processing department, and identifies the principal peripherals surrounding the processor, and in most senses overshadowing it. Fig. 1.6 does not show the off-line equip-ment supporting the computer system: pre-processing equipment such as data preparation devices and post-processing equipment such as bursters, collators, and envelope fillers. Fig. 2.2 shows a typical complete machine system in EDP, and an extension of the flowchart of the gas billing calculation of Fig. 2.1, illustrating the changed balance of computing in data processing.

Business systems are also procedural systems of great width and depth; a typical gas billing system contains many other functions beyond the procedure shown in Fig. 2.2, and could encompass:

- transferring last meter readings to a portable computer, which the meter reader will use to produce a gas bill on the spot, and re-transferring the new readings to the main records;
- production of estimated readings;
- acceptance of charges other than gas for billing, for example, coke, fittings, servicing, etc.;
- calculation and production of gas bills plus other charges including meter rents, standing charges, appliance hire charges, hire purchase repayments, coke, fittings, and service charges;
- follow-up procedures on unpaid bills;
- production of reminder notices, final notices and arrears letters;
- maintaining and calculating interest on gas deposits;
- acceptance and allocation of cash received;
- accounting for all monetary transactions;
- setting-up and maintaining hire purchase agreements;
- updating of customer details, for example, meter changes, tariff changes, etc.;
- customer removals, their subsequent billing and follow-up;
- adding new customers to the file;
- general amendments to customer details, for example, change of name, alteration of appliance details, etc.;
- accounting and statistical analysis.

The whole system would be built around the customer master file, in a repeated cycle of processing as shown in Fig. 2.2. That is:

- read input data
- update master file record
- produce output.

The role of the processor in data processing is thus a reduced but still central one, primarily devoted to:

- the control of data input, storage and output devices;
- the running of one or more computer programs, mostly of limited computational content and rather more heavily concerned with the handling of data in files;
- the supervision of the entire operation.

In this way the use of a computer in data processing is more akin to its use in automatic control (see next section). It has led to a number of technical developments in mainframe computers of immense significance, some of which will be discussed in subsequent chapters, particularly:

Fig 2.2 *data processing and the computer*

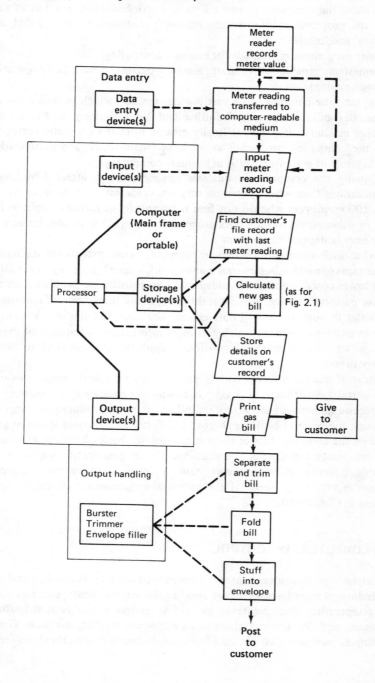

- the creation of systems software, which is a suite of programs designed to allow the computer to process its data efficiently and to act as an aid to the programmer by providing him with ready-made routines such as 'sorts' and 'merges';
- easier programming methods for business computing;
- computers capable of running many programs concurrently (multi-programming).

It exposed the computer to a vastly wider market, which in turn created economies of scale in manufacturing and led ultimately to the much cheaper machines of today. It finally created both the computer industry and the computing profession as we know them today, and particularly the key role of systems analysis in business computing.

Equally the computer in business has significantly affected business organisations themselves. There are very few organisations with more than, say, 100 employees who do not find it advantageous to use computers in one or other aspect of their data processing, and many large companies are very heavily dependent on them.

What such organisations find in computer-based systems are the basic advantages of mechanisation over manual work — speed, accuracy, reliability and lower costs — plus some added and less quantifiable benefits such as better customer service through real-time systems, integration of company activities through the use of data communications, and the ability to survive in an environment in which ever more information is required of them and in which ever more information is available to them (and to their competitors).

In turn this has affected us, the public, who are mostly employees of, and certainly customers of, computer-using organisations. As customers, we receive numerous bills, letters and other computer-produced documents through the post; as both employees and customers, records about us are held on the computer files of those organisations: banks, building societies, police, county and district councils, Post Office, gas, electricity and water boards, government departments, trade unions . . . the list for a typical citizen is very long. Some of the potential consequences of this are discussed in Chapter 10.

2.3 COMPUTERS IN CONTROL

Automatic control of machines (or automation) is a long-established feature of industrial manufacture. We are also familiar with domestic controls such as temperature thermostats in electric irons and in our central heating systems, and the timer controls in an automatic washing machine. These examples represent two classes of control. In the first case, there is a feedback from the thermostats to the heater or fan which comes on intermittently to maintain the desired temperature, known as *closed-loop control*. In the second case, there is no feedback but simply a sequence of instructions followed automatically, known as *automatic sequence control* (ASC) or *open-loop control* (see Fig. 2.3).

Fig 2.3 *automatic control and the computer*

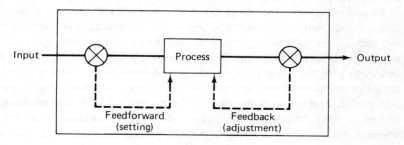

(a) *closed loop control*

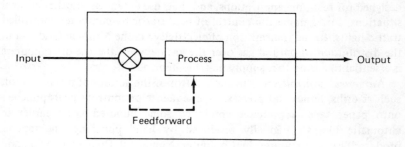

(b) *open loop control*

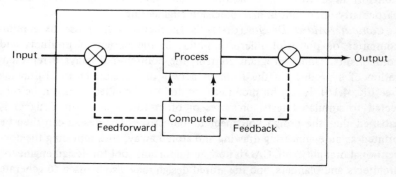

(c) *the computer as a controller*

Engineers have long been using these forms of control in manufacturing processes, and have used computers as the controlling device linked by suitable 'interfaces' (devices which enable one piece of equipment to communicate with another) to instruments ('sensors') which record production variables such as temperature, speed, weight, and to controllers ('activators') which can change some aspect of the operation of the process or machine. The most important function of these interfaces is to convert non-digital signals ('analog') into digital form, as analog-to-digital converters.

In *process control* the computer is used to supervise the operation of conventional controlling devices in large-scale continuous or semi-continuous production such as oil, chemical, paper or metal processing, or ultimately to replace them in the form of direct digital control. To do so, a computer program needs to input an instrument reading, compare it to a stored or computed value, and return a value or a correction factor to the activator in keeping with the pace of the process which it is controlling, or 'in real time'. This term is also now widely used in business computing, where it refers to computer programs which process individual transactions or enquiries on demand (while people wait), and is also known there as 'demand' or 'transaction' processing. Minicomputers were primarily designed for real-time applications, and their use extended to other control situations, for example the control of road traffic by computer-controlled traffic lights. In the transmission of electricity via the National Grid and in the distribution of natural gas over the gas network the use of computers is essential to ensure that supply matches demand.

Numerical control refers to the control of the actions of machine tools such as drills, lathes and presses, by a sequence of control signals punched onto paper tape, a principle employed some hundred years earlier in automatic looms. Originally produced by hand punching, the tape is produced by a computer in Computer Numerical Control (CNC), and eventually the signals may be sent directly to the machine (Direct Numerical Control) in a form of *Computer-Aided Manufacturing* (CAM) that is particularly important in high-precision engineering.

Computer-Aided Design (CAD) is another powerful use of a minicomputer or powerful microcomputer, in the design of products and components. Under program control, the computer displays a representation of a product in the form of a two- or three-dimensional drawing (see Fig. 4.16). It can be modified, rotated or expanded, and can be subjected to simulated tests, pressures or other forces until the designer is satisfied that the design will meet its objectives. The design can then be printed as an engineering drawing and stored away, thus replacing the conventional draughtsman. CAD is now an important tool for design engineers, architects and planners, and the stored design may also be used to generate the control sequences for CNC tools in a combination known as CADCAM, or CIM – Computer Integrated Manufacturing.

Production control is the use of a computer to plan and organise the production of parts and their assembly into goods to satisfy orders received from customers. It is really a form of data processing applied to the manufacturing rather than the administrative side of a company, and is more often called *Manufacturing Resource Planning* (MRP) in upmarket software.

Progress with minicomputers in automation was steady but unspectacular and largely unknown to the general public, until the well-publicised advent of the microprocessor – the current end-point of the on-going process of miniaturisation and large-scale integration (LSI) of electronic circuits. Microprocessors are finding widespread engineering and control applications as low-cost controllers in small domestic machines such as cars, washing machines and cameras, and finally as the control units in industrial robots and in assembly-line automation. Attempts by engineers to find a machine that could pick up and use tools as skilfully as people can, and at an affordable cost, failed until the processing power could be provided in a small and cheap form. It was the microcomputer that really pulled the robot out of science fiction into a practical reality. We now have fixed-purpose mechanical arm robots in hundreds performing welding, spraying and similar tasks (see Fig. 2.4), while the first of the general purpose robots appear to constitute the latest thing in upmarket Christmas presents for the family who has everything.

There is little doubt that the use of these computers in controlling other machines will be greatly extended as engineers learn to use them as one of their basic building blocks. For machines currently controlled by other types of device, the microprocessor is cheaper, more reliable, more flexible and has a faster response; for machines not yet taken over by the long advance of automation, microprocessors will provide all the advantages of automatic control – better quality of output and higher performance, at a lower overall cost. It is also an inevitable and long-standing consequence of automation that manual labour is dispossessed – but more about this in Chapter 10.

2.4 PERSONAL COMPUTING

The common theme running through all the different uses of computers described so far is that they are employed by public and private organisations because they can perform various tasks more effectively and therefore more economically than other machines or people; in other words they cut costs and/or improve profits. Until about five years ago the sheer

Fig 2.4 *(a) an industrial robot. (b) a domestic robot – HERO*

basic cost of a computer ruled it out as a medium of individual, educational, cultural, recreational or social enrichment. Up to that time the only opportunities for that form of non-profit-making computing was provided by multi-access computers, in which the hardware and software are designed to support a large number of simultaneously active terminals, usually by giving each terminal a short share ('time-slice') of computer time in sequence. This mechanism gives the appearance and much of the reality of continuous computer availability to terminal users. Special software also assists in making the use of multi-access terminals as simple as possible, by providing a process of question/command and answer/response between the computer user at a terminal and the computer system, a form known as interactive or conversational computing (see Chapter 7). Multi-access computer systems are highly sophisticated machines, and introduced computing to a decade of students, schoolchildren and other non-professional users. One noteworthy group of people who were able to exploit this limited and costly opportunity were a section of modern artists, who could use a computer's power to generate complex geometric patterns and create fine line-drawings, in an activity that is known as Computer Art.

However, the personal computer did not become a reality until progress in microelectronics produced the microcomputer, based on microprocessor and storage chips and interfaces to cheap and small-scale terminals. At the cheapest level there are now many models costing less than £100, using mostly TV sets or video monitors and cassette recorders as terminals. Personal computing is now a major and unique sector of the computer industry, supported by computer shops, an enormous number of magazines, cottage-style software suppliers and computer clubs. Personal computers have also made possible the growth of computing in schools; it remains to be seen whether the rhetoric which now surrounds the computer in education (see Chapter 10.2) really delivers a more educated generation. Meanwhile, the home computing mania among schoolchildren, which had reached somewhat alarming proportions, has subsided somewhat, though not to the residual level of the skateboard.

The foundation of home computing is undoubtedly the video game, employing sophisticated computer graphic displays in full colour. The common feature of a computer game is that the computer has been programmed to respond to your inputs and then display the consequences and either continue playing or even, as in Computer Chess and Draughts, make a similar move of its own. We have enjoyed computer games of a less addictive kind for many years, mostly as a diversion for bored computer programmers awaiting their next assignment, and more importantly as a means of introducing people painlessly to a computer. The computer-games manufacturers are now inventing new games of great ingenuity and technical sophistication; Space Invaders and Pacman are yesterday's favourites. The latest best sellers include computer games versions of adventures such as Dungeons and Dragons, and of quizzes and competitions such as Trivial Pursuit. The dividing line between a purely video game machine and a true home computer is a marginal one, but nearly all now allow full programming facilities.

Even at this level the personal computer permits the same type of facilities as do other and larger computers — computation, control and data handling — but obviously to a degree limited by the size and environment of personal computing. The more expensive and robust machines are therefore useful to small businesses, self-employed professional people, teachers, managers in large businesses. For this purpose they are usually sold with floppy or small hard disk devices and better-quality displays, along with pre-written programs for standard and predictable business functions.

Given the low and decreasing cost of useful personal computers and their ready availability in chain stores and even supermarkets, the supply and distribution of good-quality software remains an unsolved problem. One solution is electronic distribution of proven software from a single and central storage point — a concept known as 'Telesoftware'. This service operates over a public Videotex or other data communications facility, and transfers programs from a central 'library' computer over the link via an interface into a personal computer's memory. You need to pay a basic subscription fee and sometimes an additional sum for larger programs. There is, unfortunately, no such software supermarket for the serious adult user of a personal computer, whether for domestic, business or professional use, and the availability of software for your purpose is an essential criterion of choosing a machine from the hundreds of models available with disk storage and better quality screens for the 'business' market. At least one manufacturer (ICL), by appropriately naming it the One-Per-Desk, seeks to make it an essential piece of desktop furniture for every office desk, with software designed to assist in everyday office tasks — a business diary, jotting memos, making phone calls, preparing letters, etc. Office automation is right at the sharp end of personal computing, and is a market of enormous proportions in our increasingly white-collar economy.

Personal computing, whether for gain, leisure or pleasure, is one of the most welcome developments in modern computing, first because it offers a completely new form of leisure pursuit to help fill the increasing amount of leisure time that modern technology (computers included) will be giving us when the 35- or 30-hour working week arrives; and second because it humanises and democratises the computer as no other experience or media presentation can. When we all have a computer in the home, we will better appreciate what large computers can do for and to us, in our place of work and in the other large organisations which shape our lives.

2.5 INFORMATION SYSTEMS AND INFORMATION TECHNOLOGY

The extension of the boundaries of computing which started with the use of computers in data processing, has also been assisted by the developments in micro-electronics, two forms of which, the microprocessor and the microcomputer, have been mentioned in the earlier section of this chapter. The relative costs of this movement are interesting in that while the cost of processors has, in one estimate, been dropping at the rate of 20 per cent per year, the cost of storage has been falling at the higher rates of 30 per cent (internal storage) and 40 per cent (backing storage). The changing economics of computer hardware have been leading the computer market further away from the concept of 'processing', whether of numeric data into results or of business data onto files and documents information, and into 'information systems' of primarily information storage, retrieval and dissemination functions. The relevant French term *l'informatique* has been translated into the English 'Informatics' to attempt to redress the undoubted anomaly of 'computer' when the computation is virtually non-existent; however, the French for computer is *ordinateur*, which expresses much better the function of the computer as a rule-following (i.e. programmable) machine. It would, however, be wrong to draw too firm a boundary between data processing and information systems; most business data is also analysed and summarised in reports for use by managers, particularly in financial accounts ('Management Information Systems'), and the difference is one of balance and emphasis.

One typical and extremely common, and commercially valuable example of an information system is Circulation Control or Name-and-Address system. We are all on the receiving end of such systems, in the form of computer-printed sticky labels on letters, magazine wrappers, unsolicited advertisements, etc., and more purposefully printed at the head of apparently personal letters and circulars produced on the computer with word processing software (though sometimes with hilarious results). The sole function of this (part of a) computer application is to set up, store, select and print a (potential) customer's name and address (along with some other information relating to credit or registration status); a simplified example will be used throughout this book to illustrate some points about computer systems and programming and their impact.

Videotex is another example of an information system, whose main function in its various forms is to distribute stored information (including computer programs, as we have seen above) from a central computer to primarily domestic TV receivers via a special interface/decoder unit. Videotex systems are classified into teletext and viewdata, primarily by the form of electronic communications used. Teletext (e.g. the BBC's CEEFAX service) uses spare capacity in normal TV transmissions to send a few lines of data per cycle to build up a screen display in the interface, in a fixed sequence; the viewer may request a screenful, or 'page' of information, but has to wait until that screen is transmitted in the sequence for the interface controls to display it on the screen. Viewdata (e.g. British Telecom's Prestel service) operates over telephone lines, and sends a page immediately when a request is received. The other difference is that Teletext is currently, at least until TV is distributed through cable networks, a one-way and therefore free service, whereas Viewdata permits return of data to the remote computer, using a special Videotex (see Fig. 4.9) or normal keyboard. On Prestel, therefore, it is possible to send requests for goods or services, messages to Electronic Mailboxes, and data to a special Home Banking service run by the Bank of Scotland.

In fact, both Viewdata and Teletext primarily refer to a standard way of creating text and limited pictures on a TV screen, and that format is widely used outside the original context − e.g. in private Viewdata systems designed to use TV screens rather than other terminals and in home computers, such as the one used to compose this book, where TV monitors are also used because of their low cost. Figure 2.5 shows a typical Videotex screen.

This combination of computer technology and data communications is the essence of what has become politically known as 'Information Tech-

Fig 2.5 *a Prestel display*

nology'. This term, unfortunately abbreviated to IT, is semi-officially defined as 'the acquisition, processing storage, dissemination and use of vocal, pictorial, textual and numerical information by a microelectronics-based combination of computing and telecommunications'. Jargon-ridden as this definition may be, Information Technology does convey a change of emphasis away from conventional static computing into an acceptance that the communication of stored information is a fundamental objective of computing. Thus for a user of Ceefax or Prestel the location of the computer which holds the stored information and may accept a response is immaterial; it is the immediate availability of stored information in the home that is the essence of the service. A similar shift of emphasis is evident within Word Processing, where communication between word processors both within and between companies is seen as one of their main objectives, one of the forms of 'electronic mail' which could take us into the automated, paperless office. Electronic mail services are offered in most public Viewdata systems and by telecommunications companies such as British Telecom (BT Gold) and Cable & Wireless (Easylink), both of which can also be used in place of the long-established Telex service.

Finally, computers and telecommunications have also contributed to the objectives of *collecting and disseminating knowledge*. It is often said that automation is changing our way of life from a labour-based society to a knowledge-based society, and therefore the organisation of knowledge bases must make a significant contribution to this process. Traditionally, our formal knowledge has been written in books, stored in book libraries, with a passive information service. Increasingly, references to, and abstracts of, knowledge are stored in very large bibliographic or statistical databases, and are available for searching and retrieval via a terminal. There are both disciplinary and inter-disciplinary banks of data (databases) available, covering most branches of science, technology and business, while details of most books published in the United Kingdom since 1950 and in the United States since 1968 are available through the British Museum's BLAISE system. More recently databases of Statute and Case Law, such as LEXIS and EUROLEX, have been established to help lawyers determine points of law and legal precedents.

The extension of on-line databases to text storage and display, either on microfilm or on Prestel terminals, has led to predictions about the eventual disappearance of printed books and newspapers altogether. Without agreeing with such a far-fetched prediction, the fact that computers are bound to have some impact on our organisation, and therefore perspective, of knowledge shows how far we have come in forty years from the days of the automatic calculator. How one machine can extend its functions so far is one of the main themes to be explored in succeeding chapters.

2.6 COMPUTERS AND TRAVEL

To illustrate some of the many and varied uses of computers in our chosen sector of the leisure industry — the holiday business, let us consider a typical family arranging and starting out on their annual holiday abroad. Fig. 2.6 shows a typical sequence of activities for this purpose, in a graphical form that is not unique to computing but is very widely used within it — the flowchart (for more details of which see Chapters 6 and 7). At this stage the flowchart and what it shows should be reasonably self-explanatory. Each of the following paragraphs describes some of the more important incidences of computer usage and applications in the sequence of activites shown in the corresponding box in the flowchart.

1. Like many personal purchases, decisions about leisure travel are likely to be triggered off by the appearance of advertisements in the media, particularly on television, many of which are now created by clever computer graphics. Images are created in electronic rather than in photographic frames and then replayed in video form. There is, in fact, a major combination of these two forms, in the shape of interactive video, stored in digital form on compact discs and selected for individual replay.

   These commercials, like other forms of persuasion, exploit the situation, for instance emphasising sunshine in the middle of winter when the weather reports and forecasts so graphically show cold, wind and rain. Most weather forecasts are produced by large-scale processing of weather recordings from various parts of the world, and are brought to our screens again by an elegant application of computer graphics.

2. These holidays are offered to the public by transport and tour operators as 'packages' of travel and accommodation. Their holiday brochures contain descriptions and photographs of resorts and accommodation. Glossily and expensively printed, most of these brochures will have been created in draft form on some type of word processor before delivery to the printer. These brochures also give travel timetables — departure and arrival times of the charter flights which make it possible to offer packaged holidays at prices well below the 'normal' air ticket cost. The low cost of chartered air flight is achieved by scheduling the aircraft to be in operation for as high a proportion of the day and week as possible, and their crews to work their maximum legally permitted hours with the minimum of waiting and travelling to pick-up their aircraft. Such scheduling is often, and best, performed using complex mathematical models to evaluate the alternative schedules and determine the best schedule — something which, like the rest of this type of work ('operational research') can only be realistically performed on a computer.

Fig 2.6 *a flow chart of arranging and starting a holiday abroad*

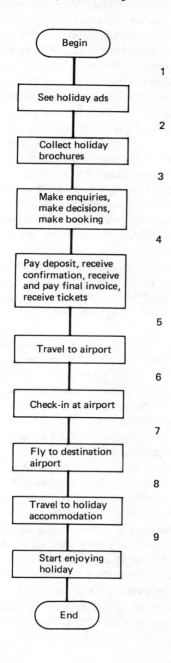

3. Descriptive information is also published electronically in the public Videotex services, or on private Viewdata systems that can also be accessed from a suitably modified TV set. Information that can be requested from the remote computer includes the holiday programmes, prices and sometimes the current availability, and the service may also be able to take requests for brochures, temporary reservations ('options') and even full bookings. Alternatively our family, or a travel agent, will be able to telephone a tour operator for advice and information, and the call will be taken by an operator sitting in front of a computer terminal which will display the required information and accepts requests.

4. At the end of this process it is usually necessary, for legal purposes, to complete and sign a booking form which has been designed, as many forms have, to make it as easy as possible to transfer data into a computer. From that point onwards virtually all of the processing of that booking will be done automatically by the computer; a record of that booking will be created, the availability of transport and accommodation adjusted, the travel agent's commission calculated and credited to his account, the family's name and address stored away separately for later use. Subsequently, at the appropriate time, the tour operator's computer will send a final invoice, print tickets, and send operating lists to the charter company, hotel manager and local representatives or couriers.

5. On the day of departure our family will have to travel to the airport. If they go by road they will probably be travelling in a vehicle designed using a CAD system, partly assembled by robots from components that may have been produced on a numerically controlled machine, along motorways with warning lights that are instantaneously set up from computer when an emergency occurs. Their car may even, if it is an expensive top-of-the-range model, have a trip computer under the dashboard and a microprocessor finely adjusting the flow of petrol and air to the engine. Alternatively they may travel in a computer-designed high-speed train through computer-generated signals, on a timetable produced by computer; or on a computer-driven underground train with computerised ticket issuing and checking devices at the station.

6. At the airport, the tour operator or charter company's check-in desk will be expecting them from information supplied by the tour operator's computer, and at the larger airports the process of checking that all the expected passengers have arrived, of identifying who is missing, and of filling any empty seats from a waiting list of 'standby' passengers, may be done by a local computer system. Similarly, the computer will accumulate the weight of passengers' luggage, both to ensure that the

aircraft is not overloaded, but mainly to compute the weight of additional cargo that can be carried on board up to the safe load limit. The airport itself will show flight arrivals and departures, and other flight information, on large displays around the passenger concourse. Similar displays may be found all around the airport, giving flight information required, for instance, by the baggage handlers, the airport police and fire service, the ground movement crews, etc., from a central source of information held on the airport's computer.

7. When all the passengers are on board, the aircraft is ready to leave, and the captain will await clearance from Air Traffic Control (ATC). At most busy airports, the air traffic controllers will use a computer to monitor the streams of arriving and departing aircraft and to maintain a correct and safe sequence among the aircraft queuing to take off and touch down. Again on most modern aircraft the flight plan will have been pre-computed in relation to the appropriate navigational signal beacons and fed to the aircraft's Inertia Navigation System, so that immediately after take-off the captain may put his aircraft on the automatic pilot. This complex of three flight computers will maintain the preset direction, speed and altitude and will signal an alarm at the point of passing the beasons on to which it has been locked. Other computer systems may, in conjunction with the arrival airport's ATC and radar systems, automatically land the aircraft using its Instrument Landing System.

8. At the destination, our family will find that the tour operator's local couriers will be expecting them and will put them on to a coach for their hotel or apartment, the operators of which will also be expecting them, in both cases from information supplied by the tour operator's computer. Holiday and travel companies transmit large volumes of data around the world, and the major airlines collectively own and operate a computer-based international data communications sytem, which, among other services, keeps a record of all personal luggage that is mislaid or lost in transit. (Our family will be happy not to need this help.) Smaller companies will mostly use the international telex service, which itself is about to be extended into a higher level Teletex service using microcomputers as sending and receiving devices.

9. Finally our family arrives, after a journey which has been smoothed throughout by the digital computer. At this point we now hope that the computer will not in any way intrude into their holiday, except perhaps when they go into a bank to change currency or traveller's cheques, where they may find the calculations performed and printed out by a small computer. For the hotelier and the charter company, however, the story does not end there; they will eventually be paid for

their services to the family on holiday by a cheque or money draft printed by the tour operator's computer, which will then be credited to their own account held on their bank's computer.

Fig 2.7 *changing your money*

```
                 BANCO  CENTRAL  S.A.
                       CIF A-28000446
                 DEPARTAMENTO EXTRANJERO CAMBIO DE MONEDA

      OFICINA NO: SUCURSAL DENIA              FECHA : 09.01.1987

                        COMPRA  DE  TALONES
         M O N E D A         CANTIDAD      CAMBIO         CONTRAVALOR
         LIBRA ESTERLINA      40.00       194.016            7.761

      T.CONTRAVALOR   COMISION     IMP.COMISION       GASTOS      LIQUIDO
          7.761     0.15+ 1.00%      350(MIN)                     7.411
                                                              =============
                        A  PABAR  POR  CAJA
         PETICIONARIO     : MR G.L. WRIGHT
         DOMICILIO        : THOMAS COOK N BC37264255
         PASAPORTE-D.N.I. : INGLES N198918B

                         THANK YOU -MERCI -GRACIAS-DANKE SCHON

       NO DE DOCUMENTO                          RECIBI
          1  /   3
```

SPECIMEN QUESTIONS

1. Explain the difference between data and information. What attributes must information possess to be of value?

2. What is meant by a real-time system and how does it differ from a conventional computer system? Give one example of a real-time system, clearly stating its hardware configuration and software requirements.   *

3. What are the major characteristics of a microprocessor? Why are these characteristics of particular value in the field of control applications?   *

4. Give a detailed definition of data processing. What additional features are implied by the newer term 'information processing'?

5. Write an account of a computer installation or application that you have studied. Include in your answer: (i) the hardware used, (ii) how and why the computer is used, (iii) two advantages that using the computer has brought for the user, (iv) any disadvantages of the application.   *

6. What is 'word processing'? Account for the origin and growth of WP as an area of computer usage.

7. Define 'information technology', and give four examples of it in action.

HOW THE COMPUTER
WORKS

The survey of computer usage in the previous chapter has emphasised the diversity of computer applications and the versatility of the computer. Three factors make this possible and this chapter deals with two of them. The first is the way that data of many different types, arising from different sources, is represented and handled within the computer; the second is the way that program instructions in a computer program are able to perform the processing of that data.

3.1 DATA REPRESENTATION

(a) The binary system

The fundamental form in which *all* information – numbers, characters, and program instructions – is handled in the computer is the binary number form.

In everyday life quantities are normally represented in multiples of ten – 'decimal' counting or counting to 'base' ten. This sytem goes back into prehistory and comes naturally to a human being who has a total of ten fingers and thumbs on his two hands. It is not the only system in general use, however, and until recently the English-speaking world used the Imperial system of measures, which has a bewildering assortment of bases:

> 2 pints to a quart;
> 3 feet to a yard;
> 14 pounds to the stone;
> 16 ounces to the pound, etc.

In the binary system, the base is 2, and it therefore has only two figures, 0 and 1. In the decimal system, there are no figures higher than 9, so whenever 1 is added to a 9 in any order (or column), the 9 is changed to 0 and 1 is added to the next higher order. In binary, where there is no figure greater than 1, this change has to happen more frequently. In decimal the orders are often called

... thousands, hundreds, tens, units

which can be represented as powers of ten

... $10^3, 10^2, 10^1, 10^0$

In binary the orders can be called

... eights, fours, twos, units

and represented as powers of 2

... $2^3, 2^2, 2^1, 2^0$

The logic of the binary system can be seen by studying the following numbers and their decimal equivalents.

	Binary	Decimal
	0	0
1 in the units column	1	1
1 in the twos column, 0 in the units column	10	2
1 in the twos column, 1 in the units column	11	3
1 in the fours column, 0 in the twos column, 0 in the units column	100	4
	101	5
etc.	110	6
	111	7
	1000	8
	1001	9
	1010	10
	1011	11
	1100	12
	1101	13
	1110	14
	1111	15
	10000	16

The use of the binary system in a digital computer is essential, because whereas man has ten fingers and thumbs to count on, it is inconvenient to represent this in electronic circuits. In the computer, only two electrical states are used — *on* and *off* — which represent, variously, high or low voltage, the presence or absence of an electrical pulse, the presence or absence of a magnetised force. This two-state system, on/off, present/absent, is eminently suitable for machine recognition and recording in both electronic and mechanical equipment.

(b) Integers (whole numbers)

It has already been stated that the byte is the basic unit of data held in a computer's memory. As each binary digit ('bit', to distinguish it from decimal digit) within the byte will be either 1 or 0 then it follows that the information coded within that byte will range from 00000000 to 11111111. In early computers only integer numbers were stored and, in fact, in the very cheapest of the modern microcomputers only integer numbers are handled. If the 8 bits of a byte are used to store integers then there has to be some order about the way in which the pattern of bits is to be interpreted. One bit has to be used to signify whether the number is positive or negative. 0 is used to signify positive and 1 for negative. This means that the largest possible positive integer stored in one byte will be represented by:

$$01111111$$

which is $2^7 - 1 = 127$. Negative numbers are represented by what is called 'two's complement form'. This involves writing the binary equivalent of a decimal number and then changing every 0 to a 1 and every 1 to a 0. Then 1 is added to the result. It sounds complicated but in fact is quite easy. For example: to obtain the binary equivalent of the decimal number −17 we proceed as follows:

Expressed in binary form the number 17 is 10001.

If we are going to express the number in byte form we pad it out so that there are 8 bits, that is, 00010001. Now changing 1s to 0s and 0s to 1s we get 11101110; then add 1 giving 11101111.

This bit pattern will now represent the decimal number −17 in two's complement form.

The largest negative integer which can be stored within one byte is 10000000 which is the equivalent of -2^7. In order to demonstrate that this system works let us add together the bit patterns for +20 and −17. +20 is represented by 00010100 and −17 by 11101111 as we have already seen. If we add them together we get:

$$00010100$$
$$+\ 11101111$$
$$00000011$$

this answer being the binary equivalent to +3, which is correct.

The rules of binary arithmetic used in this example are quite simple and are:

$$0 + 0 = 0$$
$$0 + 1 = 1$$
$$1 + 0 = 1$$
$$1 + 1 = 0 \text{ and } 1 \text{ to carry}$$

The byte can only hold a fixed number of binary digits so if there is a digit to carry when the two leading digits are added this carry digit is discarded deliberately.

In the same way we can subtract 20 from 17 using the same technique by adding the bit patterns for +17 and −20 together:

$$00010001 \quad (+17)$$
$$+\ 11101100 \quad (-20)$$
$$11111101$$

We can see that the answer is in fact the bit pattern for −3 since if we reverse the two's complement procedure:

subtract 1: 11111100

change: 00000011 giving the bit pattern for +3

The above examples use 8 bits, but most minicomputers use 16 bits (2 bytes) to store integers and by the same conventions the largest positive integer stored would be $2^{15} - 1 = 32\,767$ and the largest negative integer would be $-2^{15} = 32\,768$.

(c) Mixed numbers

The conventional way of representing mixed numbers (numbers which contain a whole number part and a decimal part) is to use what is called *floating point format*. In order to do this the number is given three characteristics: its sign, its significant digits and its size. In order to achieve a satisfactory degree of accuracy at least 32 bits (4 bytes) are needed to store a floating point number. As with integers the sign bit is the first, or more significant, bit and 0 indicates a positive number and 1 a negative number. But before a number is stored in its 4 bytes it has to be *normalised* or put into a standard form. This generally takes the form of writing the number in the form:

$$A \times 10^{k}$$

where A is a number in the range 1 to 9. This number is called the *mantissa* (familiar to those who struggled with logarithm tables at school). The power of 10, k, is called the exponent. If all numbers are reduced to this standard form then we can dispense with decimal points and the ten since their absolute values can always be calculated from a knowledge of the mantissa and exponent.

For example the number 135 can be written as:

$$1.35 \times 10^2$$

and the only parts of the number which need to be stored are the digits 1.35 and the exponent, which is 2. In fact, to make the storage of floating point numbers easier for the computer to handle, the exponent is usually stored in what is called an *excess* form. If it is stored in excess -64 form then 64 is added to the exponent and the resulting number is stored. This avoids wasting a bit to give the sign of the exponent and allows exponents ranging in size from -64 to $+64$ to be stored. As an example, the number -0.0000005438 will be first normalised to:

$$-5.438 \times 10^{-7}$$

and the number stored as:

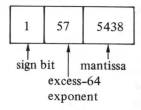

As a compromise to using the binary system — good for computers, difficult for us — much use is made in computing of both octal and hexadecimal numbers. The octal system uses the base of 8 and its numbers are expressed using the digits 0 to 7. The hexadecimal system (hex for short) uses a base of 16 and has to add the characters A, B, C, D, E, F to the usual ten digits of the decimal system. The letters stand for the numbers 10, 11, 12, 13, 14, 15. The relationship between the four systems is shown in Table 3.1.

(d) Character representation

Because of the prevalence of non-numerical data in modern computing, particularly in information processing which is almost totally non-numerical, the way we store and represent what are usually known as 'characters' is of particular importance. In simple terms a character is anything that is represented by the depression of a key on a keyboard, a pattern of holes across a punched paper tape or a pattern of holes in one column of a

Table 3.1

Decimal	Binary	Octal	Hex
0	0	0	0
1	1	1	1
2	10	2	2
3	11	3	3
4	100	4	4
5	101	5	5
6	110	6	6
7	111	7	7
8	1000	10	8
9	1001	11	9
10	1010	12	A
11	1011	13	B
12	1100	14	C
13	1101	15	D
14	1110	16	E
15	1111	17	F
16	10000	20	10
17	10001	21	11
18	10010	22	12
19	10011	23	13
20	10100	24	14
21	10101	25	15
22	10110	26	16
23	10111	27	17
24	11000	30	18
25	11001	31	19
26	11010	32	1A
27	11011	33	1B
28	11100	34	1C
29	11101	35	1D
30	11110	36	1E
31	11111	37	1F
32	100000	40	20

punched card. These characters can be numeric (0 to 9), alphabetic (A to Z), symbols such as (, ? @ / " * =), or control characters. Control characters are characters which have to be sent to devices such as printers to tell them where the printing head should go next (for example to the start of the next line — the carriage-return/line-feed character). Other characters can be sent to video screens to tell the controller to clear the screen or make certain characters blink on and off.

One of the commonest codes used for transmitting characters is the 7-bit international alphabet — American Standard Code for Information Interchange (ASCII). Fig. 3.1 shows the ASCII code and the equivalents of the binary codes for the various characters in both hex and octal form.

Fig 3.1(a) *character representation in the ASCII code*

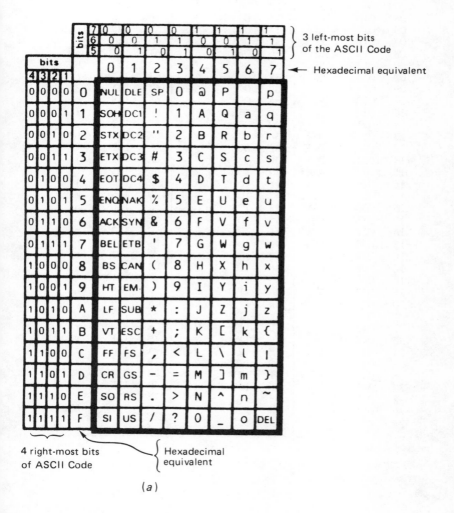

(a)

Fig 3.1(b) *character representation in the ASCII code*

Hex	7-bit Octal	ASCII	Hex	7-bit Octal	ASCII	Hex	7-bit Octal	ASCII
00	000	NUL	2B	053	+	56	126	V
01	001	SOH	2C	054	,	57	127	W
02	002	STX	2D	055	-	58	130	X
03	003	ETX	2E	056	.	59	131	Y
04	004	EOT	2F	057	/	5A	132	Z
05	005	ENQ	30	060	0	5B	133	[
06	006	ACK	31	061	1	5C	134	\
07	007	BEL	32	062	2	5D	135	]
08	010	BS	33	063	3	5E	136	↑
09	011	HT	34	064	4	5F	137	←
0A	012	LF	35	065	5	60	140	
0B	013	VT	36	066	6	61	141	a
0C	014	FF	37	067	7	62	142	b
0D	015	CR	38	070	8	63	143	c
0E	016	SO	39	071	9	64	144	d
0F	017	SI	3A	072	:	65	145	e
10	020	DLE	3B	073	;	66	146	f
11	021	DC1	3C	074	<	67	147	g
12	022	DC2	3D	075	=	68	150	h
13	023	DC3	3E	076	>	69	151	i
14	024	DC4	3F	077	?	6A	152	j
15	025	NAK	40	100	@	6B	153	k
16	026	SYN	41	101	A	6C	154	l
17	027	ETB	42	102	B	6D	155	m
18	030	CAN	43	103	C	6E	156	n
19	031	EM	44	104	D	6F	157	o
1A	032	SUB	45	105	E	70	160	p
1B	033	ESC	46	106	F	71	161	q
1C	034	FS	47	107	G	72	162	r
1D	035	GS	48	110	H	73	163	s
1E	036	RS	49	111	I	74	164	t
1F	037	US	4A	112	J	75	165	u
20	040	SP	4B	113	K	76	166	v
21	041	!	4C	114	L	77	167	w
22	042	"	4D	115	M	78	170	x
23	043	#	4E	116	N	79	171	y
24	044	$	4F	117	O	7A	172	z
25	045	%	50	120	P	7B	173	{
26	046	&	51	121	Q	7C	174	|
27	047	'	52	122	R	7D	175	}
28	050	(	53	123	S	7E	176	~
29	051	)	54	124	T	7F	177	DEL
2A	052	*	55	125	U			

(b)

(e) Graphic data representation

Representing graphic data (i.e. pictures) is based on the same principles as that used in representing moving pictures on a conventional TV screen. The screen, or an area of paper, is considered to consist of a matrix, or 'raster' of dots, just as a sheet of graph paper is made up of a matrix of small squares. Each dot is known as a 'pixel', an abbreviation of 'picture element', and for each pixel the computer must know what colour the electron gun must put in that position. In a two-colour system (i.e. black-and-white) the computer needs to know only white/not white, which requires 1 bit of information for each pixel; to show colour the computer needs to know at least 3 bits, one for each of the Red, Green and Blue guns, and additonal data is required to display different intensity and colour combinations. A powerful graphic display, such as that shown in Fig. 4.19, would contain about 1000 x 800 pixels, and the computer could hold in special memory 24 bits per pixel which would give over 16 million colour combinations per pixel. The same principles apply to graphic printers, except that the range of colours ('palette') is more limited and each colour requires an individual pen or a band on a multi-colour ribbon.

To display or print a picture it is therefore necessary to tell the computer which bit combinations are needed for each of the pixels. This would in many cases be extremely tedious, so that in some cases where less precise pictures are needed with less effort, the screen may be divided up into larger basic units usually identical to that in which one character would normally occupy, e.g. a 16 x 16 dot matrix, and a library of standard shapes is provided — square, triangle, semi-circle, etc. — to which a unique code value is ascribed. In some microcomputers it is possible to create your own set of shapes in this way. Prestel and the Teletext services in Britain constructs crude pictures on a screen divided into 24 x 40 such units, into which can be placed either a data character or a picture character. Fig. 3.2 shows the combined data and picture code used. The picture characters are composed on a 6 x 2 block matrix, and for obvious reasons are described as 'mosaics'.

3.2 THE PROCESSOR AND PROGRAMS

(a) Program instructions

We have already seen that everything stored inside or understood by a computer must be in digital form. We have also seen earlier in this chapter that all the data which the computer is required to handle can be recorded in its storage in digital form. It then follows that the program instructions held in the computer's storage prior to their execution must be stored in a similar digital format consisting of 'packets' of binary digits. A machine-code instruction, which is the ultimate form of any program instruction

Fig 3.2 the Viewdata character set

B7	0	0	0		0		1		1		1		1	
B6	0	0	1		1		0		0		1		1	
B5	0	1	0		1		0		1		0		1	
B4 B3 B2 B1 / COL Row	0	1	2	2a	3	3a	4	4a	5	5a	6	6a	7	7a
0 0 0 0 0	NUL		Sp		0		@	NUL	P	DLE	—		p	
0 0 0 1 1		DC1	!		1		A	ALPHA RED	Q	GRAPHICS RED	a		q	
0 0 1 0 2		DC2	"		2		B	ALPHA GREEN	R	GRAPHICS GREEN	b		r	
0 0 1 1 3		DC3	£		3		C	ALPHA YELLOW	S	GRAPHICS YELLOW	c		s	
0 1 0 0 4		DC4	$		4		D	ALPHA BLUE	T	GRAPHICS BLUE	d		t	
0 1 0 1 5	ENQ		%		5		E	ALPHA MAGENTA	U	GRAPHICS MAGENTA	e		u	
0 1 1 0 6			&		6		F	ALPHA CYAN	V	GRAPHICS CYAN	f		v	
0 1 1 1 7			'		7		G	ALPHA WHITE	W	GRAPHICS WHITE	g		w	
1 0 0 0 8	BS	CANCEL	(		8		H	FLASH	X	CONCEAL	h		x	
1 0 0 1 9	HT		)		9		I	STEADY	Y	CONTIGUOUS GRAPHICS	i		y	
1 0 1 0 10	LF		*		:		J	END BOX	Z	SEPARATED GRAPHICS	j		z	
1 0 1 1 11	VT	ESC	+		;		K	START BOX	←		k		.	
1 1 0 0 12	FF		,		<		L	NORMAL HEIGHT	$\frac{1}{2}$	BLACK BACKGROUND	l		||	
1 1 0 1 13	CR		—		=		M	DOUBLE HEIGHT	→	NEW BACKGROUND	m		3.	
1 1 1 0 14	CURSOR HOME		.		>		N		↑	HOLD GRAPHICS	n		÷	
1 1 1 1 15			/		?		O		♯	RELEASE GRAPHICS	o			

COLUMNS 2a, 3a, 6a, 7a produced after Graphics select code
COLUMNS 4a, 5a produced after ESC code

before it can be acted upon by the computer, will probably consist of a set of bit patterns arranged in a series of 'fields':

Operation	Modification	Operand	Operand	. . .

The bit pattern contained in the *operation field* holds the code (*operation code*, opcode for short) that instructs the computer to perform one of its available operations such as ADD, SUBTRACT, STORE, LOAD, and so on. These operations are detailed in every computer's *instruction set*. This is the set of operations defined by the designer as being those he wants his computer to perform. The *modification field* will be dealt with in Section 3.2 (e). The *operand field* of the instruction can be one of a number of things. It could be:

- the address of a location of internal storage which contains the data to be processed or into which the results of processing are to be placed (or both);

- the number of a register, which is a special set of storage locations used to hold values or to hold data for significant purposes in a computer (see next section);
- a command to an external device in an I/O instruction;
- the number of a peripheral device (what is often called its 'logical' address, that is, the line printer may be device 12 and a particular disc drive device 76);
- the address of a storage location which contains *another* instruction.

An instruction may be referred to by the number of operands it contains, for example a two-address instruction or a three-address instruction. A three-address instruction might say 'add the contents of location 203 to the contents of location 467 and place the result in location 124'.

When loaded into internal storage ready for execution each instruction may be referred to by the address of the first storage location into which it has been loaded. This is because each instruction takes up more than 1 byte, and it is generally the bytes which are separately addressed, so that if an instruction takes up 4 bytes and the first byte is in address number 304 then we will refer to it as the instruction in 304.

The general sequence of events which takes place when a program instruction is executed is in two parts. These are called the FETCH and the EXECUTE phases of the instruction cycle.

During the FETCH phase the instruction address is computed, the instruction is fetched into an instruction register, the effective addresses of the operands are computed and the operands are fetched and placed into the appropriate registers. The EXECUTE phase consists of performing the operations denoted by the opcode on the operands, computing the effective address for storing the result, and storing the result.

Depending on their size, computers can have an instruction set containing as many as 350 different types of instruction, many of which are rarely used. In order to simplify the internal structure of the processors, many are now being designed with a subset of the full instruction set and are thus known as Reduced Instruction Set Computers (RISC).

(b) Registers

Registers are special storage locations within the central processing unit usually capable of storing one or two bytes at a time. The six main registers in the CPU are:

(i) *The CPU instruction register*, which holds the instruction currently being executed and has to be sufficiently long to hold a complete instruction.

(ii) *The instruction address register*, which holds the address of the next instruction to be executed. This is usually the next instruction in sequence or, if not, it will be the address of an instruction being

BRANCHED to out of sequence. This address will be placed there during the EXECUTE cycle if a jump out of sequence is made. It is sometimes called the *program counter* or *sequence control register*.

(iii) *The general-purpose registers*, often called *accumulators*, which may be used to hold data for temporary storage or for intermediate results. There is always one accumulator into which data is placed after some CPU operation, usually of an arithmetic nature.

(iv) *The storage address register* and *storage data register*, which are used to hold the address and contents respectively of a storage reference instruction prior to data being placed into a location or transferred from it. They are sometimes called *buffer* registers.

(v) *The peripheral registers*. Every peripheral device contains a register which is used in the same way as the storage data register; the I/O mechanism of these devices feeds data to, or takes data from, their register which is itself operated upon by an I/O instruction — or more precisely, an I/O instruction *starts* the transfer of data into/out of a peripheral register after/before the device/mechanism fills/uses it.

(vi) *The status register*. The CPU also contains special one-bit registers, known as *flip-flops* or *flags*. They are used to indicate the state or condition of some part of the computer. Such a condition may be an emergency or unusual situation and one which may require either hardware of software action. These flags are often grouped together into a status register, whose content at any one time will indicate the aggregate condition of the CPU and its peripherals.

Fig. 3.3 shows schematically the way that registers and storage are used to control and execute the operation of program instructions in a processor.

Registers and the program instruction cycle

The execution of a program stored in internal storage follows a very clearly defined pattern which is detailed as follows.

- **Step 0** — when a program is loaded and made ready for execution, the leading address of the storage locations occupied by the *first* instruction is loaded into the instruction address register (IAR);

- **Step 1** — the instruction to be found at that address is loaded into the instruction register, and the address of the *next* instruction (always assumed to be the next in sequence) is loaded into the IAR:

- **Step 2** — the instruction in the instruction register then proceeds through its fetch and execute phases, using other registers if appropriate to that instruction;

- **Step 3** — at the end of the execute phase, the program will either stop, if it is an END or STOP instruction, or it will confirm the address of the next instruction to be executed; if it is not the address already stored in the IAR (for example, if the current instruction is an unconditional

Fig 3.3 *registers and instruction execution*

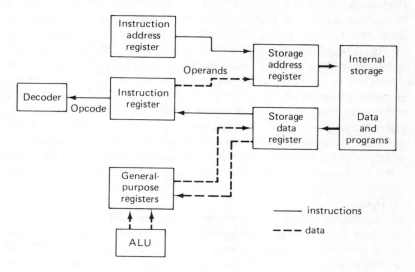

branch), the contents of the IAR will be modified to show the address of the instruction to be branched to out of linear sequence;

– **Step 4** – go to step 1.

The timing of these subsequences is controlled by time pulses issued by the system clock. The speed of the clock is a common descriptor of a processor and is usually expressed in millions of cycles per second or megahertz (MH) in SI terminology. The microprocessor shown in Fig. 1.8 has a clock speed of 16.67 MH. The number of pulses per instruction and thus the total instruction timing, is determined by the number of separate (micro) operations in the fetch and execute phases, added to the fixed times for the rest of the cycle.

(c) Operation decoding

The computer may thus be considered as a system for routing data movements and transfers between significant areas of storage and peripherals – for which purpose storage may also, in smaller machines particularly, be considered as a (special) peripheral device. Only a small number of the instructions in any machine's instruction set will entail the routing of the data through the ALU as part of the detailed action required by the operation. The exact sequence of functions required by each instruction is determined by passing the operation code to a decoder, for which purpose the construction of the opcode sometimes contains bit patterns to indicate whether for instance, an opcode is a register–register or storage–register instruction.

The physical implementation of an operation may be *either* by 'hard' electronics, or by the generation of the appropriate set of lower-level instructions known as *micro-instructions*. Sometimes a combination of these two forms is found, in which case the processor is described as having microcode assist(ance). In this respect, the decoder is itself designed to be rather like a CPU. In certain machines, these micro-instructions may themselves be available to a programmer who may use them to write complete programs or to compose his own equivalent of basic machine instructions. Such machines are known as microprogrammable computers, and microprograms written to implement special machine instructions are known in the trade as 'middleware' or 'firmware' because they represent a middle position between 'hardware' and 'software'. Such microprograms reside in control stores composed of read-only storage [see Section 3.3(d)].

(d) Data buses

The significant sections of a computer, both internally and externally, are linked by data buses or data highways, each register being connected to one or more buses of parallel wires or printed circuit tracks, and a CPU can be also considered to be a system of data buses. Data transfers occur by the opening of 'gates' from registers to the buses. The arrangement of registers and buses in any computer is largely the result of the 'architecture' (that is, the operational blueprint) of a particular make of computer and represents the main way in which a particular instruction set is implemented.

Internal data buses have a width usually corresponding to the word length (the number of bits of storage in one uniquely addressed location of internal storage), and there will be several buses depending on the maximum number of operands that can be contained in an instruction. In Fig. 3.4 there is a main bus connecting all the registers, and a subsidiary bus from the storage data registers to the ALU. The storage bus connects the storage registers to internal storage.

(e) Address generation

The contents of the operand field(s) are of course one of the significant pieces of data that are transferred from storage to registers along the data buses, and the length of the fields therefore needs to conform to the common structure. Thus it is very unusual for an operand field to be greater than 16 bits wide. Nevertheless it has to 'contain' the numerical value of any storage address location and of any register and peripheral device address.

Since there are usually no more than 16 registers, 4 bits are enough to contain a *register address*, so that a storage–register or register–storage instruction is sometimes known as a $1\frac{1}{2}$ address instruction. Eight bits will be adequate for a device address. However, even 16 bits will not be enough to contain directly the whole range of storage address values. The maximum value that can be held in 16 bits is $2^{16} - 1$ (assuming all values to be positive), which is well below the storage capacity of most computers today. In fact, all addresses start from the value 0 upwards so that a 16-bit register can directly address the full complement of 2^{16} locations.

There are, therefore, several ways in which the operand field can indirectly contain the information which will enable the real or 'effective' address of an operand to be generated (by using other values contained in one or more registers, or even in other storage locations) outside the range which it can directly address itself. These methods are of interest to computer programmers writing programs in machine-code instructions. The use of the modification field in an instruction is to indicate which type of address generation is to be used (usually by hardware) to calculate the effective address.

(f) The processor and the ALU

From these descriptions of how program instructions are performed, it is evident that the significant parts of a processor are:
- registers and gates;
- data buses;
- instruction or micro-instruction decoder;
- ALU.

Fig. 3.4 shows a highly simplified structure of a processor linking all these features. The list of features shows the ALU as only one of the functional subunits of a processor, through which only a proportion of instructions are routed. Additional subunits may be provided for particular purposes, for instance hardware floating point arithmetic, and even fast array (non-serial) arithmetic units for enhanced arithmetical work. The ALU is however the most complex unit in the processor, and computer arithmetic is one of the most difficult tasks for the processor because of the range of number types, and because of the conditions which may occur during arithmetic, for example, rounding, justification, overflow or underflow, or attempting to divide by zero. The ALU therefore uses the condition flags [see Section 3.2 (b) (vi) above] to signify error conditions occurring in the course of arithmetic and logical operations.

(g) The processor and the transistor

A transistor is an electronic device that was invented in 1948, and has subsequently been the fundamental building block for all types of processor. It relies on the peculiar qualities of a class of material known as a semiconductor — halfway between an insulator and a conductor. A thin

Fig 3.4 *a simple processor*

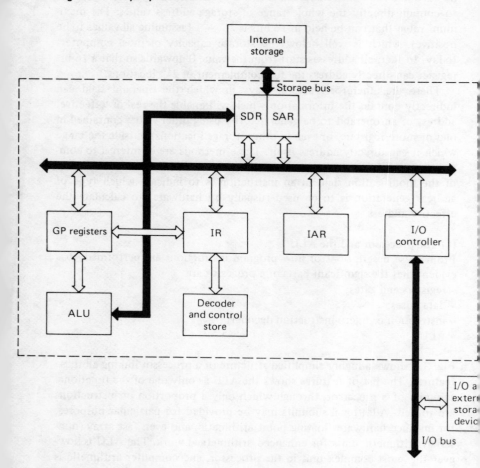

wafer (about 1 micron thick and 5 mm square) of this material — silicon, germanium or gallium arsenide — is coated with a metal oxide which is then etched away to allow a pattern to be formed on the surface of the wafer. This treatment produces three regions with different atomic characteristics, such that when an electric current is passed through them the device can act as a very fast and low-energy switch, and can also amplify and retain a low-value signal. The transistor could therefore be used, in computers just as in our radios, to replace the original thermionic valves of the first computers.

Since then, engineers have found various ways of combining transistors to form the basic logical circuits of a processor, and of aggregating them to hold binary data as registers and ultimately for use as internal storage (see next section). They have also been able to manufacture these combinations of transistors, along with the connecting buses, in an ever smaller and denser ('integrated') form on a single wafer, with the result that all of the structure of the processor shown within the dotted lines in Fig. 3.4 can be produced in the same medium, on a single chip. This is then mounted on a ceramic tray with connector pins which fit into sockets on a circuit board for connection to input and output buses.

3.3 INTERNAL STORAGE

Internal storage, or 'main memory', is used to hold information for temporary or semi-permanent use inside a computer, in particular the following types:

(i) programs that are currently or intermittently active;
(ii) data read from external storage being processed;
(iii) intermediate results of calculations ('working storage');
(iv) tables of values that are required continuously, e.g. days of the week and months of the year;
(v) other software and data required by the computer ('system software').

The principal operational requirements of internal storage are that the information, once placed into internal storage ('stored') should be safe and unharmed as long as it is wanted for use, and secondly that it should be retrievable immediately on valid request. Various forms of electronic devices have been used in the past for this purpose, but all have been swept away in the last few years by storage composed of the same type of material used in the microprocessor — banks of transistors made in highly integrated form and known as 'solid state' memory or 'semiconductor' storage. In fact this term covers a range of different forms, or families, of transistor-based logic, and one reason for its superiority over earlier types of storage such as magnetic core is the way in which different types of semiconductor storage can be selected to meet specific needs and match up to differing performance requirements.

(a) Performance criteria

(i) Speed

The access time of a storage system is the time interval between the receipt of a request for a storage reference from the command and the completion of the operations required to place the data in the storage data register. The access width is the number of bits retrieved in a storage reference request, which when multiplied by the access time gives the memory speed in bytes per second. The cycle time of a storage system is the minimum time interval between two such operations on the same storage location. Access time is typically of the order of 10 to 500 ns, and is the same regardless of the storage address, even in large memories of 16 megabytes or more (a concept known somewhat misleadingly as 'Random Access'). The access time of a storage system needs to match the internal speed of the processor (regulated by the processor clock) and semiconductor storage provides such a range of speeds.

(ii) Retention of data

It is necessary for internal storage to retain the binary data values stored in it for as long as a running program requires to use them. It is also highly desirable for the storage not to lose its values during an involuntary or unavoidable loss of electrical power, or even a brief surge in the voltage such as that caused by a flash of lightning overhead. Storage that loses its data immediately power is lost is known as volatile; the opposite is permanent or non-volatile. Volatile storage can be given a temporary extension of life by building a small rechargeable battery into the processor power supply arrangements.

(iii) Power and heat

Electrical power is needed to create and retain binary states in electronic storage. Static storage retains its data once set, but requires a higher initial power level, while dynamic storage has to be frequently and regularly refreshed but uses less power overall. Dissipation of the heat generated in a processor is a considerable problem for a computer designer; large computers, such as that shown in Fig. 1.6, are most likely to have a water-cooling arrangement. Solid state memory, with low distances for the pulses to travel and no 'moving' parts, creates much less of a problem, but finding a method of designing faster storage without a correspondingly greater heat output is still a priority for electronic research.

(iv) Density

A processor with a 32-bit word can address 2^{32} unique locations of memory. Assuming, as is the usual case, that each location holds 8 bits of data, then the total (potential) memory space contains 32 gigabits. Fully exploiting this capability is physically impossible and logistically undesirable unless the data storage can be constructed of a size comparable to the processor which can address it. At the moment 256 Kbit dynamic storage chips are widely available, so that up to 2 megabytes of storage can be accommodated on a single circuit board (see Fig. 3.6), and in the near future 1 megabit and 1 megabyte storage chips will be appearing inside our larger computers.

(v) Cost
The same considerations apply to the cost of storage. One of the consequences of integrating circuits is that it is possible to apply a considerable
degree of automation in their manufacture, and thus to reduce their cost
by an unbelievable order of magnitude. Currently 256 Kbit chips can be
obtained, in bulk, for a few pounds. However, it also has to be said that
the low cost of the non-automated parts of chip manufacturing is achieved
by subcontracting the mounting of the wafers to the low labour-cost
countries of the Third World, work that leads to permanent damage to the
eyesight in a few years. In addition, the automatic and 100 per cent testing
of chips gives a supply of guaranteed zero-defect chips, thus adding to the
overall reliability of a processor.

(b) Reusability − ROM and RAM
Most of the uses of internal storage call for the various locations to be
'reusable' − for instance a program will put some data into an unused area
of storage, and change the original values perhaps many times; subsequently when the first program has finished using it, the data will be
erased and another program will have the use of the same storage area.
Reusable, general-purpose storage is known as RAM; this is strictly short
for Random Access Memory, but it is easier to remember its main feature
if you explain it as Read And write Memory. RAM has its values set and
changed by passing an electric current through it, and when that current
is turned off the values are lost (i.e. RAM is normally volatile). There are,
however, some uses in which you want the same data or programs to be
permanently resident in a computer and never to be erased or overwritten,
for which purpose you require the data to be put into Read Only Memory,
or ROM. ROM has a specific pattern of data imprinted ('burnt') into it
during the manufacturing process, and thus cannot subsequently be
affected by the application or loss of electrical current.

ROM is used in particular to hold special software supplied for fixed
purposes − language compilers, word processing software, etc. The program which is being used to prepare this book (VIEW from Acornsoft)
operates from a ROM chip, as does the system software, the BASIC interpreter, and some Graphics software, while the text which I am entering,
changing and subsequently printing is held in RAM. ROM used for this
purpose is often known as 'firmware'.

Several intermediate forms of ROM are also available to the computer
designer, though not normally to the computer user.

(i) Programmable read-only memory (PROM)
PROM is ROM in which programming is available to the programmer with
the use of special electronic equipment itself known as a PROM program-

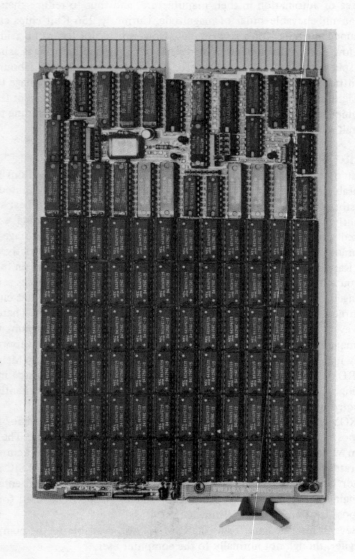

Fig 3.5 *semiconductor memory*

mer, but still cannot be changed subsequently – a process known as 'blasting' because it involves blowing 'fuses' to represent one of two values in each bit location.

(ii) Erasable-PROM (EPROM)

EPROM is PROM which is reversible by exposure to an intense ultraviolet light source. The device may then be reprogrammed, and re-erased indefinitely. *Electrically alterable PROM* (EAROM) and *electrically erasable PROM* (EEROM) both allow complete or selective writing of bits electrically, but are more difficult to use and are slower in operation.

(e) The organisation of internal storage

Whatever the form of technology used, over which the customer has little control within an individual machine (that is, it comes as part of the black box), internal storage will have its own set of electronics to control the processes of READing and WRITEing, particularly for the purposes of decoding an address directed to it, via the storage address register, from the processor. The way in which the unit or units of internal storage are organised relative to the processor may have as significant an effect on the total access capability as the technology involved, and since this is one of the most important design features affecting computer performance, a number of significant alternative forms are used in computers. The arrangement as shown in Fig. 3.4 is common in mainframe computers and has internal storage directly under the control of the processor, which means that *all* data transfer passes through the processor between internal and external storage. This can both degrade the performance of the processor and limit transfer rates. The alternative arrangements shown in Fig. 3.6(a) and (b) permit direct transfer of data between internal and external storage – a feature known as *direct memory access* (DMA) though this is also achievable by special mechanisms in the previous structure.

The range of addresses which can be used in storage depends on the size of the address registers (see p.60). In its simplest form this means that if an address register consists of, say, eight bits the lowest address would be 00000000 and the highest address would be

$$11111111 = 2^8 - 1$$
$$= 256 - 1$$
$$= 255$$

This means that an 8-bit address register can address memory locations numbered from 0 to 255. However, this restricted range of addresses can be increased by organising storage in separate modules, with the first n bits of the address field of an operand representing block number and the remainder the address within block. Such a feature can also improve the transfer capability in the form of *interleaved storage*, in which the total storage capacity is provided in two or four modules, with the storage addresses spread across them rather than within them. In two-way interleaved storage, the odd addresses are in one module and the even in the other, thus providing simultaneous access to two more adjacent addresses.

Sometimes special ultra-high-speed storage is provided in small volume to hold the most frequently used data and program instructions. Internal storage may be seen as part of a hierarchy of storage in a computer system, and high-speed storage, known as *cache* or *scratchpad*, bears the same logical relationship to internal storage as internal to external. Similarly, special-purpose storage areas known as *stacks* are sometimes used to control software; stacks are groups of locations with the characteristic that they can be filled only from the bottom up, and read from the top down, and the top of the stack is the only location that is available to a READ; it is similar to a conventional queue, and has the same kind of uses in a computer.

The most difficult concept to explain in respect of internal storage in large computer systems is that of *virtual storage*. 'Virtual' means that it appears to be there to the user, but is not actually (all) there; as a description it can be applied to machines and terminals, and in every case it means that an appearance or illusion is given to the user, by hardware or software, of something that is actually not physically there. Virtual storage allows the programmer to use more storage than is physically available to him, either because the full addressable memory space has not been provided, or because his program is having to share the available memory with other programs. The systems software initially loads only the first part of a large program, into a few small fixed sections of memory ('pages'); and then, while the program is running, it will detect if the non-loaded part of the program is needed, in which case it will load that part of the program into another page that is not in use at that instant, adjusting the memory addresses referred to in the newly loaded program.

The need for virtual storage, even in the face of widely available cheap storage technology, is one indication of the dependence of computer power on the immediate availability of very large volumes of information. The total volume of internal storage is one of the few aspects of this part of a computer system that the user can specify, usually in units of 64 K or 128 K up to the addressable limit available on a machine. If this is not sufficient, add-on or extended storage is often available, with cost and performance intermediate between internal and external, and with special electronic control circuits. Finally, the various developments under way in backing storage (see Section 4.1) may mean that the distinction between internal and external storage are becoming somewhat blurred.

Fig 3.6 *alternative arrangements of internal storage*

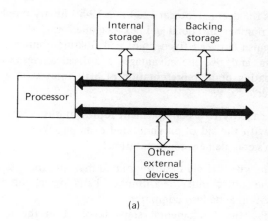

(a)

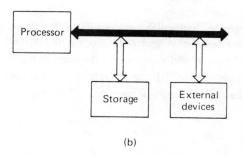

(b)

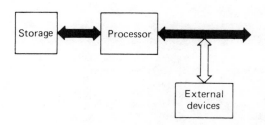

(c)

72

SPECIMEN QUESTIONS

1 (a) Express the decimal integer 1234 as a 12-bit binary number. Convert the binary number into octal and hexadecimal form.

(b) Distinguish between fixed point and floating point representations of numbers, and give the advantages and disadvantages of each form. Why is floating point representation of little interest to a commercial programmer? *

2 What is meant by two's complement representation? State an alternative form with the aid of an annotated example. What are the benefits of the two's complement representation? *

3. (a) Explain, with the aid of an annotated diagram, the interrelationship between the control unit, the arithmetical and logical unit and the main memory within a modern computer.

(b) Describe the fundamental steps involved in the fetch–decode–execute cycle by considering instructions which:
   (i) transfer control unconditionally;
   (ii) perform input or output;
   (iii) access the main memory. *

4. In a microcomputer, distinguish between ROM, RAM and PROM. *

5. Distinguish between direct and other forms of addressing, and show how different forms of addressing affect the range of addressable storage. Give one example each of (i) one address, (ii) two address instructions, and indicate the consequences of each type of instruction. *

PERIPHERALS AND
THE COMPUTER

The final reason why a computer can be tailored, or 'configured', to satisfy so many diverse needs is the range of devices which can be attached to the processor as 'peripheral' devices. The term peripheral is misleading, first because these devices are *essential* to the use of a computer, and secondly because there are two distinct classes, with different characteristics and functions, subsumed within it. One class is that of *backing storage devices*, the other *input/output devices*. Backing storage devices are:

- usually local to the processor;
- connected to it by high-speed parallel communication lines;
- high capacity, high-transfer-rate machines.

I/O devices are:

- very often remote from the processor;
- connected to it by slower serial data communication facilities;
- usually low-capacity, slower-speed machines.

As a result, backing storage can usually be considered as part of the central computer, particularly as it bears a relationship to internal storage, while I/O devices can be considered a conceptually separate subsystem related as much to the user and his world as to the computer itself [with the sole exception of one I/O device which is always close to the processor and is used as the operator console by the (human) machine operator].

The only way in which peripherals can be considered as one class is that their control by the processor, and their use by a program, is again through a READ or WRITE operation instigated by an I/O instruction which initiates the data transfer in the appropriate direction. The form of the instruction, and the way that it is handled, will in most cases be different.

Fig. 4.1 shows how these two classes of peripheral devices are usually (except in the very smallest computers) connected to the processor, and also shows the logical structure of external connections with data buses,

74

Fig 4.1 *connection of external devices*

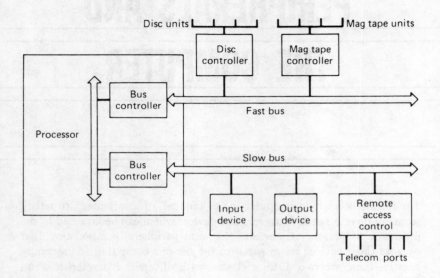

bus controllers, device controllers and the devices themselves in a highly organised and differentiated arrangement.

4.1 BACKING STORAGE

Backing storage devices are designed to provide permanent storage for large volumes of data, and to permit retrieval of that data by the processor ('access') when required.

They can be classified into three groups according to the recording principle or media employed — magnetic, optical (video) and semiconductor states respectively — giving a range of cost and performance characteristics from which the system designer, and to a lesser extent the customer, may select. Figure 4.2 shows how different types of storage device, to be described below, offer significant combinations of capacity and access. The exercise of choice is limited by the normally processor-specific interface that is required, but there is a growing movement towards standard interfaces giving increased interchangeability of storage devices with the same processor.

(a) Magnetic storage
All forms of magnetic storage use the same or similar principles of recording two-state values as are used in magnetic core. A small magnetic spot is deposited on a magnetisable material in one direction or another, depend-

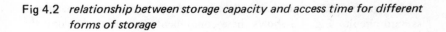

Fig 4.2 *relationship between storage capacity and access time for different forms of storage*

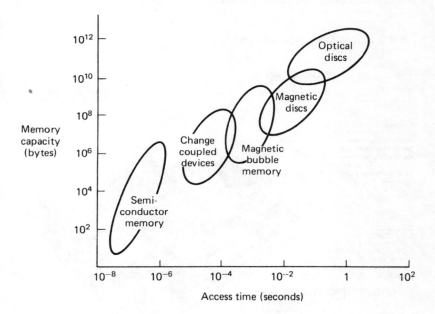

ing on the direction of the electric current in a coil in a *read/write* (R/W) head, and its state is determined by switching off the current and using the head as a magnetic detector. In all magnetic storage devices the recording medium is mobile, and is passed through or under a fixed or stationary head. The R/W head either touches the surface or floats immediately above it. These principles, and the mechanisms themselves, will be familiar through the domestic equivalent of magnetic storage – audio or video cassettes, recording tape, video and audio disc records.

(i) Magnetic discs

Magnetic disc storage devices use these recording principles on a wide range of magnetic disc media. The devices vary in size from a large composite device with about the same dimensions as two sideboards placed on top of each other (see Fig. 1.6) down to a 'Hardcard' measuring 12 in × 4 in × 1 in that fits inside a personal computer box. A disc storage device, however large or small, will contain one or more *drives*; each drive can accommodate a disc volume rotating on a spindle driven by the drive motor, with a retractable or fixed R/W mechanism containing (at least) one head per recording surface of the volume. The drive operates under a hardware controller which usually contains microprocessor units as well as hard circuits. Fig. 4.3 shows these components in a small disc unit the size of a domestic tape cassette player.

Fig 4.3 *a small magnetic disc unit*

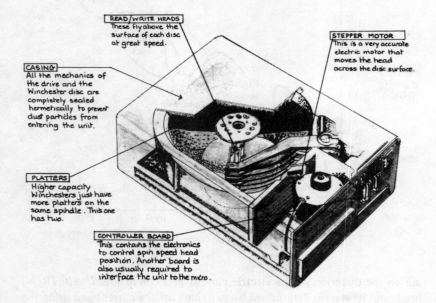

The discs themselves are made either of a light alloy or a polyester plastics material coated with a magnetisable layer of ferrite, and data is stored in concentric tracks on the surface(s) of the disc, serially bit by bit around the track. The R/W head or heads 'float' a few micrometres or less above the surface of the disc as it rotates at high speed — up to 5000 revolutions per minute — for which reason it is known as *rotating storage*. The technology required to make disc drives capable of reliable operation at such demanding precision is one of the most remarkable in computing, and is one of the reasons why it is necessary for high-performance disc drives to operate in sealed or environmentally controlled conditions.

Disc volumes (that is, individual disc media) come in a variety of shapes, sizes and characteristics:
- single/multiple recording surfaces;
- hard or soft;
- fixed or removable;
- formatted or unformatted.

Hard(rigid)/floppy Traditionally discs have been composed of rigid material in order to provide the required clearance for the R/W heads. One of the most remarkable developments that occurred simultaneously with the microcomputer, and indeed may be even more significant, is the appearance of soft floppy disc devices, of lower operating characteristics but nevertheless capable of full backing storage work. Floppy discs were originally invented as flexible data input media (see section 4.2) capable of surviving the rigours of the postal system, containing both user data and special software from computer manufacturers. There is now a range of floppy and mini-floppy disc devices mainly used with smaller computers.

Recording surfaces There may be up to ten distinct discs ('platters') connected into a single volume (known as a disc pack or storage module) by a central spindle. The outside surfaces of the pack will generally not be used; the top surface, known as the servo surface, is used to control the precision of the R/W operation. Ten-platter and three-platter packs are standard for removable discs. Cartridges are two-platter discs usually within an almost-sealed cover. Single platter discs may be used on one side (single-sided) or both (double-sided). Discs may be from 3–14 inches in diameter.

In a multi-platter volume, the set of tracks on each surface with the same track number (that is, those vertically above each other) constitute a *cylinder*, numbered in the same way 0 to *n*. An individual track will thus be identified by cylinder number and surface number within cylinder. A cylinder is also that set of tracks which can be accessed by a set of R/W heads when it is in one position, and related data is stored cylinder by cylinder on such a disc for reasons of faster overall access. (See Fig. 4.4.)

If the drive number, track number and cylinder number of a particular piece of data are known then it has a unique address, just as a piece of data in internal storage has a unique address, and this is used by the device controller to position the R/W mechanism directly to that address — a concept known as direct access (also, but most confusingly, as random access). Discs, and some other storage devices which allow the same facility, are sometimes known as *direct access storage devices* (DASDs). Note that direct access only takes the head to the addressable location; the data required may be anywhere on that track and has to be sought.

Fixed/removable Some disc devices contain both a drive and a disc volume as one integral unit in which the disc volume is fixed and irre-movable. The total capacity of such a unit is limited to the capacity of that single volume. Removable discs can support unlimited total storage, but the amount of data available to the computer at any one time is limited to the volume(s) currently loaded in the device's drive(s). There are two types of fixed disc: *head-per-track* discs in which there is one R/W head per track on each recording surface, and *Winchester* discs (so called after the IBM code used in their development) which have the

Fig 4.4 *multi-platter discs and the cylinder*

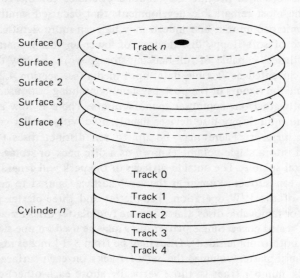

normal retractable head per surface but are sealed units to permit greater reliable recording density. Head-per-track discs give a reduced access time (see below), but are much less used now than in the past because removable discs and Winchester discs have themselves improved their access times. The main disadvantage of fixed or sealed discs is that you need another storage device on which to take a copy of the data stored on a fixed disc, as a security against the disastrous situation which happens when the R/W heads actually come into contact with the surface of the disc. Normally the heads 'float' a few millionths of an inch above the surface and when contact occurs we have the situation known as a 'head crash'.

Removable discs are, as their name suggests, devices in which the discs can be removed and reloaded. Removable discs can support only one R/W head per surface, which has to be disengaged into a safe position before a disc volume can be removed. The operation of moving a retractable head to a track for reading/writing adds to the access time for that device.

Formatted/unformatted Each recording surface of a disc contains a number (up to 1000) of numbered concentric tracks, packed at a density of up to 1000 tracks per inch, in the outermost area of the surface. Although the innermost track of the recording area is shorter than the outside track, each track is used to store the same quantity of data (up to 30 K characters or bytes), the timing of each operation being identically controlled (by the servo surface track in a multi-platter disc) regardless of the track number. Each track is therefore used for data storage as a fixed length storage location (see Fig. 4.7). Recording density is up to 15 000 bpi.

Discs in which the entire length of the track is available for data storage are known as *unformatted* discs. Some discs units have a subdivision of the tracks, known as a segment or sector, as the lowest-level addressable unit of storage, numbered sequentially round a track and from track 0 to track n, and are known as *formatted* discs (see Fig. 4.5). Formatting may be performed by software or by notches or holes in the disc. It reduces the searching operation for data. An intermediate form, known as *self-formatting*, is where the disc controller packs data into a special format which aids the operation of data retrieval but reduces the amount of storage available.

Fig 4.5 *recording surface layouts*

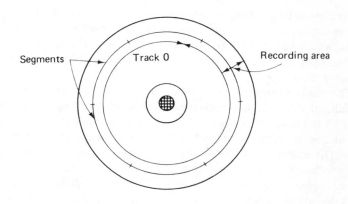

(ii) Magnetic disc storage – performance

Total storage capacity The storage capacity of a disc volume will vary from about 1 megabyte to 500 megabytes; currently the upper limit is 150 megabytes per disc surface. This means that if we use the fact that 1 byte of storage can hold one character – one letter, digit or punctuation mark – then such a disc volume could store the contents of fifty novels each of 300 pages. Capacity per device depends upon the number of volumes/drives. On-line capacity depends upon the number of devices installed; the largest available disc has a capacity of 2.8 gigabytes. As with other equipment, there is a trade-off between capacity and speed of access. The nominal capacity of a disc may not all be available to the user, mainly because it consists of multiples of fixed-length locations, in each of which there may well be unused space which cannot be aggregated.

Speed The *access time* is defined as the time taken to locate and then transfer data from a disc into internal storage. It includes three elements:
- movement of R/W head to required cylinder/track ('seek');
- scan of track to find data record ('search');
- transfer of data.

On average, the search time will be half the revolution time ('latency'), and the transfer time will be the appropriate fraction of revolution time depending on how much data is transferred. A revolution speed of 2000 rpm would give an average search time of 15 ms and a full track transfer time of 30 ms.

The seek time is typically the largest element (0 to 250 ms) and is avoided through the use of head-per-track discs. In practice the *write access time* is longer than the *read access time*, as defined above, because of a read-after-write convention to check the correctness of a write operation, which adds a further revolution time. A rough approximation of read access time for a wide range of discs is 50 to 150 ms (one-twentieth to one-sixth of a second).

The *transfer speed* is in general defined by the revolution time and the amount of data which can be transferred in one read operation. In principle all the data under a set of R/W heads at one time (that is, a cylinder) can be continuously transferred at the rate of track-length per revolution time. The actual unit transferred is ultimately software-specified, the unit being a 'block' of data, usually a multiple of data records of up to the physical capacity of the track or sector. For the unit defined above, with a track length of 20000 bytes, the nominal transfer rate would be 660 K bytes per second.

Developments in disc storage. The disc storage device is under continuous and unrelenting development, primarily to increase the density of the storage process and thus the capacity of the device. The Winchester disc is being pushed to the very limits of physical science in packing density, platter size and head gap, and thus new techniques are being sought, of which one is vertical recording, in which the magnetised bits, instead of laying horizontally along the track, are turned through 90 degrees so that they stand vertically in the magnetic material. Bernoulli discs are a similar revolutionary invention; the disc is held and spun within a hard plastic cartridge, but not by a motor-driven spindle; instead the disc is lifted and spun by injecting air into the cartridge at high speed using the principles of laminar flow and pressure discovered by Daniel Bernoulli. The discs are thus removable and have other operational advantages.

(iii) Magnetic tape

Magnetic tape storage uses reels of half-inch Mylar tape, 600, 1200 or 2400 feet in length as industry standards, on which one or two characters of data have been recorded across the width of the tape by a tape drive into which the magnetic tape has been threaded. Magnetic tape drives hold one working reel at a time on a 7 or 10 in. spool, but a number of drives (usually up to eight) can operate under one controller. The reels are removable, and total off-line storage is limitless.

Tape drives operate in bursts as the tape is unwound from one spool and wound on to another, past the R/W head, at speeds of up to 200 inches per second. Reel-to-reel (Fig. 4.6) drives operate directly, with high-precision tensioning mechanisms, but for higher speeds vacuum buffer drives are used, in which tape is moved into a buffer column in loops. It is then moved from one loop past the R/W head into an output buffer, also in loops, from which it is rewound on to the output spool. The loops in the buffer columns are controlled separately, by sensors, from the capstan drives which move the tape past the R/W head in response to a R/W command. The drives are capable of virutally instantaneous starting and stopping, but a space, called an inter-block gap (IBG) has to be left to allow for acceleration to full tape drive speed/deceleration to stop, data being transferred only when the tape is moving at full speed. The unit of a read/write operation is thus a block of data, whose length is ultimately software specified, each block preceded and followed by an IBG of about half an inch (see Fig. 4.7).

The data recording density comes in one of a series of industry standards: 800 bpi, 1600 bpi or the latest models at 6250 bpi. Bits per inch (bpi) here refers to the bit width of a frame (seven or nine tracks across the tape width) and thus means characters per inch; this is not so with all other tape-like media (see next section). Fig. 4.7 shows the layout of data on a magnetic tape.

Unlike magnetic disc, the areas of storage on a magnetic tape reel are continuous (at least within a data block defined by the computer programmer) and are not addressable. Data blocks are written to a tape in serial order (one after another) and are read in serial order from the beginning of the tape. The beginning and end of the used area of a tape will be physically signalled by reflective marks, and there may also be header and trailer records to indicate the contents and date of use. These ensure that a reel of tape does not become accidentally unthreaded. The normal mode of use is to read through a tape from beginning to end and then to rewind it

Fig 4.6 *magnetic tape units*

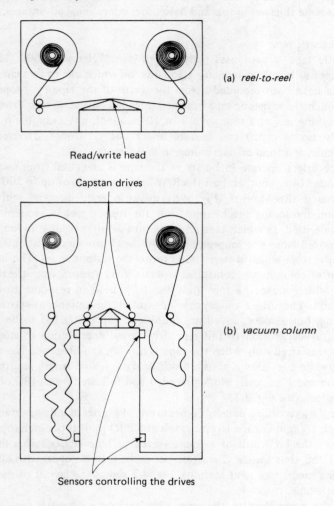

(a) *reel-to-reel*

Read/write head

Capstan drives

(b) *vacuum column*

Sensors controlling the drives

for reuse. It will be necessary to do this to find more than one record on a tape *unless* the records have been placed there in a particular sequence which allows *sequential* rather than merely *serial* access (see Chapter 5 for a discussion of what this difference means).

Magnetic tape recording can be effected in several different ways whose initials are used to characterise the devices — the standards are NRZI, PE and GCR.

NRZI (*non-return to zero incremental*) is a recording mode in which the direction of magnetisation (the 'flux') changes only to signify a 1 bit,

Fig 4.7 *layout of data on magnetic media*

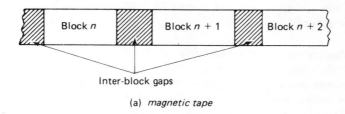

Inter-block gaps

(a) *magnetic tape*

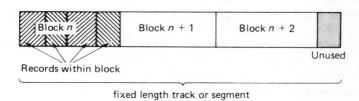

Records within block

Unused

fixed length track or segment

(b) *magnetic disc*

the absence of a change between bit positions indicating a 0 value. This is economic and reliable but demands high precision of speed movement, or a track to clock the pulse (that is, to separate one bit value from another).

PE (*phase encoding*) uses a positive flux change to represent a 1 value and a negative change to represent a 0 value. PE can support the greater packing density but requires a fluctuation-free drive speed.

GCR (group code recording) uses additional electronics to increase the packing density (up to 6250 bpi). Four bits of data are encoded into 5 bits on the tape, basically as for NRZI but using only the binary combinations of five bits that have no more than two consecutive zeros. Any other combination is detected as an error.

The continued popularity of magnetic tape storage rests on its unchallenged position in cost per character stored, at the low end of the capacity/ speed trade-off. A tape reel (2400 feet) costs a few pounds, and assuming only 50 per cent space utilisation at 1600 bpi density can hold 25 million characters. It is ideal for long-life storage, and for data, a high proportion of which is required in any run of a computer program, such as employees' accumulated pay and tax paid information needed in every weekly or monthly payroll run. The transfer rate depends on tape speed and recording density; for example, a unit with a tape speed of 125 ips and a recording density of 1600 bpi will transfer a block at 200 K bytes per second. Access time depends on search time, which for one record will be approximately equal to the block read time multiplied by half the number of blocks on the file; the block read time being block transfer time plus start and stop time. For the same unit and a block of 1000 bytes, the block read time will be about 25 ms.

(iv) Magnetic tape cassettes and data cartridges

Full-scale magnetic tape drives, however, are storage devices available only to medium and large computer users. For smaller computers, modified (or at the lowest level, unmodified) forms of domestic audio cassettes and tape recorders are used, with lower capacities but still surprisingly high performances. (Occasionally minitapes are also found.) *Digital cassettes* contain up to 300 feet of 0.15 in. computer grade tape, storing one track of data at 800 bpi serially, on both sides of the tape. *Data cartridges* hold up to 450 feet of 0.25 in. tape, at densities of up to 6400 bpi in four tracks, up to 16 megabytes per reel. Transfer rates are up to 200 K bits per second. In both cases data is stored in fixed length blocks.

Most data cartridges (and some small versions of magnetic tape) operate in 'streaming' mode rather than 'start-stop' mode. Streamers are not capable of stopping in an IBG, but operate from the processor at a rate which will keep it constantly in motion. When it is necessary to stop, a streaming drive repositions itself by coasting to a stop, backing up over a section of tape previously processed, awaiting the next command and accelerating to a running start.

Cassettes and cartridges are used primarily as back-up devices to fixed/sealed Winchester discs, and also for long-life storage. They are also used as data input media (see next chapter), and on the smallest home computers may be the only form of external storage available. The cost of the media (£4 approximately for a digital cassette, about £15 for a data cartridge) makes them extremely cost-effective storage devices for small computers.

(v) Mass storage

Mass storage devices offer very high ('archival') on-line storage capacities of the order of hundreds of gigabytes, with access times of a few hundred milliseconds. Such systems are essentially made up of complexes of small sections of magnetic tape or card strips arranged in cells. Cells or cell groups are addressable, data then being retrived serially within the tape or card strip. Their function is likely to be taken over by optical storage devices in the very near future.

(vi) Magnetic card

The only example now remaining of small strips of magnetic tape attached to card is the small strip on the reverse of cashcards and credit cards, on which is stored the Personal Identification Number (PIN) and other data.

It used to be a common form of storage in small office computers known as Visible Record Computers because, completely differently from the credit card, the ledger card showed in clear print the same data that was stored on the magnetic strip. Magnetic cards, however, suffer several drawbacks: they are easy to copy, have a small storage capacity and have to operate on line. An intelligent card is the same size as a credit card but contains a microprocessor and memory built into the card in one or more chips, bonded into a carrying frame and encapsulated into the plastic frame. For use the card is inserted into a slot in a terminal, which provides power and communication links via metal contacts on the surface of the card. The processor in the card can then be used in a much powerful way to authenticate the presenter of the card and the outstanding credit balance, and since the card has its own intelligence it can operate off line from the main accounts computer, to which the terminal may send batches of transactions periodically. The intelligent card is much used in France, where, encouraged by a Government initiative, they have been issued to bank account holders. These cards give much greater protection against fraudulent use than do conventional magnetic-strip cards. In the UK they are beginning to be used to hold a patient's medical history.

(b) Semiconductor storage

These magnetic recording devices have been followed on to the market by storage devices built using semiconductor techniques in VLSI. The most significant of these new products are magnetic bubble memory (MBM), charge-coupled devices and the solid-state disc.

(i) Magnetic bubble memory

This type of storage is already on the market and devices are available in chip form. This is a form of non-volatile storage based on iron garnet (a crystalline material) which has the property of creating magnetic domains known as bubbles when a magnetic field is applied. These tiny domains can actually be created, destroyed and moved about tracks on the chip by variations in the magnetic field. The presence of a bubble represents the presence of a bit (1) and absence means a zero (0). If the magnetic field is rotated the bubble will collapse and disappear, thus giving the propensity for 1 and 0 values. Magnetic bubbles are now available in 1 M bit chips organised on to memory boards. The total organised capacity is limited, at the moment, making it suitable for microcomputers and intelligent terminals, but there is no doubt that it has a magnificant future; it is non-mechanical, non-volatile, consumes very little power, is compact, very reliable and will, in mass production, be very cheap (the 4 megabit MBM chip being already under development). Access time is 1 to 4 ms to the first bit, but is serial within a module. Transfer rate is about 150 K bytes per second; as such, it will not yet rival magnetic tape or disc, but it is at the very beginning of product-life. It is already used in some portable computers, and in applications where robustness and non-volatility outweigh the higher costs, for instance in the computers which control the Space Shuttle.

(ii) Charge-coupled devices

These are similar to bubble memories with electric charges replacing magnetic bubbles. Although they have their place as storage devices their common use at present is in TV cameras where a pattern is used to build up a picture.

Access to the data depends on the data circulation rate, but can be as low as 100 μs to the first bit, subsequent access being serial. Because of the simpler organisation of the minute cells, CCD chips can be constructed several times *more* densely than the conceptually similar RAM chips, but several times *less* densely than magnetic bubbles. Access times and transfer rates are much faster than magnetic bubbles, and CCD is seen as a potential rival to both disc and cache memories where direct access is not a prime requirement. A cache storage is a very fast serial storage device forming part of internal storage. Its great use is when large blocks of data are to be read from internal storage and processed serially.

(iii) Solid-state discs

The plummeting cost of RAM chips (approximately £1 for a 64 Kbit chip), and the arrival of CMOS technology which requires a very low power supply (a watch battery will suffice) and gives off very little heat, makes it economic to treat a battery-powered board of RAM chips as a small capacity replacement for floppy discs, organised by software to appear to the processor as a conventional disc (for which reason the device is sometimes known as a 'virtual' disc). A more revolutionary proposal is to leave all the chips on the wafer in which they are made and wire up the single wafer rather than split up the chips and wire them separately. The advantage of all forms of solid-state discs is access time of up to 100 times faster than revolving discs.

(c) Optical storage

Optical storage uses a low-power laser beam to induce permanent changes on the surface of a disc or card, such that the changes can subsequently be detected as a difference in reflected light (see Fig. 4.8). Several different medium coatings are currently in use — photographic film, polymer coating in which a bubble is induced, thin metal film in which a hole is burnt. The advantages of optical memory are immense:

(a) a vastly increased storage capacity — up to 5000 Mb/surface at 20 000 tracks/inch — 10 to 100 times that of magnetic storage for the same access characteristics as floppy discs;

(b) optically stored data is virtually inerasable, and the surfaces can be protected within a sandwich of clear plastic or glass; as a consequence the media are non-reusable, and optical discs are often described as WORM discs (Write-Once Read-Many). However, non-erasable optical discs are under development and may appear at the end of the decade;

(c) optical data is readily copyable, by pressing, in either plastic or metal;

(d) unlike magnetic strengths, optical marks do not decay with age;

(e) reading optical data can be performed with a very much larger gap (1000 microns typically) between read head and media surface, and optical discs are therefore removable and expect fewer head crashes.

Fig 4.8 *optical disc format and read/write head*

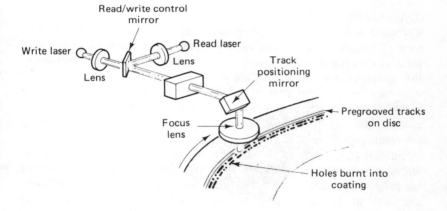

Several types of optical disc are available, mainly based either on the Compact Disc or Video Disc format, both pioneers of non-data optical storage. The current capacity of a 14 in disc (the 'Gigadisk') is 4 gigabytes; by comparison, the human brain is thought to have a storage capacity of about 1000 gigabits, in an area of about 40 cubic inches. One disadvantage of optical discs is a higher read error rate, and the Gigadisc has a two-level error detection and correction feature.

Even more of a revolution is the Lasercard, a small plastic card the size of a credit card or bigger, containing a layer of silver particles suspended in a gelatine and protected by two sheets of plastic, on to which a laser burns tiny holes. Currently about 5 megabytes can be stored on a credit card size — enough for 2500 A4 pages or three copies of this book. As such they are currently being investigated for holding personal medical histories for use in accidents, for software distribution and more generally for paperback book publishing.

4.2 INPUT/OUTPUT DEVICES

I/O devices are the immediate interfaces to the computer — the ways that the user gets his data in and results out — in fact, how he uses the computer. The operative stages of Input are data capture, (optional) temporary data storage, and machine recognition/data conversion; and of Output, data generation, (optional) temporary data storage and data display. Data capture and data display respectively can operate from/to a variety of sources and media.

(a) Data capture

(i) Keyboards
Keyboard devices such as typewriters, teleprinters and flexowriters date back 100 years. Keyboards of various types remain the most widely used form of data input, both onto recording media for subsequent re-input to the computer, and by direct data entry. However, most keyboards now work not by physical contact but by setting a magnetic, electronic or photo-electric switch attached to or positioned by/underneath the key plunger, the output from which is interpreted as a specific character by intervening electronics.

Further gains in robustness are provided by 'touch-sensitive' keyboards without individual moving keys; they generally consists of a membrane sandwich of insulating sheets which contain contacts on the outer layers and holes in the middle layer through which contact is made when the appropriate key printed on the overlay is touched. Many keyboard operators miss the audible 'click' and the feel of the key moving which tells them that they have hit the key ('tactile response'), and the click and movement are often artificially reinstated for that reason. The principle of contact induced by pressure on a membrane has more recently been extended to devices in which the various positions in the tablet can be made, by program, to select values or options which are printed on the overlaying template and which the user operates by touch.

Most keyboards still contain:
- *alphabetical* keys in the original layout known as the QWERTY layout, along with
- *numerical* keys, both above the alphabet and in a separate optional group;
- *special character* keys;

- *control* keys, for example, shift keys, return key, cursor control on a VDU (the position of the cursor, usually a blinking marker, indicating where the next character will be printed);
- *function* keys, to invoke processing functions that may be continuously used by a program (e.g. a Delete Line function in Word Processing software).

Since keyboards of some type are provided with virtually all computers and on most terminals, keyboard skill is a necessity for all computer users. Keyboard skill is easily transferable from typewriters (at least from those with electric or electronic keyboards). To those of us without nimble fingers they are an unavoidable burden — until they are replaced by an input method more appropriate to the rest of a computer system. Fig. 4.9 shows a typical layout. Standard layouts exist for most of these keys, but there are infuriating differences between the placing of the control keys on different devices.

Alternative layouts for full key content can also be found, designed to permit faster keying rates, but the vast proportion still use the conventional QWERTY layout. Special reduced-scale keyboards (keypads) also exist, mostly in small-scale portable terminals, such as those used with videotex terminals, usually a numeric key only with a few character keys. A revolutionary device known as a Microwriter permits full alphanumeric input (that is, all the 10 digits and 26 alphabetic characters) with five figure keys.

Because keyboards are so prevalent, keyboard skills are important to all computer users. We used to suffer from a prejudice against keyboarding from 'executives' who believed that it was 'clerical' and women's work, but the advent of a computer-literate generation of younger managers (and exposure to their children's home computer) has changed the climate to such an extent that an executive-style terminal on a desk is something of a status symbol.

(ii) Handproduced input

Because of the cost of a keyboard unit and of associated input media and equipment (and also its slowness and clumsiness), many alternative input methods have been sought. The conceptually simplest is the use of hand-produced input, which can take several forms
- marking/ticking designated spaces;
- hand printing;
- line drawing.

Optical mark recognition (OMR) entails the use of a pencil to make machine-recognisable marks on a pre-printed sheet or card, in such a way that a recognised mark in a specified position indicates to the computer a positive piece of information. Fig. 4.10 shows a typical form in which digit

Fig 4.9 *fullscale and restricted keyboards for data input*

(a) *a typical terminal keyboard*

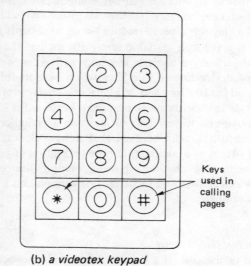

(b) *a videotex keypad*

positions are shown for input use. OMR is often used in social survey work, or in sales recording, and generally in situations where it is possible to use only paper and pencil.

Handprinted input is a special form of character recognition with input devices which will recognise either a subset or full set of handwritten (but not yet cursive) characters. The processing required in the recognition process has until recently made this form of input relatively expensive, but the use of LSI components is now making it a realistic proposition.

Fig 4.10 *an OMR form (courtesy of the Open University) (see also Fig 4.13)*

Line drawing devices provide the user with a special pen or stylus whose movements are recorded as the pen is moved along a line or is used to make any drawing on a special 'table'. The co-ordinates of the pen movement are recorded continuously and can then be used either to produce a graphic display or they can be stored away for future use. Also known as digitisers, these devices are particularly used for inputting maps and engineering drawings for subsequent manipulation or output. Special forms of pressure-sensitive tablets are also in use for signature validation — it has been found that although visual signature forgeries are possible, the profile of signature pressure is usually unique to the owner of the signature.

(iii) Printed input

Business documents such as invoices, credit notes and sales orders are a universal vehicle for business data. Such documents contain a mixture of fixed information and variable information that the user has to originate. To avoid other forms of inputting the fixed information it is possible to print or code characters in such a way that they are uniquely machine-recognisable either by the optical or magnetic waveform that they produce under a scanner, or by other measurements of shape and characteristic features.

Mark recognition is merely the same principle as used in hand-originated OMR, but with pre-printed digit selection. Documents can be printed from a computer with fixed information pre-selected in this way, and variable data can then be marked in and the whole document re-input — called a 'turnaround' document.

Character recognition is the use of specially designed printing fonts that can be recognised optically (OCR — *optical character recognition*) or magnetically (MICR — *magnetic ink character recognition*). The latter is universally used on cheques, the former in a wide variety of applications. MICR and OCR input can be read by fixed and mobile devices; in the case of MICR there is also a range of combined reader/sorters and other large machines, designed for and used by banks for cheque handling. OCR is more flexible, since OCR fonts can be printed by some printer terminals, and some document readers can handle both OCR characters and OMR marks for variable input on the same form. Fig. 4.11 shows some uses of MICR and OCR.

Bar-codes are sequences of bars and spaces, each of 1, 2, 3 or 4 units width, in which a space unit is treated as a 0 and a bar unit as a 1. The sequence is optically interpreted as a bit sequence, in which successive groups of 4 bits are logically treated as BCD or other numeric codes. The two most significant uses of bar-codes at the moment are on virtually all consumer products sold in retail shops and supermarkets, and on books — on the inside cover for use in computer-based library systems, and on the back cover for use in stock control (look at the back cover of this book). In both cases the bar-code can be scanned by a small mobile 'wand' or 'light pen', connected to the controls by a lead. For full-scale supermarket use, bar-codes can also be used with low power laser beams through which the products are passed at the checkouts. In both applications, international standards apply: in the retail market a European Article Number (EAN) code contains fields for manufacturer and product, for libraries there is an international standard book number (ISBN). Fig. 4.12 shows these bar-codes and an optical wand.

Other pre-printed data may be in the form of punched/perforated *cards or tags*, or on short strips of magnetic tape stuck on to the back of *plastics cards or badges*, or on *merchandise tickets* (see Fig. 4.13). Plastic cards or badge cards are used to input personal data that can be checked against stored data in order to authorise some action that has personal or security implications; for example, payment of cash at a 'Cashpoint' terminal, entry to a restricted zone (such as a computer room), or crediting production and therefore pay to a factor worker. Pre-punched ('Kimball') cards or tags are widely used in shoe and clothing shops, as a way of inputting sales. The card or tag associated with a pair of shoes or clothing is detached at the point of sale and sent to a computer for processing or read by a portable reader attached to a point-of-sale terminal [see Section 4.3(c)].

Fig 4.11 *some computer-readable characters on financial document*

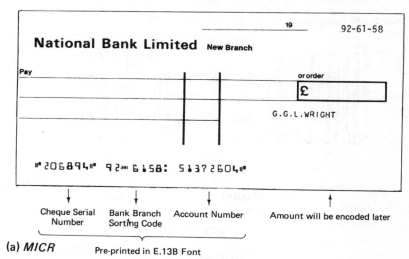

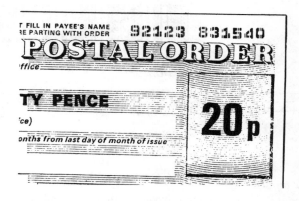

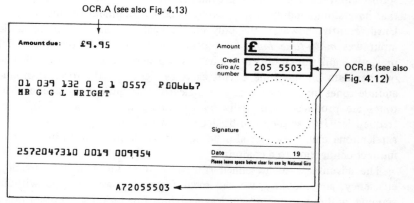

(b) *OCR*

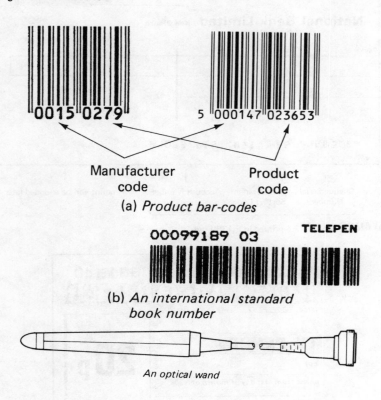

Fig 4.12 *bar-codes*

Manufacturer
code

Product
code

(a) *Product bar-codes*

00099189 03   **TELEPEN**

(b) *An international standard
book number*

An optical wand

(iv) Voice input

Audio input to a computer provides a directness and 'user-friendliness' that have stimulated extensive research and development for many years. Until recently, however, the only commercially available form of audio input was *multi-tone input* (not officially permitted in the UK under previous regulations). Multi-tone hand sets generate both dialling code and number data on the same circuit as voice signals in the form of unique audible tones, one for each digit in a clearly distinguishable sequence. The tones are produced electrically by generating sound waves of different frequencies. Just as they can be deciphered by switching devices to set up a telephone call, they can also be converted to digital form in direct or indirect connection to a computer.

The advantages to be gained from true voice input include urgency, efficiency, and mobility; we can speak faster than we can type, without training, without sitting down, leaving hands free or in use on other tasks.

Fig 4.13   *pre-printed cards and tags*

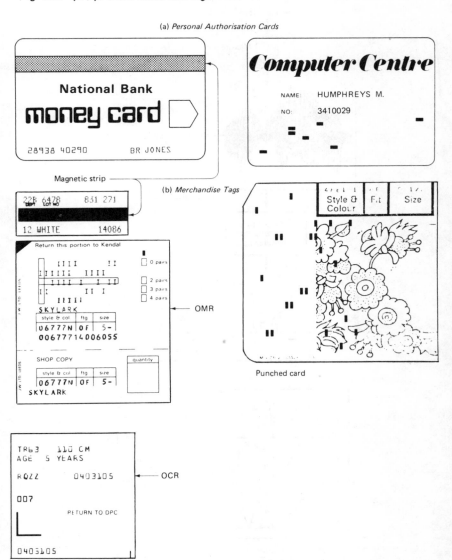

(a) *Personal Authorisation Cards*

Computer Centre

National Bank

money card

28938 40290   BR JONES

NAME: HUMPHREYS M.

NO: 3410029

Magnetic strip

(b) *Merchandise Tags*

22B 6478   831 271
DEPT LOT NO

12 WHITE   14086

Return this portion to Kendal

SKYLARK

style & col	ftg	size
06777N	OF	5-

00677714006055

☐ 0 pairs
☐ 2 pairs
☐ 3 pairs
☐ 4 pairs

OMR

SHOP COPY

style & col	ftg	size	quantity
06777N	OF	5-	

SKYLARK

Style & Colour	F.t	Size

Punched card

TR63   110 CM
AGE 5 YEARS

RQZZ   0403105

007

PETURN TO DPC

0403105

OCR

Voice input devices work by comparing a spoken word against a library
of stored word images. The voice waveform (see Fig. 4.14) is digitised and
its significant features analysed using electronic filters and mathematical
techniques. The data thus derived is then matched against similar data that

Fig 4.14 *the principles of voice input*

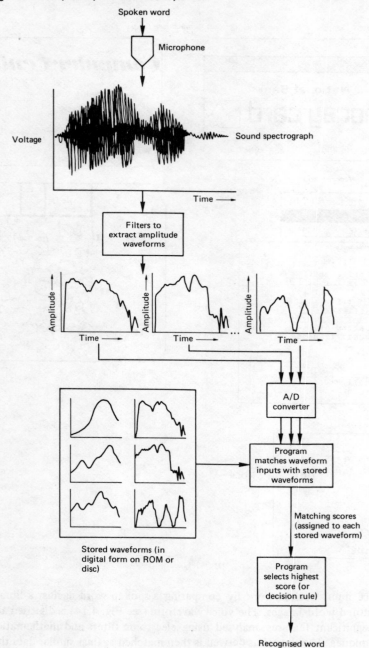

Spoken word

Microphone

Voltage — Sound spectrograph

Time →

Filters to extract amplitude waveforms

Amplitude → Time →   Amplitude → Time →   ...   Amplitude → Time →

A/D converter

Program matches waveform inputs with stored waveforms

Stored waveforms (in digital form on ROM or disc)

Matching scores (assigned to each stored waveform)

Program selects highest score (or decision rule)

Recognised word

has previously been input and stored, either for whole words or for the phonetic constituents of words – 'phonemes'. The stored data whose characteristics most closely match those of the input data is taken to represent the required word provided that its score exceeds a minimum target value. The principal problem remains that voice is an identifying characteristic of a person, and a 'voiceprint' is nearly as unique as a fingerprint and can be used in the same way. Speaker-dependent voice input means that the person whose voice is being input has previously to create the stored library of words, or 'vocabulary'; speaker-independent vocabularies are usually created by combining a variety of voices into one version, but the matching of a unique voice input against stored data is either less certain or slower. The matching process may be improved in two ways: by limiting the size of the vocabulary, or by restricting the vocabulary to a particular application area and then interpreting matching scores according to the sense of the context, e.g. a railway timetable enquiry, and also by the rules of grammar. Most voice input machines at the moment can therefore 'recognise' only a few hundred words within an acceptable response time (about a quarter of a second), but there are strong forces driving further research – the military and security agencies (for automatic surveillance of radio and telephone messages) and in the so-called Fifth Generation Computer projects (see Chapter 1), one of whose original objectives was for the computer to be able to recognise a vocabulary of 50 000 words. For the Japanese, who originated the idea of the Fifth Generation Computer, there is the added benefit from voice input of being able to dispense with a keyboard, which in their case has to be able to handle an alphabet with over 5000 characters!

(v) Direct data input

Like the human voice, most other forms of physical data that are measured by instruments such as weighing machines or voltmeters can be converted into a form that is suitable for handling in a computer. For this purpose the instrument, or 'sensor', is connected to a device which converts the data in its original, or analog form, into digital form; the device is therefore known as an *analog–digital converter* (ADC) or *digitiser*.

An illustration of the two forms is best given by reference to a thermometer; the analog value is the level of the mercury and the digital value is read from the scale of 0 to 100 °C (for normal domestic use). In order to make the conversion possible, it is necessary that the instrument presents an electrical signal to the ADC. This form of input is often known as signal input, and its processes as signal processing. It is of course the form of input used primarily in process and machine-control and in laboratory and patient-monitoring systems, and in data-logging generally. Full signal processing and the use of digitised input and output calls for careful and skilled systems engineering, but simpler examples can be developed on many microcomputers, with built-in a–d converters and ports that are programmable as memory locations; and practical interfacing to computers is now becoming a mainstream activity in computing as a result.

(vi) Computer vision

The process of computer vision consists, similarly to voice input, of two stages — image acquisition and image processing. Machine vision systems acquire images with special cameras of the type used in television news gathering. The acquired picture image is converted from the analogue state into a digitised image, by assigning a digital value to each pixel of the camera frame. Most cameras have a pixel grid of between 126×126 and 1000×1000 pixels. The size of the digital value generated for each pixel depends on the characteristics of the camera, particularly black and white/colour. The digital images are stored in RAM ready for the next stage of image processing. The stored digital values are subjected to computer processing to compress the digitised data, to tidy up and enhance the image contrasts and to extract significant features and finally to match the analysed image against patterns stored in memory. Optical character recognition (see section (iii) above) is one of the original and simpler forms of image input and recognition; we are about to use computer vision to identify different parts (nuts and bolts, etc.), and the ultimate objective is robot vision.

(b) Input media

The results of data capture are in many devices transcribed in the first place on to a temporary recording medium which then acts as an input medium into a further device. The reasons for doing this are partly historical and partly for efficient use of the computer since secondary input from a recording medium is very much faster than primary input from a keyboard, and much less demanding of the processor. Against this must be set the time-delay in processing the data, since data temporarily stored in this way represents a batch of input data accumulated over a period of time. The process of keying input on to a recording/input medium for re-reading was originally known as data preparation. The alternative, of entering data directly into the computer at the stage of capture, is known as direct data entry.

(i) Paper media

The original and widespread input media was paper in the form of discrete punched cards and continuous paper tape, into which data is punched in the form of small rectangular or round holes, with a variety of codes used to convey numeric, alphabetic and special characters. These holes were

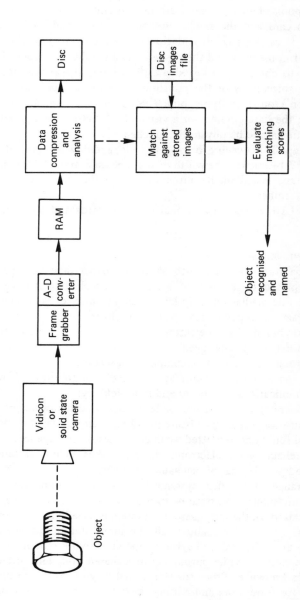

Fig 4.15 *computer vision*

then recognised mechanically by brushes or by photo-electric cells, in card/tape readers which could operate at high read rates from card hoppers or tape spools. Punched cards are now found in two standard sizes — 80-column card and the smaller 96-column card — and miscellaneous tag and ticket sizes (see page 95). Mechanical card punches (e.g. the IBM 029) had no buffer memory and their speed was limited by the operation of the keyboard, to about 8000 key depressions/hour. It was also necessary to check the correctness of the punching by a repeat operation (known as 'verification') on a verifying punch. Modern card punches are buffered and retain the data entered for a visual check before the operator finally commits the data to be physically punched.

Paper tape is between 5/8 and 1 in wide, and data is recorded in frames of 5, 6 or 7 bits across the width of the tape, in a 'frame'. The importance of paper tape rested on its automatic by-production in telex and other business machines.

Figure 4.16 shows conventional punched cards and paper tape input media.

(ii) Magnetic media

Data preparation using punched cards and paper tape have been almost totally replaced by equipment systems in which data is keyed directly onto magnetic media — usually known as 'key-disc' or 'key-tape' systems. There are several impelling reasons for this change:

(a) the keyboards are all-electronic and permit the operator to work at his or her full keying speed;
(b) the storage media is more compact and secure;
(c) data can be re-read from magnetic media, or transmitted over a data communications line, faster and more reliably;
(d) the decreasing cost of microelectronics-based hardware provided real financial savings over existing punches, even before allowing for additional functions permitted by microprocessor intelligence;
(e) the reliability of electronic devices makes their maintenance cost much less than that of mechanical punches.

A wide range of key-disc systems is now to be found, from one-one replacement single workstations to multiple workstations sharing a single output station. In the latter case, the system is usually built around a minicomputer, whose power allows all the input stations to operate simultaneously at a fully trained keyboard operator's work rate of about 12 000 key depressions/or while outputting to a shared disc. This arrangement is sometimes known as Processor Controlled Keying. Software may also be provided for formatting and editing the data before the file is manually or directly transferred to the main processor.

An even further stage in the revolution in data preparation is to make it

Fig 4.16   *punched cards and paper tape as input media*

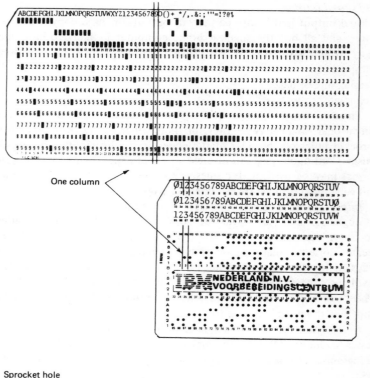

One column

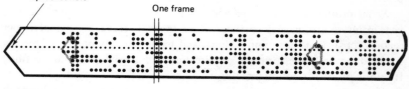

Sprocket hole

One frame

a function of the main processor itself (usually in a small business computer) in which data entry software can operate in parallel with other tasks, if it is a multi-tasking machine, or in a sequence of data entry → validation → processing tasks in a single-shot machine.

Meanwhile data capture has been expanding in other direction; we now have a range of portable, microprocessor-powered and hand-held terminals, with a reduced keyboard tailored to the particular needs of the job, and data output onto a cassette or non-volatile bubble memory, from which it can subsequently be output to a full computer for processing.

(c) Data display

(i) Printed output

Printed output is the only permanent output, or 'hard copy' from a computer, and all but the smallest home computer is likely to have one, or more, from the variety of types available. Printers may be characterised as:

- impact or non-impact;
- serial, line or page;
- character or matrix.

Their common characteristic is that an electric drive moves paper by pinch-roller, as in a typewriter, or more generally by sprockets engaging sprocket holes on the sides of the paper, past a horizontal printing mechanism. Continuous pages or discrete sheets of paper (blank or as preprinted forms) may be used, with a linespace of between 80 and 144 characters, and generally 66 single-spaced lines per page.

Impact printers create images by physical contact on to the paper through a ribbon (on to the top copy) and via carbon sheets interleaved or treated no-carbon paper for the other copies. The physical impact creates noise — a major nuisance and even a health hazard. Many different ways of handling the print heads are found; on continuous chains, on a revolving sphere ('golfball'), on spokes around the hub of a wheel ('daisy-wheel') or as a combination of retractable pins, with appropriate ways of impelling the print heads on to the ribbon.

Non-impact printers create images only on one copy, by various processes including ink-jets, thermal effect on treated heat-sensitive paper, xerographic and laser beam printing. They are much quieter than impact printers.

Serial printers print one character at a time, *line* printers one line, and *page* printers one page at a time. Their speed is rated in characters per second (cps), lines per minute (lpm) and pages per minute (ppm) respectively. Line and page printers require line and page buffers to be filled from the processor before printing.

Character printers contain a separate and distinct print key for each character (like a typewriter), and produce a continuous image. They can print only one size and one font at a time, although alternatives may be fitted. Matrix printers and non-impact printers create a character by filling the necessary positions in a print matrix, similar to the way that a character is created on a screen (see Fig. 4.20), and if you look hard enough, or under a microscope, you can see the dots. They select the appropriate combination of dots under firmware control, and usually offer a choice of fonts and print sizes (see Fig. 4.18). The matrix size varies from 5×7 to about 300×300 on the fast laser printers, at which point it is very hard to detect the individual dots.

Fig 4.17 *a matrix printer (courtesy of Epson (UK) Ltd)*

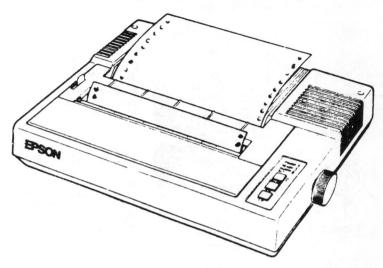

The *character set* of a printer is the range of alphabetic, numeric and special characters that it can print. Fast impact printers may have 'reduced' character sets for economy and efficiency; matrix printers will generally have a full ASCII set with selectable national variation (e.g. £ instead of $). Lower case characters are an advantage (compare your gas bill with your bank statement) and sometimes a necessity. Intelligent printers may also allow the programmer to create special characters for graphical purposes within the scope of a matrix. Foreign language characters and different alphabets can be produced in the same way.

Print quality is concerned with the visual clarity and intensity of the printed image. In general, top quality is required for personal documents to rival that of the best typewriters — known as Letter Quality or LQ for short; intermediate quality is NLQ (Near Letter Quality) and ordinary quality as 'draft'. In general there is an inverse relationship between printer speed and quality — LQ from 20 cps to 100 cps, NLQ 100 cps to 300 cps and draft upwards — and some printers can be set to produce varying quality by changing the speed of the machine. Laser printers are the exception to the rule and can produce exceptional quality at speeds of up to 20 000 lines per minute; they have been correspondingly expensive, but the first models of more modestly priced laser printers have recently appeared.

As with keyboards, the demands of reliability and quietness are taking the edge away from impact printers, with considerable benefits to the quality of computer room and office environments.

Fig 4.18 *printing mechanisms, and print images (a) impact dot matrix (9-pin print head) (b) laser*

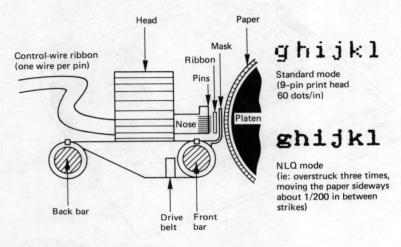

(a)

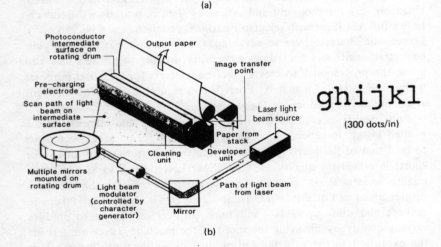

(b)

The most important characteristics of a printer are its sheer versatility and utility. The *volume* and *variety* of reports and forms printed by the computer can be illustrated by the following list of items printed in a typical well-developed payroll system, weekly and monthly except where indicated (a payroll system being normally considered as one of the first and easiest of a company's procedures to be computerised). The list includes output on pre-printed forms and on plain ('listing') paper, reports for internal and external use, reference reports and action reports, and some statutory and quasi-legal returns.

Adjustments listing.
Payroll record cards.
Additions, deletions and amendments list.
Salary advice and coin analyses.
Salary advice (industrial) and coin analyses.
Time sheets.
Cheque list.
Bank Giro credit transfers.
List of Bank Giro credit transfers.
Summary of Bank Giro credit transfers.
National Giro list.
National Insurance contributions not
deducted due to absence.
Summary of overtime and additional salary
costs.

4-weekly SAYE listing	Monthly
Monthly SAYE listing.	Monthly
Monthly statutory sick pay return	Monthly
Payroll control.	Monthly
Analysis of superannuation contributions.	Monthly
Analysis of trade union subscriptions.	Monthly
Employee deductions analysis.	Monthly
Benevolent Society/HSA deduction analysis.	Monthly
National Savings control register.	Quarterly
National Savings statement of Premium Bonds/Savings Certificates.	Quarterly
National Savings substitute form.	Quarterly
National Insurance card change schedule.	Quarterly
Income tax statement P9/P11 and P60.	End of year
Combined schedule of graduated pension contributions, and PAYE income tax form P35.	End of year
Cumulative superannuation contributions.	End of year
Listing of back-dated rise details for current employees.	As required by pay rises
Listing of back-dated rise details for ex-employees.	As required by pay rises

Computer listings on the familiar paper with sprocket holes are thus an inevitable part of office life, and the maintenance of a regular and reliable source of stationery is an important part of running a computer (see Chapter 9).

It is to be regretted that the speed of most normal printers is such that the computer can be comfortably used to generate much more printed output than most people need, thus contributing to the paperwork which chokes our offices and letter-boxes. One significant alternative to printed paper is *computer output on microfilm/fiche* (COM), in which semi-permanent text (for example, book references) are printed in very small form on either film strip or cards. Microfilm or microfiche can subsequently be viewed in magnifying readers which expand the text to normal size on VDU-type displays.

One further way in which computer output is already contributing to the paper explosion is via *computer-controlled typesetting*. Newspaper reports can be set to full-page layout from a terminal, and the page layout can then be either printed from the buffer or printed out to be repro-duced by a dry-printing process, in both cases bypassing the traditional hot metal process. Unfortunately the threat to our procedures from computer-generated paper may be further increased by developments in the electronic office; IBM has already introduced the *computer-controlled photocopier*, connected to a word processor through which multiple copies of printed output can be commanded.

Plotters, or graph plotters, are line-drawing devices which move a pen under computer control in such a way that continuous lines and curves can be drawn. They are known as graph plotters because the movement of the pen is directed by x and y co-ordinates from a nominal origin at the bottom left hand of a sheet of paper, as in a graph. Graph plotters are of two types: drum plotters, in which the paper is continuous and drawn across a drum, and flat bed plotters in which sheets of paper are separate.

Plotters may be regarded as hard copy graphics, and are often used in conjunction with graphic displays (see Fig. 4.19). The more sophisticated devices are capable of working to great precision, and in colour. Computer art is usually output on plotters, and any other output demanding con-tinuous high-precision line drawings, for example maps, engineering draw-ings, mathematical curves. An interesting development is the production of overhead transparencies. Lower precision graphics may also be printed by some matrix printers in 'graphics mode', which requires intelligence within the printer, and even (at the level of Snoopy Dog) on line printers.

(ii) Visual output

Visual output is easy to absorb, immediate and environmentally acceptable. It is the fastest growing form of computer output, particularly in the VDU (see next section), for which reason one example is shown on the cover of this book as the single most characteristic shape associated with the com-puter today.

Fig 4.19 *graphic display and graph plotter*

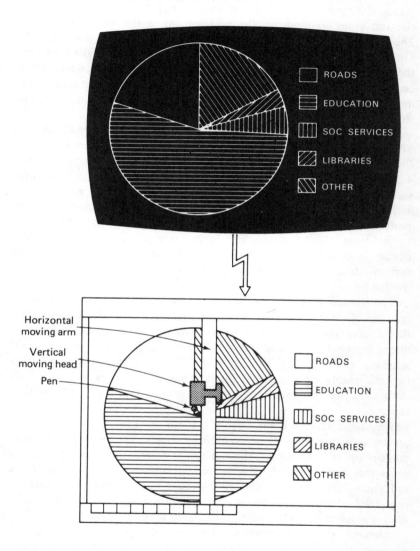

Most forms of visual display use some form of *cathode ray tube* (CRT) as the display medium, and it is the tube which gives the VDU its distinctive TV-type shape. The visual display is created on the face of the tube, which is coated with a phosphor surface which emits light when bombarded by an electron beam produced by an electronic gun. The light is either transient, in which case it has to be re-energised, or 'refreshed' by the beam scanning from top to bottom of the screen, line by line, approximately 50 times per second; or, with a special form of phosphor and electron beam arrangement, the light remains on the screen until erased. The former is known as a *raster scan display*, the latter as a *storage tube*. The type of phosphor determines the background colour of the screen and the foreground colour of the image; white on black, black on white, amber on brown or light green on dark green. The background/foreground colours may often be reversed by keyboard or program instruction into 'reverse video'.

The image produced on the face of the tube may either be in the form of characters (*alphanumeric* displays) or in free-line drawing (*graphics*). Characters are pre-formed on the framework of a dot matrix (see Fig. 4.20), usually 7×7, created by a character generator from data presented to it from the screen buffer store. There must therefore be a buffer store at least equal to the character capacity of the screen, and each character position on the screen is identified with a separate storage location in the buffer, from which the refreshing process originates. The form of identification is via the cursor — a square or line which moves, or is moved, to be underneath or on top of the character position actually being read from/ written to.

The 'standard' screen contains either 12 lines of 80 characters or 24 lines of 80 characters (1 K and 2 K screens), but high-quality screens that display the equivalent of an A4 page (A4 screens) are being introduced in word processing systems. Screens designed to meet the ANSI standard X3.4 may also be used with 132 characters per line, and thus interchangeably with normal printers. These lines of characters are built on a screen of 600 scan lines. Videotex screens have a 14×40 character fomat.

Graphic displays are addressable spatially, treating the surface of the screen as a two-dimensional co-ordinate graph. The vertical scale may contain up to 800 points, the horizontal screen up to 1000, and any point may be referenced by a pair of x (horizontal) and y (vertical) co-ordinate values. The scale is detailed enough to produce a continuous line composed of very small points. Many alphanumeric screens may also be used in graphics mode but with much cruder scales (e.g. 100×80).

Alphanumeric displays may also be used to draw representative pictures or maps using combinations of a set of character shapes, but the precision of graphic shapes on true graphics screens is much greater because the fundamental unit is the point, and images can be composed of arrangement of points known as 'pixels', (in much the same way as photographs are printed in newspapers or transmitted and reproduced from space). In 'memory-mapped' displays the current contents of each pixel (including the colour code in a colour display) are stored in an unique area of the processor's memory or in a data buffer in the display itself.

Fig 4.20 *a CRT display and character matrix*

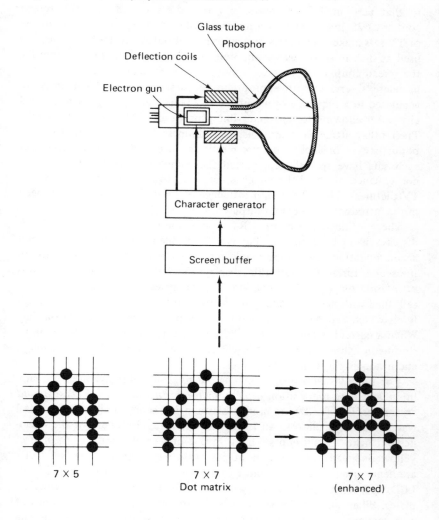

The graphic screen can be considered as a blank area in which images are created by software. Two-dimensional images can be developed easily in conventional programming languages, but three-dimensional images require complex software, and a lot of computer processing, to calculate perspective and shading. The author regrets that the black and white format of this book will not be able to convey the breathtaking beauty of full-colour three-dimensional images that can be created in this way.

The raster scan method of creating and refreshing displays is similar to that used in TV screens, except that the standard (UK) TV screen contains 625 lines and uses a lower-persistence phosphor. The cheapness of TV sets makes them attractive as computer output devices, and they are used as such in small microcomputers, and as slave video displays copying the screen content of the master video screen. Similarly, they can be used in teletext services with appropriate decoding interfaces. Characters are generated in a sequence of about ten (TV) line scans, giving a screen capacity, after allowing for character–line gaps, of up to 48 lines of characters. Their other attractive feature is their slimness, which accounts for their popularity as business videotex terminals on crowded office desks, but such sets have specially engineered flicker-free screens — flicker being a consequence of the different phosphor used to avoid blurring on *moving* TV pictures). The other major influence of TV on visual displays has been in the introduction of colour displays.

The continued use of the CRT tube as the basis for computer system displays is an anachronism that creates problems of bulk, mobility and accommodation, and considerable research effort has been expended in the search for an alternative flat display. The only previous alternative was *gas plasma* display, which contains an arrangement of character cells, each cell filled with neon gas, and with an arrangement of wires running through it on which can be traced, by a selection process, any character outline. When a current is applied, the selected character shape glows like a miniature neon light. The principle is widely applied in some calculator displays and in the displays on petrol pumps.

For small visual displays, such as the single-line displays used in many input and data preparation devices, *light-emitting diodes* (LED) or *liquid crystal displays* (LCD) are used. LEDs and LCDs are familiar from digital watches and calculators. An LED is a solid state equivalent of the incandescent light bulb; it emits a light, in one of several colours (red, orange, yellow or green) when a current passes through a diode. However LEDs are heavy users of current, and give a poor display in bright natural light. LCDs are constructed by sandwiching a liquid crystal between two glass plates. When an electric field is passed between electrodes at the ends of any segment, light is prevented from being transmitted which makes the segment appear black. LCDs thus also need either a reflective backing or an illuminated rear light. They have the advantage of virtually zero power requirement, but the control arrangements are more complicated.

Both devices work by selecting the appropriate combination of the seven segments which make up the full display field, as shown in Fig. 4.21, to make up an alphanumeric character. Extensive development is under way to produce full flat screens based on solid state LCD components, one for each character display position, and these will undoubtedly come on

Fig 4.21 *the basis of LCD and LED characters*

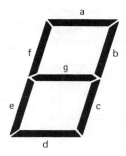

the market in the next few years. They are to be found in portable computers and terminals (see Chapter 1), but their quality is currently very poor. Meanwhile a lateral alternative form of flat-bed display is about to be launched, in which a CRT tube is retained, but with the electron beam deflected sideways at 90 degrees by an ingenious arrangement of mirrors and lenses.

(iii) Voice output
Voice output or voice response systems have achieved a higher rate of acceptance in computer usage than has voice input. There are basically two methods used to generate speech output: the first is by converting words into digital form, by sampling the waveform, storing the bit patterns, and recalling them as required in any sentence or phase (the speaking clock works in this way). An output message is thus assembled from word equivalents stored on ROM, converted back to the original analog waveform and amplified to a loudspeaker. This is expensive on storage, but a small number of words will suffice for a wide range of recognisable messages, as alarms, travel announcements, responses to telephone or keyboard enquiries, or merely as a talking clock or speak-your-weight. Fig. 4.22 shows a typical speech output process.

The second method is to generate speech artificially, either by using a library of phonemes and concatenating phonemes into complete words, or synthetically from stored voice parameters previously created by electronically filtering a spoken word into twelve components associated with the process of producing speech. This class of voice output method is much more economic on storage, but tends to produce the flat monotonous voice associated with robots and the Daleks.

In a less serious vein, the same mechanisms may be used to generate other sounds: computers programmed to produce crude music, in sounds of different frequencies, have been the star attraction of many computer

Fig 4.22 *principles of voice output*

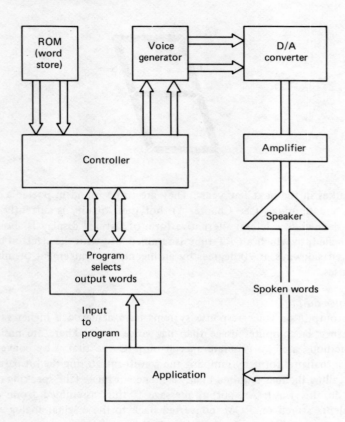

room visits, but more serious attempts are now being made in the area of electronically synthesised music.

(iv) Direct output

The corollary of direct (signal) input to the computer is direct or signal output in which the computer produces a bit pattern which sets, or changes the setting, of a mechanism controlling the operation of another machine or servo-mechanism. Signal output is usually produced subsequent to a signal input via an *analog-digital converter* (ADC) and returned via a *digital-analog converter* (DAC), which will convert digital values into, say, voltages or pressures (see Section 1.1). Increasingly, however, control devices are being produced which respond *directly* to digital signals with their own in-built microprocessor.

4.3 TERMINALS

By terminals we mean devices intended for use:
- at the workface;
- at the source of data;
- by the creator/user of data;
- remote from (central) computers.

They therefore contain *both* an input mechanism designed for 'non-professional' use at human (low-speed) rates of performance, *and* an appropriate output mechanism in the same device, along with a data transmission interface. They are mostly multi-function devices for multi-function use.

Some particularly important types of terminal are:
- keyboard/printer terminals;
- VDUs;
- point-of-sale (POS) terminals;
- data collection terminals.

(a) Keyboard/printer terminals
The original computer terminal was the teletype or teleprinter, but this was so slow and noisy that it has now become almost obsolete. However, its popularity dictated a form of interface and operation that set a standard followed by other keyboard/printer terminals (silent teletype, DECwriters, etc.) and also by the cheapest and lowest-level VDUs. A variety of other terminals containing both a low-speed serial printer and a keyboard are on the market. The printer is used both for pure output and also to record keyed input ('echoed' back from the computer), so that it contains a full record of both input to and output from the program.

(b) Visual display units
Visual display units, also called visual display terminals, contain both a display (usually a cathode ray tube) and a keyboard. The lowest levels are teletype-compatible, which means that they work in the same mode as a teletype, even to the extent of scrolling display on the screen (print lines moving up the screen and disappearing off the top), but of course with faster display speeds (usually switch-selectable according to transmission line speed). VDU's may also contain other input facilities − a light pen which can detect light emanating from a point on the screen; and touch input, in which a finger touching the screen can be positionally recognised as it breaks a grid of infra-red rays running across the screen, or causes an impedance change on a fixed conductive coating. Increasingly, the VDU is provided with 'intelligence' in the form of a microprocessor and ROM containing a fixed set of functions that can be used both by the programmer

and by the keyboard operator. At a minimum these will include clearing the screen, moving the cursor, changing the intensity of the image, reversing the screen background/image colour, flashing the cursor and 'ringing' the bell. An ANSI terminal, such as the model shown in Fig. 4.23, contains a much fuller set of 150 commands.

Optional extra facilities may include:
- *line buffer(s)* so that the VDU may receive and transmit data in block rather than character units;
- *addressability* to permit linkage of more than one terminal to a line;
- non-impact printer/screen copier for *hard copy*, and interface sockets for printer and slave monitor screens;
- *split screens* to allow presentation of more than one functional output at a time;
- *processing functions* such as form display, data validation;
- *switch options* to work in different modes and to different processors ('compatibility').

Most of these options permit the VDU to be described as an intelligent terminal, effected by microprocessor and ROM storage (see below).

Fig 4.23   *typical general-purpose terminals*
            (a) a visual display unit (courtesy of Digital Equipment
            Corporation)

Fig 4.23   *(b) a point of sale terminal (courtesy of W. H. Smith Ltd)*

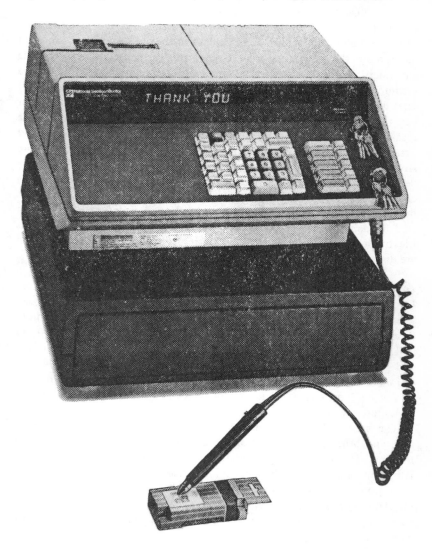

The size of the VDU, determined by the depth of the CRT tube, provides more than adequate space for building it up into a complete computer, in the form of the desktop personal microcomputer. A terminal that can also operate, for certain limited purposes as a local processor, and at the same time has the power to control additional devices is now sometimes described as a Workstation.

(c) Point-of-sale terminals

Unlike VDUs, which may be used in any environment, POS terminals are designed for use at the point of sale – in retail shops and supermarkets. They are the modern electronic equivalent of the old cash register, and still incorporate the same functions of keying-in cash received and printing customers' receipts. They also store cash and item data on a storage medium and/or transmit it centrally to a processor. They may also input sales data in other ways – optical scanning of bar-codes by a wand or laser beam is the latest method (see Fig. 4.12). When used in conjunction with a local computer they can be programmed to extract the current price and description of an item from a data record, and to deduct sales totals from stock totals. An in-store POS system can be extended to transmit the details of a non-cash transaction either to a cheque drawer's bank or to a credit card-holder's account; in each case the amount owed may be deducted directly from the computer record. You may find such systems on trial in many places, in garages, stores and some railway stations. This is Electronic Funds Transfer (EFT) in action, some consequences of which are discussed in Chapter 10.

(d) Data collection terminals

Data collection terminals are used to collect information of different types, usually in a factory or manufacturing location, where robustness and multi-function simplicity are the keys to efficient data capture and storage. They will include: keyboard functions and displays, badge readers, time recorders and pulse recorders (for automatic item counts). The environmental conditions and user requirements are among the most demanding that computing equipment face, which is one reason why the first commercial exploitation of fibre optics is to be found in this area.

The latest addition to the range of data collection terminals deployed in this, and other similar operational areas, is the battery-charged portable terminal. This is essentially a hand-held terminal the size of a large calculator containing a simplified keyboard, an optical light wand (optional), small-scale storage (cassette or magnetic bubble) and data communications interface for subsequent downloading. It is designed for use by an operator walking or moving or driving about his normal job, in warehouses, factories, sales or wherever mobility is essential.

(e) Compatibility and interfaces

It has long been an objective of computer users to be able to connect any device to any processor. This has not been largely achieved except in the case of terminals connected by data transmission (see below).

Connectability of local high-speed devices to processors is almost entirely manufacturer-specific, except where another processor manufacturer makes his device 'plug-compatible' to IBM processors; it is not uncommon to find an IBM processor with discs and magnetic tapes from such a supplier. There are two parallel interface standards for relatively high-speed devices, but the dominant manufacturers are not enthusiastic. The situation is, however, better at the lower end of the market, where in any case most microsystems are assembled from bought-in components. There are several standard bus structures (e.g. S100 and Multibus, and several disc and printer interfaces (e.g. SCSI, Centronics), through which a wide range of independently manufactured devices can be subsequently connected to many different microcomputers; the matrix printer shown in Fig. 4.17 is one such example, made in Japan but used with nearly every model of microcomputer, including the one on which this book is being drafted.

Interconnectability for data transmission, and thus for low-speed devices attached via data transmission lines, has been largely achieved by CCITT (International Consultative Committee for Telephony and Telegraphy). CCITT standards are coded Vnn for equipment (e.g. the V24 standard for terminal/modem connection) and Xnn for procedures (e.g. the X25 standard for the operation of Packet-Switched Networks (see Section 4.4). A wider and integrated set of standards is now being sponsored by the ISO (International Standards Organisation), in the pursuit of Open Systems Interconnection (OSI), through which it will be possible for any terminal to connect to and use any computer, just as it is possible for any telephone user to connect and speak to (at least in the same language) any other telephone over most of the world.

4.4 DATA TRANSMISSION

One of the significant characteristics of a terminal is remoteness from a computer, which thus implies the transmission of data to and re-transmission of results from the computer. To do so requires:
- access to a data communications medium;
- selection of a data transmission service;
- provision of additional hardware and software.

(a) Data communications media
In principle any form of data communications medium used to carry voice (for example, the telephone network), pictures (for example, CCTV) or non-computer messages (for example, Telex) can also be used to carry digital data. Our freedom to use these media is limited by the scope of the public telecommuncations network — landlines, land or sea cables, microwave channels, earth satellites, and switching centres and exchanges. In

most countries, a national government agency or publicly-supervised corporation (in the UK effectively the Post Office and British Telecom) operate the Postal, Telegraph and Telephone services (such agencies are generically known as PTTs), and exercise some degree of statutory responsibility over the usage of an attachment of devices to the public network. Within a building or a site, however, users are not subject to any external controls over their private internal data communications, and data communication networks in these circumstances are known as Local Area Networks (LANs). Here, in addition to the media which public networks (often now called Wide Area Networks) can use, networks have been constructed using short wave/infra-red waves, electricity cable and all types of copper cable.

(b) Data transmission services

Typically, data transmission services on offer over the public telecommunications network provide a range of facilities:
- line speed from 200 to 4 megabits/sec;
- transmission mode — synchronous/asynchronous or block/character mode;
- traffic simultaneity — half/full duplex (one way or both ways together at a time);
- leased for private use or shared via dialling.

The services offered included a line and an interface. In services which use telephone lines as the carrying medium (currently still the general case), digital traffic has to be converted into the same *analog* form as voice traffic (for example, a fluctuating waveform). This is achieved by an interface device at the start of a line which generates a carrier (sine) wave and then superimposes on it (modulates) the bit on/off pattern coming from the digital source. A similar device at the other end works in reverse to demodulate the wave, i.e. convert it back to the original digital form (see Figure 4.22). This device is known as a *modem*, and has other important functions. For slow line speeds a much simpler device may be used at the terminal end — an acoustic coupler — which recognises the modulated waveform acoustically through a telephone handset. Portable terminals are available fitting into a business case with a built-in acoustic coupler — all you need is a telephone to connect to a remote computer.

Modulation is not required for *digital data networks*, on which both voice and data are sent in digitally coded form and on which, conversely, voice traffic has to be converted to bit form, generally in the local exchange. Most countries are planning for their Integrated Digital Networks during the 1980s, in conjunction with a new generation of computer controlled exchanges and switching centres (the UK version known as System X). A simpler interface known as a Network Interface Unit (NIU) is required to

Fig 4.24 *a modem*

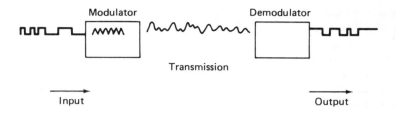

Input   Output

transmit data at a specified rate over digital lines. The advantage of IDNs is a much greater carrying capacity over the same physical lines, and greater line speeds in the absence of the bottleneck effect which modems impose.

The growing importance of data traffic has stimulated most PTTS to invest in services solely for data transmission, sometimes also on dedicated networks, including a faster and improved version of Telex, known as Teletex (not to be confused with Teletext).

Packet switching works on a different principle from circuit switching. In a telephone call, the circuit from source to receipt is open throughout the call; in message switching, of which packet switching is a variant, the destination need not be available at all, the message being sent via a series of switching centres which have some form of intermediate storage. The only open circuit that is required is that between the one switching/centre/ source and the next, or the last switching centre/destination. Message switching treats an entire message as one unit; telegrams may be thought of as an example of pre-computer message switching service. In packet switching, messages are sent in a series of fixed-length packets, each packet being dispatched and handled separately.

Facsimile transmission (Fax) is a special form of data transmission originally devised to send (low-precision) pictures over telecommunications lines by scanning the image line-by-line and sending bits to signify the presence/absence of a mark in the appropriate positions along each line. It is ideally suited for the transmission of text, which it performs on the same basis. There are three international standards now available for Fax; there are regular international services between large cities, and a number of internal users, including newspapers, send copies of pages set in one location to be printed in another. In addition, several European countries are planning widespread internal FAX networks for electronic mail.

Electronic mail allows users to enter letters and other messages at a terminal and be stored in a 'mailbox' (i.e. in a computer store) until the recipient also accesses the same computer; in fact many services provide a much wider range, including access to Telex. They are an example of customer services using and based on the data transmission network, known as Value Added Networks. Prestel, British Telecom's Viewdata service is another example. Their role in disseminating knowledge is further discussed in Chapter 10.

(c) Data transmission hardware and software

A single terminal is treated by the processor like any other slow I/O peripheral, but a distinguishing feature of most terminal-based systems is that there are many potentially connected terminals, and most of the additional hardware and software required for 'teleprocessing' is there to remedy the special problems that a multiplicity of terminals poses.

(i) A data communication controller is normally attached to the slow I/O bus, containing a fixed number of 'ports' (multiples of 8 or 16), each port being a plug-in point for one serial external line. A line may either support one slow terminal, or several more sophisticated terminals 'multidropped' on one line but with a unique logical 'address' on that line.

(ii) A device called a multiplexer may be used intermediately to pack a number of slow terminal traffics on to a faster line; the controller may also contain a demultiplexer to distribute the data back to the original terminal source.

(iii) For all asynchronous traffic (that is, character-by-character), the processor has to handle each character (by interrupting its current work) and then build up the incoming messages from each of the connected terminals. This burden may be eased by 'concentrating' characters into message blocks in an intelligent device either intermediately, or immediately prior to the processor in a subordinate processor known as a *front end processor* (FEP); this may also support some of the extra I/O software required by this type of input data.

(iv) The processor (main or front-end) has to run software that ensures that each terminal has a fair and equal chance of being able to send data when it is ready; that the data as received has not been corrupted in transmission; that data sent by the computer actually get to the specified terminal and so on. This software, aided by firmware in the terminal and other intervening hardware, is collectively known as 'protocols'; most protocols have been designed separately by the computer manufacturers, which is one of the reasons why it is difficult to switch terminals from one computer to another of a different make.

(d) Wide and local area networks

These components are used to construct large-scale networks consisting of terminals on one side and central computers on the other, such as the nation-wide networks of terminals inside and outside banks to the central computers which hold bank account records. The design and operation of these networks is a demanding task in modern computing. Fig. 4.25 shows a typical example of a terminal network of this type.

A simpler approach that is feasible where all the system lies within one building or site is a Local Area Network (LAN). This uses low-cost cables to send small packets of data in bit form over short distances (up to 100 metres between nodes), and at very fast rates (up to 10 megabits/sec). Each terminal and processor is attached to the network by an intelligent interface ('node' or 'transceiver'), which will ultimately cost a hundred pounds or so. The protocols used can be designed from scratch and, using VLSI technology, are built into the nodes; one particularly elegant, and British-invented solution relies upon the simplicity gained by organising

Fig 4.25 *multiple terminal networks*

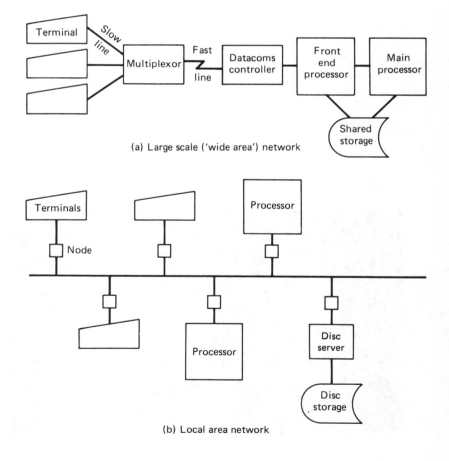

(a) Large scale ('wide area') network

(b) Local area network

the network as a continuous loop or ring. A LAN, as well as being a communications network, can also be seen as an alternative way of arranging devices together ('systems architecture'), and is widely used to allow low-cost microcomputers to share the use of an expensive hard disc or good quality printer.

(e) Computer networks

Even the degree of connectivity described in the pervious section is not enough to meet modern industry's needs for data communication, and many large companies and organisations have built networks of communicating computers to transfer large volumes of data between computers — from one company site to another, from one country to another, from one bank or airline to another, from one government department to another. Most computer networks carry data in packets, using land channels rented from their PTT and satellite links rented from the satellite operators such as Comsat. Fig. 4.26 shows an example of an international computer network.

(f) Bulletin boards

These are the electronic equivalents of public notice boards — a computer containing stored messages which are accessible and readable from terminals or other computers. Some hardware and software suppliers use them for posting errors and their solutions, but they are mostly used by computer clubs or for 'exchange-and-mart', like postcards in a newsagent's window — or merely as a correspondence column.

Fig 4.26 *an international computer network*

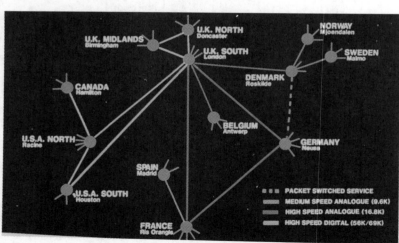

4.5 USING COMPUTERS IN THE TRAVEL TRADE

The message of this chapter is that computer peripherals are the computer's ears and eyes into the real world and its store of information about the real world. The power of the computer largely rests upon our ability to plug it into so many different situations, via the enormous variety of input/output devices that are now available or being developed. Furthermore, the reasons why we wish to get in touch with a computer in this way may be only to gain access to the computer's store of information, or to go through the computer back into the real world at another place, using the computer more as a switching centre and data controller than as a 'processor'. To illustrate how one group of users organise their access to computers in this way, let us examine the travel trade as the chosen sector of the leisure industry.

(a) Travel agents

Travel agents are the retail end of the travel trade, operating in the real world of the high street to sell to the public the services of the transport and accommodation operators, directly or via packages of both organised by tour operators. For this purpose they need to display information about these services, and they need to be able to contact the providers of the services.

The display of information still largely depends on printed material — brochures and posters, leaflets and reference books. These sources of information suffer from several defects — firstly they are expensive to produce and distribute, secondly their supply is exhaustible and not instantly replenishable, thirdly they take up storage space, fourthly, they can easily become out of date, and lastly they contain only static information. For dynamic information it is necessary either to write to or telephone the source, with all the delay and aggravation which this causes. Most travel agents first came into contact with computers when the tour and travel operators started using Prestel and the Teletext facilities to supplement their printed information display, in the form in which all Videotex was originally conceived, as an electronic bookstall which could also accommodate frequently updated dynamic information. Prestel also had an advantage over the telephone, in that a Prestel call cost less than a telephone call of the same duration, and Prestel is always there, not needing a lunch hour or going home at 5 p.m. Furthermore, there was nothing very frightening about the Prestel set, originally looking very much like a television, and you could get information about many different providers from one place/on one telephone number, with auto-dial and repeat dialling; and customers did not get as flustered as they did with long telephone calls and impatient operators on the other end of the line.

When it came to the process of transacting the sale of their services to a customer, however, travel agents were largely limited to the telephone and post for UK business, and to the international telephone and Telex services for international messages. The original Prestel set, as still with most domestic Prestel/TV sets, has only the numeric keypad for sending back data to the Prestel centre and thence onwards to the information provider, and the conventions of the Prestel data layout on 'pages' and screens of limited character content, made it difficult to input the large volume of data needed for a sale.

This situation has been changed out of all recognition in a period of about five years, to a point at which the Viewdata set can now perform a much wider range of the travel agent's communication needs, in the following ways:

(i) The public Prestel service itself has not changed, but it can now provide a linkage from the Prestel computer centres to computer systems of the tour and travel operators, a facility known very sensibly as a 'Gateway' and organised as a numbered 'page' in the normal way;

(ii) Other public data communication services are also accessible from the Prestel service in the same way — electronic mail, Telex and the PSS, all of which contain international data links;

(iii) The Closed User Group feature of Prestel permits information providers to restrict access through the use of passwords to information of a confidential nature, thus turning it into a 'private' system. This has made Prestel attractive to a wider set of users who would not otherwise have made their data available to full public inspection;

(iv) The success and presence of the Prestel set as a 'user-friendly' terminal has encouraged tour and travel operators to set up their own private Viewdata systems, or to use systems organised by third parties;

(v) Business Viewdata sets now have full keyboards and simple screen printers, and the capacity to hold many telephone numbers for auto-dialling to different private Viewdata systems.

There have been other solutions to the problems caused by the multiplicity of tour and travel operators whom the travel agent may wish to contact. In other types of business, and still today in the financial centres, you end up with an array of separate terminals on a desk, each connected to a different source of financial information, and your desk looks like an airline pilot's cabin. The travel trade does have a limited and expensive solution to this problem, in the shape of a special terminal which could be made, using a set of stored protocols, to look like many different terminals which then could access the different computers used by the world's large airlines. This facility is now being extended into the Travicom Skytrack system, in which the airline computers are accessible from a

Viewdata set through a Prestel gateway into a specially-constructed centre containing interfaces to the airline systems.

Thus the modified Viewdata terminal (see Fig. 4.27) can become the hub of a very wide information display and communication network, as shown in Fig. 4.28. Currently, there are more than 10 000 Viewdata sets installed in UK travel agents, 350 tour and travel operators are accessible from a Viewdata set in one or other of the routes shown, and about 70 per cent of business with the biggest operators is transacted in this way.

What the Viewdata terminal will not do for the travel agent is to print the various travel documents needed by the customer and keep the travel

Fig 4.27   *a business Viewdata terminal (courtesy of Sony UK Ltd)*

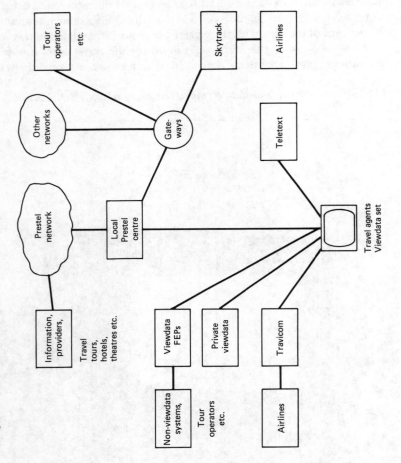

Fig 4.28 *Viewdata and travel systems*

agent's books, because the terminal does not have any local intelligence of its own. In fact, the first failing is only a problem when the customer is travelling immediately, in which case the travel agent has to fill in a blank ticket by hand. It has taken the world's airlines several years to agree on a common layout for their tickets, and it is at last possible for tickets to be printed out direct on a special terminal linked to the central reservation service referred to above; for agents who do a lot of business of this kind, this somewhat simple exercise produces great savings in storage and ticket costs, just as the same facility does in theatre booking systems. More generally, however, the way ahead for the travel agent is to buy a small computer which can run various accounting programs, print out documents and at the same time act as a Viewdata terminal. Such systems are now widely available and are discussed in the next chapter.

Meanwhile the travel agent is being tempted to subscribe to rival value-added networks currently being established in the industry, providing a faster service than the current Prestel facility and based on high-speed digital trunk lines.

(b) Tour and travel operators
The needs of the providers of travel and holiday services are to reach as many customers as possible either directly or through the retail agents, and to provide a fast competitive system for processing actual or potential sales thus generated. There are four ways in which the average family can be seen as accessible in their own right, at home: through the TV set (owned by 85 per cent of families), through the telephone (80 per cent), in newspaper and magazine advertisements, and by direct mailing. Providing information is a significant part of their operations, and using the various computer-based Videotex services is just one part of a wide-ranging advertisement campaign that can be employed to reach the TV/telephone owners. Also significant is the number of 'repeat' customers — those who come back to the same airline/hotel/tour operator, and a data base of names and addresses of previous customers is widely used to produce a mailing list for selling campaigns; this in itself requires a large volume of data storage. That data base also contains the customers' telephone numbers (in case of enforced last-minute modifications by the operators), and thus the potential for telephone selling; luckily, the previous regulations prevented the sort of direct telephone selling common in the USA, but careful readers of this chapter will have noted the advent of both voice input and voice output devices — put them together and you have the basis for the telephone as a computer terminal. The computer accesses each customer record in turn, auto-dials the telephone number in it, sends a synthesised message and responds to the customer's reply, triggering some further action on the strength of the eventual outcome.

Most advertising, and full information in brochures, is still carried on paper, and for all these purposes the larger operators will seek the assistance of word processing in some form or other. The need to carry glossy colour photographs, however, almost always means that WP is used only to prepare the draft text which is then made up in the normal printing processes. This limitation is now being removed by the advent of 'desktop publishing' systems — 32-bit microcomputers with image processing and laser printers, plus software to compose pages with text and illustrations. The process of making up brochures often involves the 'enhancement' of photos to make the sand yellower and the sky bluer, to remove intrusive buildings and even to incorporate artistic impressions of what it will look like when it is built. Such activities are intrinsic capabilities of image processing by computer, and I have no doubt that it is being investigated. TV advertising already makes widespread use of computer-generated images and computer-processed images; and travel operators are already using both static and interactive videos to supplement the normal broadcast opportunities, and offering their services through video hire to the large proportion of households owning a video player. Fig. 4.29 summarises the ways in which travel operators use computers, via specific computer peripherals, in reaching their customers.

Fig 4.29 *reaching the customer with the computer*

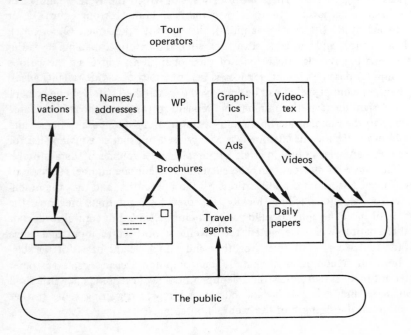

For processing actual or potential sales, and to answer specific enquiries, travel operators need to be accessible both to the public and to the travel agents. A few operators only sell directly to the public, or through their own agents, considering the commission paid to travel agents unnecessary and excessive, and most will provide telephone access to the public and a few, mostly the larger airlines, also have their own 'shops' in large towns. Curiously, direct booking by Viewdata does not seem to be generally available to the public. For most operators, the important feature of their computer system is to be accessible directly or through an intermediate telephone service to the retail travel agents and to their own local sales offices; and since the data base of holidays/flights/rooms is almost always held on the operators' central computer systems, a major objective of their computer operations is to facilitate immediate access via a data communications network which, like the services themselves, operates worldwide.

The large international airlines were, in fact, the pioneers of large-scale terminal networks of the type that are commonplace now, but using a variety of hardware and software that meant, until the advent of the 'common interfaces' described above, a consequential variety of terminals for the independent agents. These networks were directed initially at their own sales offices throughout the world, and particularly at the large international business centres. To reach across the world they had either to rely on international public telecommunications, or to construct their own private network; and most still use the airlines' own network, SITA, even though public services internationally have improved enormously since then through the use of communications satellites.

Travel operators also need large volumes of disc storage to hold information about their services on offer and about their current and potential customers (see Chapter 6 for a further discussion); and they need high-speed and good-quality printers to produce the various transaction and travel documents that are sent direct to customers or via travel agents. In most commercial organisations, documents and letters that are sent to customers are an important element of that organisation's corporate style and image; until recently there has been an unfortunate conflict between speed of printer output and quality of print, but the new breed of laser printer achieves both at the same time, and I confidently predict an improvement in print image quality in our travel documents in the next year or so.

Typical computer systems for travel operators are also widely available in the computer industry, and their content and features are discussed in Chapters 5 and 8.

CHAPTER 5

SYSTEMS ANALYSIS –
PUTTING THE
COMPUTER TO WORK

The previous chapters have covered the basic functions of computing – input and output, processing and storage – and have described devices used to perform those functions. In order to make *profitable* use of the computer it is necessary to adapt these functions and embed them into the fabric of the commercial, industrial or governmental situation whose efficiency we wish to improve through the use of a computer. The main part of this process is known as *systems analysis*, and computer professionals who are employed for this purpose are known as *systems analysts*. The term 'systems' implies a co-ordinated set of activities, in which computer functions will perform only part of the total task, so that it is more correct, and more specific, to talk about computer-based systems, or computer-assisted systems, as an organised and integrated set of man-machine activities in the wider context of a business organisation, for example.

Developing and installing computer-based systems in these circumstances is a critical and sensitive task, calling for business judgement, personal acumen and technical ability, a combination rarely found in equal proportions. This is one reason why so many computer applications are either technically correct but don't meet their functional objectives, or are working to meet their users' needs but in a technically incompetent manner. A proper balance and compromise are required, although it must be accepted that the full capability of a computer is *not* met merely by requiring it to perform mechanical equivalents of human tasks.

5.1 DECIDING WHAT YOU WANT THE COMPUTER TO DO

A computer-based system for any purposeful use, or 'computer application', will contain, as its core, a set of computer programs as its distinctive dynamic feature. It must be said, however, that the writing of these programs (computer programming) is one of the last and lowest levels of the activities in the development of a system, and only one of the interconnected activities in operating a system. (Computer programming is therefore dealt with in Chapter 6.) To use the analogy of building a house, computer programming can be seen as part of the construction work — perhaps the brickwork. Before this stage an architect has to be engaged and given his brief; the size, layout, style, contents and features of the house have to be decided on; plans and drawings and specifications of materials made; planning permission sought and approved; a site found and prepared; builders engaged; materials acquired; contracts placed, and so on. In practice, however, there are few people who can afford the luxury of an architect-designed house built to meet their exact and individual needs (and perhaps some who can afford it who do not have enough faith in architects to do so). Instead we buy either new houses already designed and under construction, or older houses from their previous owner, houses that were probably built en masse to a general standard but speculatively for sale as fully finished product. Custom-built or made-to-measure cars, suits, and software are all much more expensive than their off-the-peg ready-made equivalents, which have the added advantage of being ready for use or wear without waiting. For many computer users, therefore there is little choice other than finding the most suitable 'package' of off-the-peg software (and then find the appropriate hardware on which to run it).

The process of establishing a computer-based system in a company in place of a manual system, regardless of the eventual source of the software, starts with a decision to make some change from the present arrangements that is triggered off either by immediate problems and deficiencies, or in accordance with the current stage in a previously agreed long-term plan — the systems plan.

Experience has taught us that this work is best approached in an orderly way through a series of stages shown in Fig. 5.1, which is sometimes known as the systems life cycle or project life cycle, since the task of developing a computer-based system is a typical project activity. It is possible, of course, to acquire working computer programs without going through all these stages, but all the evidence from our previous thirty years' business use of computers is that you ignore them at the peril of wasting your time and your company's investment. Of course, the time and effort that you expend on them will depend upon the size of the scheme and of the projected investment which it will incur.

(a) What is the problem?

Although it has been repeatedly emphasised that the computer is, through the computer program and I/O devices, a highly flexible and multi-purpose machine, it cannot be assumed that it is the answer to every problem occur-

Fig 5.1 *the stages of systems development*

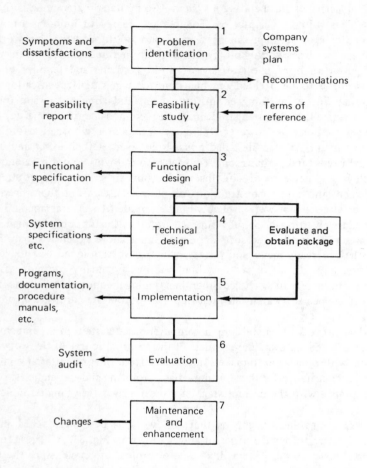

ring in the running of a business; unfortunately no such universal panacea exists (except in the minds of computer salesmen and consultants). When a request, suggestion or command is received to computerise some business activity, it is advisable to undertake some analysis of what the fundamental difficulty is in the present set-up. Chapter 2 has itemised some business problems which may well be within the true scope of information technology, but the would-be user should be aware that there are other solutions to some of these problems – perhaps with a simple redesign of paperwork or clerical jobs that O and M or work study officers are qualified to carry out. Even inside the information handling area, there will be activities in which the computer may play a very restricted role:

(i) those requiring individual/expert skill;
(ii) those involving human counselling and advice;
(iii) those in which the alternatives and procedures are not standardised or are enormously complex;
(iv) those involving one-off decisions;
(v) those involving complex matching and pattern recognition;
(vi) those involving very low volumes of activity.

As a consequence it may be necessary or advisable (though not necessarily politic) to reply to certain requests that the computer is not the (best) answer to this problem. Company management may however decide that for other reasons it would still be preferable to press ahead; that decision is properly a business decision taken in the full light of the best technical and professional advice.

(b) The feasibility study

Having passed this hurdle it is necessary, in principle, to be satisfied firstly that the computer can meet the operational targets required of it, (*technical feasibility*), and secondly that it can also meet those requirements in a financially acceptable manner (*economic viability*). These two interwoven factors can be investigated, if required, in a feasibility study. However, in most cases both technical feasibility and economic viability can be assumed:

(i) when it has been done before (on the same type of equipment);
(ii) when your competitors (or similar organisations) have done it.

A feasibility study is needed when completely new applications are being investigated, or when the application is critical in performance (life-dependent systems such as air traffic control, defence systems, hospital systems).

Technical feasibility is investigated by examining the demands made on the proposed systems, primarily in terms of speed of response to input (real-time response) and its capability for bulk handling of input and output, by the foreseeable traffic load. (A computer system has to be designed to cater for the maximum likely level of work on a system, which may call for statistical analysis of current and previous trends; 'system overload' is perhaps the most serious and most difficult operating problem likely to be encountered). There is obviously a trade-off between the cost of a proposed system (see below), and its performance on the one hand and its viability on the other.

Economic viability is concerned with the cost-benefit analysis of a proposed system (one which meets its operational objectives) or the relative cost-performance trade-off of a range of alternatives. The *cost* of a system is calculated from two factors:

– the initial cost (hardware plus software plus implementation/installation)

written off over the period of years assessed for its operational life (less any scrap value at the end of life);
- the running costs per year (staff, materials, services).

Benefits are harder to quantify and must be sought from the following list:
- staff savings;
- speed and accuracy;
- less lost revenue through stock-outs, machine down-time, non-utilisation of plant;
- improved management;
- greater competitiveness and share of the market;
- capability of expansion and change.

The evaluation of costs must conform to the accounting standards used for the appraisal of *all* investment within a company. The *feasibility report* should contain clear conclusions and recommendations presented in a convincing manner, so that management (often the Board of Directors) can reach a decision based on the report.

(c) System definition

When it is assumed (or demonstrated) that a satisfactory application is envisaged, it is then desirable to draw up, after some investigation and discussion, a system definition or functional specification. This is a semi-legal document, which may in fact form the basis of contracts, containing a specification of what the system is to do, and the volumes and other given information. It is not a technical specification, and therefore does not specify how it is to be done unless that is particularly relevant to the case at issue.

It is at this point that some careful judgement is required by the systems analyst. He is strictly the agent of the user concerned, and must therefore have a more limited knowledge of the work area concerned, so that the user's requirements must be considered as paramount. However, most users are not fully aware of all the computer's capabilities, and will be setting out their needs in terms of their current operations. A careful synthesis of the two interests is needed. The most sacrosanct part of the specification is the output: the results are what only the users themselves can lay down, and it is then normal to work backwards from that point, to work out what input (from data input or data storage) is needed, and what are the processes to provide those results.

As a document that may be used to gain competitive tenders, and as the terms of a contract, the system definition must contain all the information that a tenderer and potential contractor needs to know about the users' requirements (in the Civil Service it is known as a Requirements Specification):

- statement of objectives and scope of the system;
- performance objectives and justifications;
- a verbal or diagrammatic description of the system showing the flow of data and logical content (see also Section 5.5 below);
- description and examples of output from the system;
- description and examples of input to the system;
- (additional) hardware requirements;
- data specifications;
- processing and calculations;
- controls;
- departmental responsibilities;
- glossary of terms;
- enhancements and potential growth.

For large computer applications both feasibility studies and functional design are high-level computing tasks, often carried out by external consultants. They require a high degree of technical knowledge and experience, a full understanding of, and sympathy with, users' needs and a sound judgement in assessing standards — by profession, across industry or industrial sector, by application, etc. As do further stages of systems analysis, they will call upon fact-finding and documentation skills, dissection/analysis of findings and problem solving/synthesis for solutions.

At the same time, the importance of joint user–computer staff work at this stage cannot be over-emphasised. In order to ensure this, a professional approach of *participative systems analysis* has recently been put forward after long exploratory studies, based on the thesis that nobody has the right to design a work system for somebody else. Participative systems analysis requires formal joint working groups at all levels (not just the user management and computer project leader), and jointly determined objectives and decisions. It clearly owes much to ideologies of industrial democracy, and while it is clearly apposite at the stage of system definition, it is harder to envisage its working successfully at the next stage, which takes off from the system definition into full-scale technical design.

It is also appropriate, particularly if the system is to be produced on contract, to accompany the functional specification with a prescription of what will constitute the acceptance test for the system, since acceptance will totally depend on specific performance of the functions and the operational targets defined in the functional specification.

5.2 ACQUIRING A PACKAGED SYSTEM

At this point comes a major divergence between acquiring a working system (either from external contractors or your own computer staff) by designing and producing the software from scratch, and seeking your solution from packaged software. In very many cases there is no choice at all; bespoke software is not even a consideration when you buy a home computer, or a small business or educational microcomputer at the cost of a few hundred pounds; and in a tiny proportion of cases it may well be that because of the near uniqueness of the circumstances no packaged software can be found at all (software for lighthouse keepers or polo players??). Where a choice in principle exists, the considerations that may apply are summarised in Table 5.1.

Table 5.1

Advantage of package	Disadvantages
Saves staff	Requires 'customising'
Saves time	Likely to be less efficient
Provides expertise	Difficulty of buying
Should be cheaper	The 'not-invented-here' syndrome
Avoids 're-inventing the wheel'	Cost of multiple copies
No possible alternative	May still require changing your procedures

Since the packaged outcome is statistically more likely, this section deals with packaged software; bespoke systems are discussed in Section 5.3.

(a) Cost
Good quality bespoke software is expensive, because it is still a labour-intensive product — you can expect to pay between £5–10 per program instruction for good-quality work. It is possible to find cheaper sources of bespoke programming, but the poor quality programs that usually follow are one of the reasons why bespoke software has a bad reputation among many companies. The cost of packaged software depends on the volume of the expected market (the more copies you expect to sell, the smaller will be each customer's share of the original production cost), and to a lesser extent on what the market will bear, leading to the infuriating situation of paying more for the same package if it is to be used on a large computer than on a smaller and cheaper computer. Even with modifications, however (see Section (iv) below), you can expect a package to be at the very most half the cost of bespoke software.

(b) Delivery
Packaged software is available off-the-shelf, while bespoke software takes time to produce and test. It is a mistake to produce software in a hurry, as what will be left out in the latter stages of testing and what will be left

in are errors which will you discover over a period of time, and according to Murphy's law, at the worst possible times. For the same reason, you should be careful about being the first customer of a new package, at least without negotiating extended warranty and immediate repairs; preferably you should aim to have allowed time for previous customers to have discovered the most obvious errors.

(c) Customising

Customising is the process of tailoring a package to meet more closely your exact requirements. It is reasonable to expect a well-designed package to have built-in facilities to do this, without additional programming or cost, for the following purposes:

- putting the company name on displays, reports and documents;
- formatting computer output on preprinted documents which form part of your company's or personal image — (letter-heads, cheques, invoices, payslips, etc.;
- inclusion/exclusion of optional processing features, e.g. trade union subscriptions in payroll, VAT eligibility in invoicing, discounts in sales;
- setting alternative process variables, e.g. maximum customer credit, period allowed for payment of bills;
- selection of major parts of a package and integrating what you have selected.

You should look for a feature in the package that allows you to make these changes or choices, often called a system setup facility, without requiring any software knowledge whatsoever but merely by taking you through a series of questions-and-answers or by allowing you to select from a list of alternatives (see Fig. 5.2).

More serious structural changes to a package, or extensions to the standard facilities, will normally be performed under separate contract by the software producer, if they are willing to undertake this type of work. Even if you have the staff and time to do it, you will probably find that the software producer is unwilling to give you the source code as there is so little protection against the illegal copying and 'pirating' of software at the moment. There is a point of view, however, that you should think very seriously as to whether such changes or extensions are absolutely necessary, as in any case you may find the company totally unable or unwilling to do the work themselves or help you to do it yourself.

(d) Maintenance

If the procedures contained in the package are subject to significant structural change of a type that cannot be ignored, then your package will have to be changed, often at short notice. Such changes usually result from government legislation or orders in council, and are often announced in

138

Fig 5.2 *a typical commercial package (courtesy of BOS Software Ltd)*

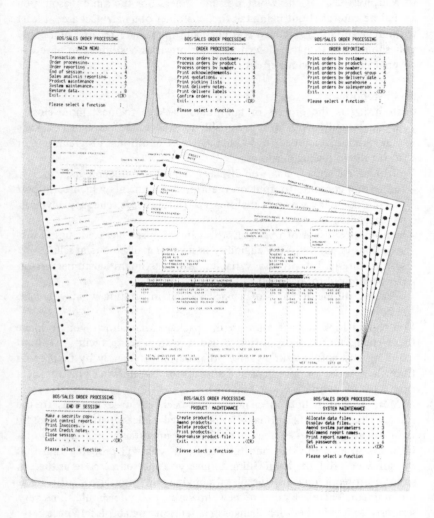

the annual budget. Without the change your package may subsequently be invalid. A 'good' package will not leave you in the lurch, provided you have taken advantage of any maintenance contract that is offered. This particularly refers to packages containing tax procedures – income tax deduction in payroll packages, income tax relief in mortgage and insurance payments, VAT and Excise Tax. Under a maintenance agreement you will either receive a completely new copy of the package incorporating the enforced change, or an item of software containing the change along with instructions on how to affect the change. A maintenance contract may also cover you against basic errors in the software itself.

(e) Availability

Packages are likely to be available, and relevant to a recognisable market, where the functions to be performed are fixed or standardised:

- by country-wide legislation – taxation (income tax, national insurance, VAT), sick pay benefits, company law, etc.;
- by general commercial practice – e.g. accounts, sales order processing, stock control;
- by industry type (e.g. manufacturing or local government);
- by 'vertical market' such as holiday tour operators or travel agents;
- by standard formulae – engineering calculations, general maths and statistics;
- by common functions such as graphics, word processing, spreadsheet manipulation, sorting;
- by company or trade group policy on behalf of all parts or members.

The generality of the contents of packages will vary according to the sanctions behind the standardising agency. There are, however, some applications where it will hardly ever be necessary to go outside the package industry, and correspondingly you will expect to find a range of highly acceptable alternatives;

- word processing, spreadsheets, graphics, data management (see section 6.6 below);
- general accounts, sales and purchase ledgers, payroll;
- engineering design/CADCAM and engineering production (larger microcomputers upwards).

(f) Sources

Packages are available from a number of sources, with corresponding costs and advantages or disadvantages.

(i) Commercial packages

These are packages that have been produced specifically, or developed from an original set of programs, for the purpose of selling at such a cost, and in such quantities, that both the producer (usually a software/systems house) and the vendor/licensee make a profit. They are available primarily from software houses and service companies, and represent the major *raison d'être* of many such companies, and a major source of excellence in software.

140

(ii) Manufacturers' packages

These were primarily produced as a service to customers, in order to attract them to buy in the first place, and thus were sold at a nominal price or provided free, included in ('bundled' with), and disguised in the overall cost of the hardware along with system software (see Chapter 7). This practice has now largely disappeared in mainframe computers with the introduction of 'unbundling', and manufacturers' software operates at the same sort of level as commercial software, though not necessarily at the same profit levels, and not necessarily at the same level of excellence.

(iii) Program libraries

Many computer manufacturers, users' organisations, and some professional institutions have build up extensive libraries of computer programs, usually contributed on a mutual self-help basis, and usually programs written for specific purposes. The contents of libraries are described in library guides, and a program, with minimal documentation, is available for the cost of a magnetic tape, or disc, on to which the required program is copied.

Programs obtained from program libraries are mostly unguaranteed, and language/machine specific, but at the same time very cheap. For a commonly required utility function or application program you will almost certainly find what you want from these sources, provided you can accept the uncertainty associated with it.

There are, however, a very few quality-controlled libraries available, usually for a higher entrance fee. The Numerical Algorithms Group (NAG) Library and the International Mathematical and Statistical Library (IMSL) are particularly good examples, and if this is your line of business, you cannot do better than to purchase subscription rights.

(iv) Software brokers and indexes

The scope for using existing software, however, extends well beyond the capacity of organised libraries, and more organisations have been tempted to make their software available, at a fee, to external users, through the agency of commercial software brokerages and indexes. Smaller software houses also use such agencies as selling outlets. Software obtained in this way usually has a higher guarantee of reliability, and the National Computing Centre operates a carefully thought out software verification scheme for software available on its computer-held index.

(v) Small business systems

In the minicomputer and microcomputer market, packages come with the computer, and to a large extent the package sells the computer (see Chapter 8) and not vice versa. Many packages are available on a number of different computers, but there is not always a wide range, if at all, of alternative packages for the same function.

(vi) Free software

Free software is to be found from a number of sources — computer clubs, bulletin boards, magazines, and from the free market culture of computer enthusiasts everywhere, although often of an unpredictable quality. Because of the high price of software and the avarice of some software producers, there is also a natural temptation to copy any software that you can get your hands on, and there is almost a black market of software circulating in this way. Also, but regrettably very rarely, an institution may as a matter of policy put into the public domain software produced by them; for instance there is a file transfer program named Kermit produced by Stanford University, USA, which performs the invaluable function of transferring data between a wide range of otherwise incompatible computers (see Chapter 4.4). No computer installation should be without a copy. Lists of public domain software are available from computer clubs and even from some suppliers.

5.3 DESIGNING BESPOKE SOFTWARE

The production of a computer system relying on bespoke software is the bread-and-butter work of most computer professionals, and means designing and implementing the computer programs, and the framework of data handled in them. This is essentially design work, and like any design work consists of 5 per cent inspiration and 95 per cent perspiration. The systems designer's specific brief is the functional specification previously prepared and agreed, and to ensure that the eventual system meets that specification it is highly desirable that the specification has been drawn up in a way that leads on to further analysis and design without a major interruption of thought and effort. There now exist several Systems Design Methodologies (known like nearly everything else by acronyms such as SSADM) which require a functional specification to be prepared using specific verbal and/or diagrammatic techniques that enable system design to proceed by expanding the original into greater detail and subsequently (and at the latest possible moment) adding the technical dimension. Some of these techniques are examined in Section 5.4 below.

At the same time as ensuring that a system meets the exact terms of its functional specification, a system designer also has to adhere to a general brief to produce a well-behaved system that is:

(i) economical (that is, cost-effective) compared with alternative systems;

  (ii) accurate, to ensure that all outputs are correct;
 (iii) timely, to meet the schedule of outputs;
 (iv) flexible, to cope with unforeseen requirements;
  (v) robust, to cope with all errors in input;
 (vi) secure against loss, fraud or failures;
 (vii) maintainable and intelligible (that is, well-documented);
(viii) implementable with current skills;
 (ix) compatible with existing systems;
  (x) portable over a range of hardware/software configurations;
 (xi) efficient in use of hardware;
 (xii) acceptable to company standards.

From these starting points, the systems designer has to make reasoned decisions on all aspects of a computer system:

-- data to be output — content, format, device/media;
- data to be permanently or temporarily stored in the system — content, organisation, device;
- data to be input — content, format, device/media;
- content and organisation of software;
- programming language and methods of software development and testing;
- selection and organisation of computer (if appropriate);
- selection of data communication methods (if appropriate).

These are weighty problems, pursued with the aid of the Systems Methodologies, working from what is fixed and given, through successive stages of transformation from what is given to what is required, and preferably delaying irrevocable decisions until the last possible time. The three major groups of topics — data, software and hardware — are treated in more detail in the following chapters.

The end product of Technical Design is a System Specification followed by a series of lower-level specifications. The system specification is the ultimate technical reference, and contains detailed descriptions of all aspects of the computer system, hardware, software, and operating procedures (which is why it has sometimes to be subdivided), and may be regarded as the final plans and blueprint for the system. The lower-level specifications are for the detailed implementation work, primarily for the production of working programs and for other operational requirements.

An outline of the contents would be as follows:

- system summary; brief description, including relationship with other systems;
- systems diagrams and other relevant forms of documentation;
- data preparation and output procedures;
- data communication procedures;
- computer procedures;
- document and I/O specifications;

- file and record specifications;
- operating requirements;
- program list and software;
- references to lower-level specifications such as program specifications.

5.4 MAKING A SYSTEM WORK

(a) Implementation

The detailed construction of the system calls for a number of parallel activities, and is the most demanding and intensive part of the project, particularly as by this time, detailed project planning to achieve the target date is in operation. Programming is perhaps the most urgent and intensive activity (unless pre-packaged programs are used) but acquisition of hardware and particularly services such as data transmission facilities and stationery are perhaps more troublesome because they depend on outside agencies. (Subcontracting programming is also a common practice at this stage.) Fig. 5.3 shows a diagram of typical activities undertaken at this time, from which the variety of work can be seen. The processes involves in the production of working *programs* are described in Chapter 7.

Another significant group of operations is concerned with final planning for the introduction of the system — (recruiting and) training staff, briefing manager and customers, producing working and informative documents — all of which, along with the final approval and acceptance of the results of the programs, also places a heavy premium on relationships with the users/ customers.

The process for the final testing and introduction of the computer-based system generally moves through the following substages:
 (i) internal program and program run testing;
 (ii) conversion of permanent files into computer form;
 (iii) full-scale systems test on historical data;
 (iv) parallel running on live data *or* pilot-trial running on selected part of the organisation;
 (v) partial or total changeover.

At some stage, a formal acceptance test (which has been defined before-hand, preferably as part of the 'contract' or agreement with the systems development team) will be run and the results used to determine whether the system is contractually acceptable.

This ends the first part of systems development — with a bang not a whimper — but it should be remembered that subsequent activities of review, enhancement and maintenance may, in a system of a realistic life of say ten years, add as much content and work load as in the original phase of development.

144

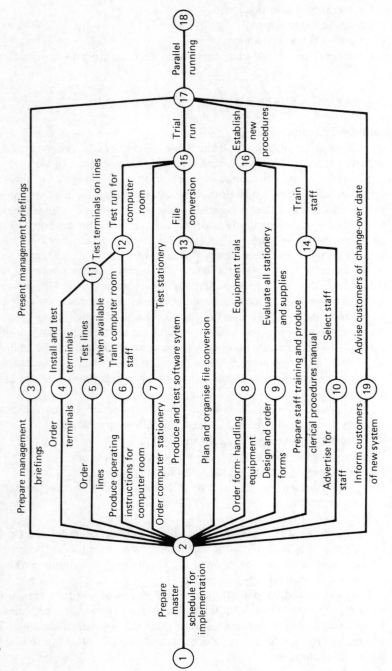

Fig 5.3 *implementation activities*

(b) Audit and review

After the system has been taken over and run for a few months, it is common to hold an audit and review operation to consider whether the system really is working as required, and to consider whether any shortcomings can be put right. (It may be considered to be the equivalent of a warranty period.) One of the greatest problems in designing systems is that managers only realise what the computer can do when they see it working and then they want it to do more than they originally asked for — one of the reasons for Parkinson's law of computers, which states that the demands on a system always escalate to the full capacity no matter how much spare provision you have prudently left. That is why it is important to produce an unsophisticated mock-up of important points of the system (mostly the fully interactive stages and terminal/screen dialogues) well in advance of the design being frozen, as it must be at some point in the technical design stage. It may be prudent, if very troublesome, to allow formally for some type of evolutionary design to emerge during the first few months of operation and then finally (?) to confirm the system at this point.

(c) Maintenance

One of the greatest hopes of computer departments is for systems which go into operation on time, are trouble-free and never need attention. Alas, the facts of business and commercial life are never static, and changes to working systems (known as maintenance) now account for up to 50 per cent of the time of progammer and analyst teams. If you have subcontracted your design and/or programming work you will need to make another contractual arrangement for maintenance. Some of the factors which call for programs to be changed are:

(i) changes in the law (for example, Statutory Sick Pay, EEC procedures, tax changes);

(ii) changes in business practice (metrication, inflation accounting);

(iii) changes in company organisation;

(iv) change of company style and documents;

(v) new and irresistible requirements by managers.

The predictable changes (such as wage rates, product costs) should be provided for in the sets of working programs. Only unpredictable events *should* cause program changes.

Other causes for reprogramming are to bring old programs up to new standards (such as those brought about by trends such as structured programming), or to convert programs to run on new machines when changing hardware.

The need to amend and rework old programs is the main reason why standards of program construction and documentation need to be so high. Nearly as troublesome, but arising from a different source, are requests to add to, or *'enhance'* a working system. Users change their minds, or extend their horizons, very quickly once a system is successfully working, and such requests are undoubtedly legitimate. Computer staff, however, having emerged from the traumatic stage of implementation are more likely to wish to leave well alone unless they have to make enforced maintenance changes, and this is a cause of friction in many organisations.

5.5 SYSTEM DOCUMENTATION

The need for full information about what a computer system does and how it works is evident from the previous sections of this chapter. If you are buying a packaged system, you normally have no direct contact with the authors of the software, nor can you read it yourself, so that you are dependent on formal descriptions of the product. If your software is being produced by your designers and programmers you will have to provide full information about your wishes and receive full information back about the system in the same way when it is ready for use. Information about computer systems is carried in systems documents, whose creation and care are important parts of computing, both as integral elements in the work of analysts, programmers and managers and also as the main elements of technical authors' work.

Fig. 5.5 shows a typical 'hierarchy' of systems documents, most of which at the lowest level will be created at or immediately prior to implementation. Most systems documents are of course formal (typed) documents on paper, but computer-based text-processing methods are increasingly being used, and many terminal-based systems are self-documenting (see Chapter 7).

An important feature of systems documents is the use of various types of diagrams, firstly on the general principle that a picture speaks a thousand words, and secondly because diagrams can convey formal structures and relationships that are indispensable in some formal Design Methodologies. A diagram is a graphical representation of a procedure, showing the constituent activities of the procedure within box symbols, and connections between the activities by connecting lines which may indicate flows from one activity to the next. Flowcharts of various types are widely used by engineers and work study officers. They may in particular be used to describe existing or proposed clerical and computer procedures at any level of detail down to the internal processes of computer programs. Many of them are prescribed in official standards, such as the Systems Documentation Standards of the UK National Computing Centre, and others form part of the systems methodologies or are deeply enshrined in custom and practice. Templates and preprinted chart forms are useful for drawing them.

Fig 5.4 *the documentation of a computer project*

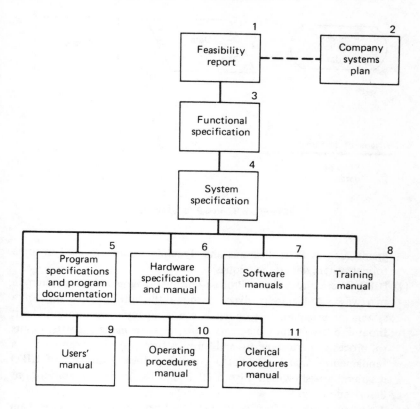

(i) a block diagram shows all activities in undifferentiated block symbols – for an example see Fig. 5.1;

(ii) a data flow diagram shows the flow of data within a system, from source to files and processes, and then to their destination; a variation is a document distribution chart. See Fig. 5.5 for a definition of symbols and Figs 5.8 and 5.9 for examples;

(iii) a system flowchart shows the flow of control (sequence of activities) within a computer-based system, generally at the level of programs, input, output and files. Fig. 5.6 shows an approved set of system flowchart symbols, used in an example in Fig. 5.13;

(iv) a network or arrow diagram, showing activities and events usually in a once-off job, or 'project' in general, is a common method used in the planning of all types of work involving multiple activities in parallel, and an example is shown in Fig. 5.3; special forms of network dia-

Fig 5.5 *data flow diagram conventions*

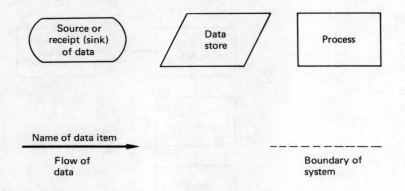

(See Figs 5.8 and 5.9 for examples.)

grams such as Petri diagrams and dynamic graphs are used in some formal system design techniques;

(v) HIPO (Hierarchy + Input–Process–Output) diagrams show a system in two ways. A hierarchy diagram shows the internal structure of a system or program, very much like a company's organisation chart. Input–Process–Output diagrams show, as their name suggests, inputs to, processes performed by and outputs from a system or module – a fundamental model of what a computer does. Examples of HIPO diagrams are shown in Figs 5.10 and 5.14, using the conventions described in Fig. 5.7.

(vi) A System Outline Chart very simply but very clearly shows the main structural features of a system, with the addition of the main Data Files held in the system (see Fig. 5.12).

(vii) Some systems can exist only in a fixed set of states (e.g. a telephone is either engaged, unobtainable (i.e. out of action) or ready for use). A state diagram shows each state and the conditions under which the system changes from one state to another (see Fig. 5.16 for a somewhat atypical example).

Many of these diagrams are shown in the following section. Other types of diagrams are used for documenting programs and are discussed in Chapter 7.

The presentation of the textual part of Systems Documents is also aided by the use of formal preprinted forms for describing the contents of reports, records and files, examples of which are given in Chapter 6.

Fig 5.6 *computer system flowchart symbols*

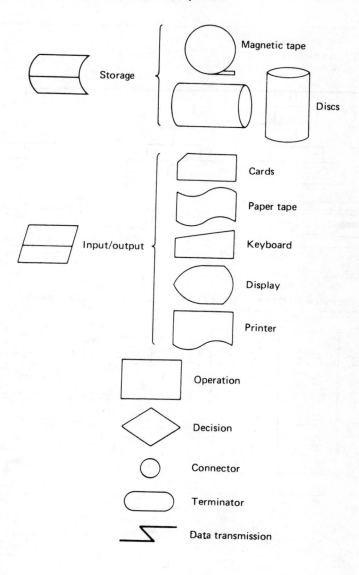

150

Fig 5.7 *HIPO diagrams*

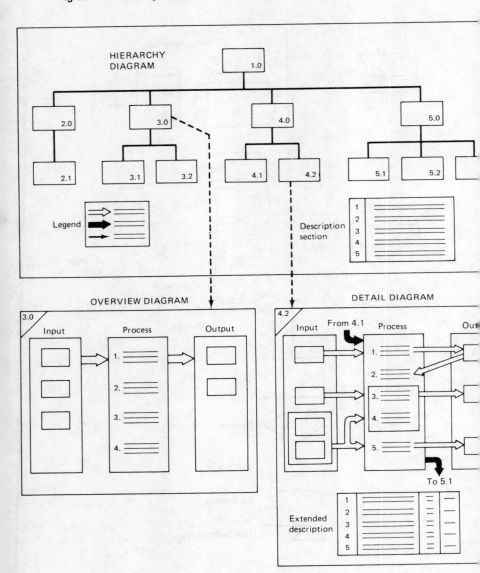

5.6 DESIGNING COMPUTER SYSTEMS FOR THE TRAVEL TRADE

(b) The market
The travel trade represents a distinguishable 'vertical market' to the computer business, with some characteristics which have made it a specialist area for the development of computer applications. Some of these characteristics relate to the structure of the trade, and have been mentioned earlier in this book at the end of Chapter 2:
- the division between the travel operators, tour operators and the retail travel agents, with a relatively small area of overlap and 'direct selling';
- competition between tour operators;
- the dependence of profits on selling all the seats;
- operational procedures largely 'standardised' by competition and through trade standards;
- small size of most operators in both sectors;
- a few very big operators who set the pace.

Objectives for people designing new or acquiring packaged computer systems in this area mostly follow from these market characteristics:
- systems must be able to reach as many retail outlets/travel operators as possible, and fast;
- systems must be able to hold/access a large volume of data and report on it in a variety of ways;
- systems must accommodate a large number of different processing rules, which may need to be changed very frequently;
- systems must encompass the standard features and procedures common to the trade;
- systems should be able to expand upwards in capacity;
- systems must be reliable;
- systems must incorporate a Viewdata element;

(b) The scope
Fig. 1.12 showed a diagram of the travel trade and its constituent components, in a form subsequently defined as a data flow diagram. For the purpose of detailed examination of computer applications, it is necessary to further narrow the field of study, by defining the Holiday Business as comprising the tour operators and the travel agents. Most operators distinguish two main operational sub-systems — front office/selling and back office/administration and accounting. Figs 5.8 and 5.9, which are data flow diagrams for a typical tour operator and travel agent respectively, show the boundary between back office and front, which is no more than that which exists in most organisations between the administrators and the doers! As in any other type of business, there is clearly a considerable interaction between the two areas. Historically, computer systems tend to

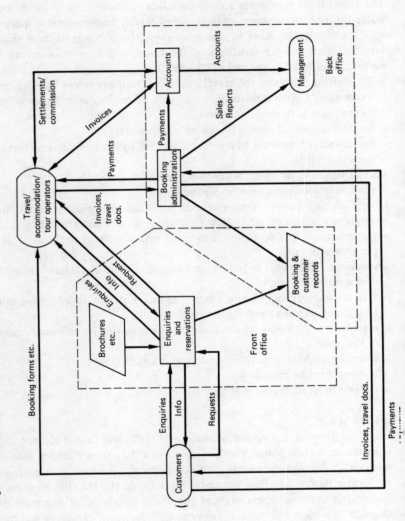

Fig 5.8 *a DFD of a travel agent's system*

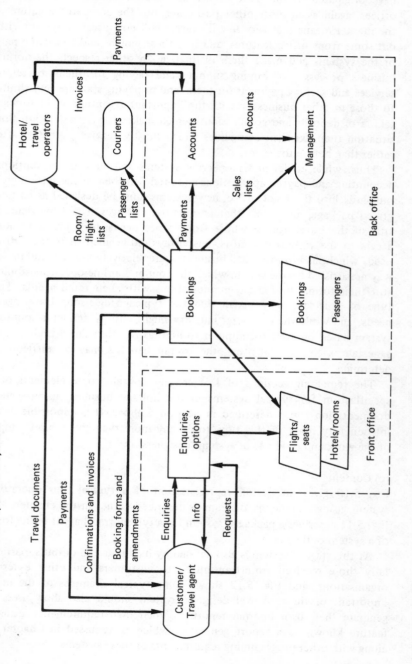

Fig 5.9 *a DFD of a tour operator's system*

have originated in the back offices and then expanded into the front offices, again as in most other businesses, but the competitive nature of the market means that very few operators will now accept a system without some front office features, and it is these which tend to set the pace of the systems and make them distinctive. In other respects the normal business processes of buying supplies and paying for them, of selling services and seeking payment for them, and of paying staff are very similar to those in other businesses; with the important exception of the forward taking of deposits and commissions, which makes for an easier cash flow situation than exists in companies which mostly receive payments after rather than before the event.

Thus, while earlier and pioneering systems started with conventional accounting and payroll applications and modified them as the system grew outwards into the front office, new systems must be designed as an integrated package, albeit one that permits use in stages. This is particularly true of the travel agents, whose front office needs, for communications access to the various operators, has always outweighed their back office needs which, as in most small businesses, are relatively modest, and in any way are assisted by the way in which the tour and airline operators administor their formal business communications with their retail agents. This type of assistance may be all that the typical single-shop travel agent needs, and while the computer industry might wish to sell an accounting system based on a microcomputer to him, as to other single traders such as estate agents or solicitors, the overall benefits may be difficult to determine.

The remaining sections of this chapter contain some elements of a specification for typical systems in the holiday business, using system doumentation forms described in Section 5 above. It is impossible in an introductory book of this type to do any more than give a brief sample of the work and products of systems designers.

(c) Contents

Fig. 5.10 gives an overall representation of a typical tour operator's system, using a hierarchy diagram as described earlier in the chapter, and Fig. 5.11 describes a packaged system for a typical travel agent in the form of a system outline chart.

At this stage, a system is also defined by its inputs and outputs, particularly those received from/transmitted to customers and other external organisations, and Fig. 5.12 shows some typical examples of the most important of these. A well-designed system should also allow users to generate their own internal reports to their own requirements, using a feature known as a report generator, which is discussed in Chapter 7, along with other programming requirements of these systems.

Fig 5.10 a HIPO hierarchy diagram of a tour operator's system.
(Abbreviated in interests of simplicity of presentation)

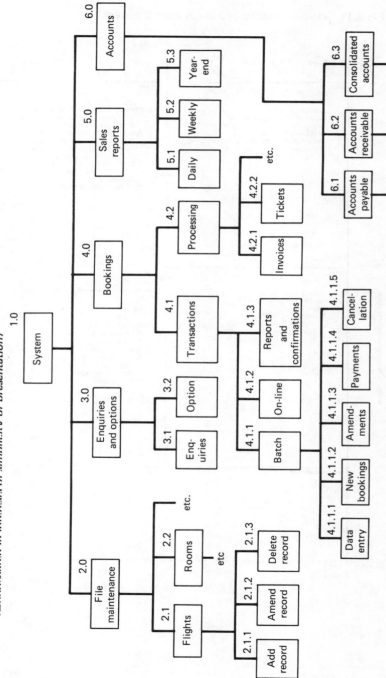

156

Fig 5.11 *a system outline of a travel agent's system*

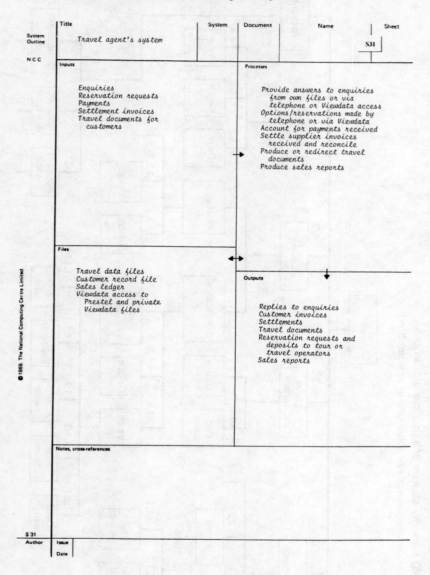

157

Fig 5.12 *some travel documents (courtesy Intasun Ltd)*

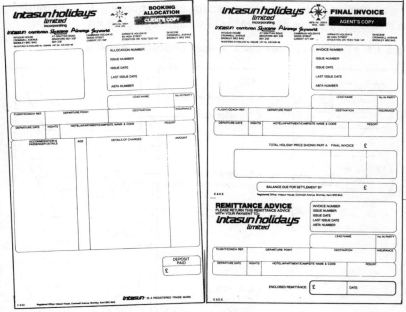

In order to provide the necessary outputs, a system must be based around a powerful and flexible data storage facility, the features of which are discussed in the next chapter.

(d) Processing

The most critical processing of inputs within a system relates to the two stages of making a holiday booking — firstly taking out an option, and secondly the confirmation of a booking with a deposit and full information about all passengers. Figs 5.13 and 5.14 contain a typical specification of these processing procedures, the first in the form of a HIPO detail diagram and the second in the form of a flowchart.

The progress of a booking through a system passes through a number of stages, each of which changes the status of that booking. It is appropriate to record the progress of a booking as a state diagram, in Fig. 5.15.

Fig 5.13 *a HIPO detail chart of a holiday booking procedure*

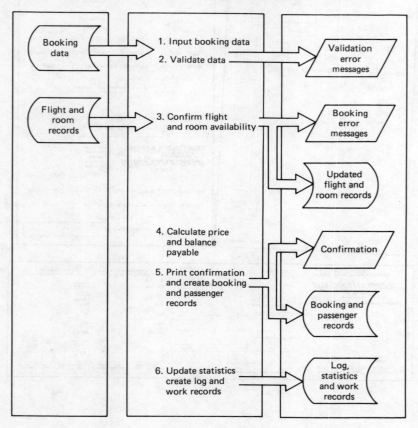

Fig 5.14 *system flowchart of holiday booking procedure*

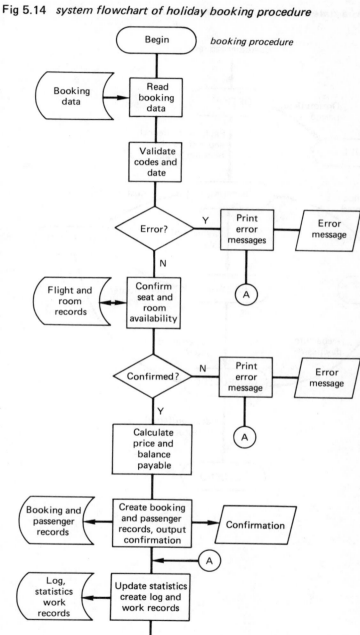

Fig 5.15 *a state diagram of a holiday booking*

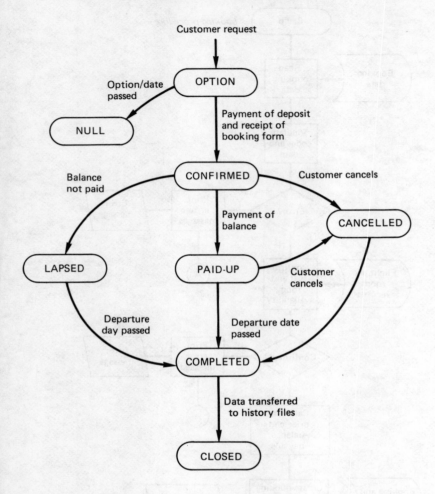

DATA AND RECORDS

There are two reasons why it is important to examine and analyse data as part of the process of setting up a computer system. Firstly, data is the raw material of a large proportion of purposeful computing; the older term of data processing and the more sophisticated version of information processing express this fact explicitly. It would not be surprising, therefore, that poorly arranged and organised data leads to inefficient and unsuccessful computing. This might be described as the theoretical or logical reason why data is important. Secondly, the processing of data or information (or perhaps the processing of raw data into refined information) involves a mixture of Read/Write commands, which set off a sequence of external device operations (but not in every case — see below) measured still in tens of milliseconds, and of other commands which are executed within the processor at nanosecond speeds — a speed differential of one million! In these circumstances the run time of a program is effectively the sum of its I/O operation timings, and computer systems are 'I/O bound', the resolution of which phenomenon is a major preoccupation for hardware and software engineers. This might be described as the practical or physical reason why data is important to efficient computing.

6.1 DATA ANALYSIS

Data analysis is concerned with the source of data and the fundamental relationships between data. Data is the values of properties or characteristics of things, or 'entities', that are permanently and structurally significant in a particular situation. Thus in a company which manufactures products for sales to customers, the significant entities would include:
- the products made;
- the parts or raw materials from which the products are made;
- the machines or processes on which the products are made;
- the operators of the machines;

- the suppliers of the parts or raw materials;
- the customers who buy the products.

Each occurrence of an entity can be described and/or identified by certain ongoing properties, which are either fixed/constant or changeable/variable. Thus the entity 'supplier' might be said to have the following properties which describe and identify and/or describe an individual supplier:

- the name of the supplier or supplying company;
- the supplier's main address;
- the supplier's company registration number at Companies House;
- the names of the company's directors;
- the company's VAT number;
- and so on.

These properties do not change very much over a reasonable period of time. Other characteristics, however, change more frequently and can be described as variables;

- the quantities and value of goods bought within the last year;
- the value of goods received but not yet paid for;
- how long the supplier takes to deliver parts or raw materials ordered;
- etc.

In any situation, the relevant entities are connected together by relationships which reveal themselves in significant transactions or messages, the content of which may affect a variable of interest; so that the entities 'parts' and 'suppliers' are connected by the following transactions:

- an order on the supplier;
- a bill from the supplier;
- payment of the bill by the manufacturer;
- goods returned to the supplier as faulty;
- a credit note from the supplier for faulty parts;
- etc.

Fig. 6.1 shows a diagram, known as an entity–relationship diagram, of a situation in which a customer orders goods from a company, the bill for which is sent separately to the customer at a later date from the company's head office (a typical mail order procedure).

The second part of data analysis starts from the basis of entities and transactions identified in this first exercise, and proceeds to define each entity/transaction in terms of their descriptor variables, of which one must be selected as an identifier, or key variable, whose value must be different for each record. This is not always easy; sometimes there is nothing that uniquely identifies, for instance, an order for goods, and sometimes an identifier exists that is either unwieldy or not necessarily unique. For instance, your name is not a unique identifier since there may be other people with the same name, and some way must be found of making it unique, either by linking your name with your date of birth, or with your

Fig 6.1 *entity–relationship models*

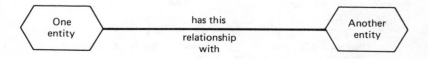

Example:

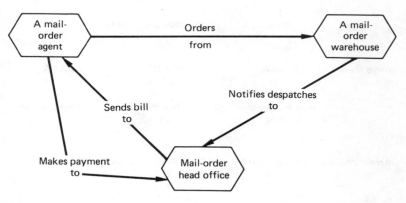

address. This combination, or 'concatenation' of name and other personal information is used, in a scrambled form, inside a driving licence. The alternative is to use a numerical code that merely acts as a convenient and unique 'label', such as the publisher code and book code within an ISBN book code, or a code that contains some discernible information, such as the post-code. Most identifiers used within computer-based systems are a combination of both principles, e.g. bank account number, credit card number, rating assessment number. Fig. 6.2 shows some examples.

At this point it is common to summarise the data thus selected and identified in the following form:

Dataname (*Identifier*, Descriptor-1, . . .).

Thus for the data entity 'Customer' we might have a formal data description such as:

Customer (*Customer-Code*,Name,Address,Amount-owing, . . .).

Finally it is desirable (and for some purposes, discussed in Section 6.5 below, essential) to submit all the data descriptions to an exercise known

Fig 6.2 *some common identification codes*

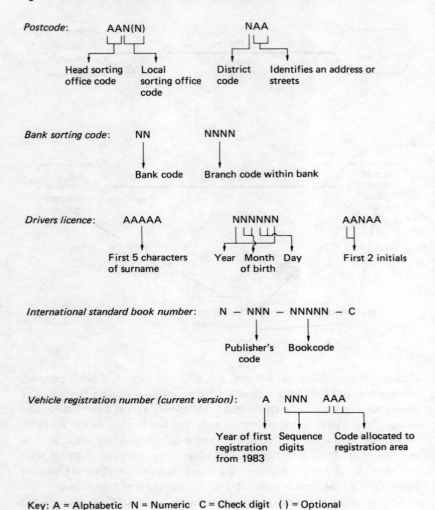

Key: A = Alphabetic   N = Numeric   C = Check digit   ( ) = Optional

as 'Normalisation', as a result of which the data will emerge in a fully cleaned-up or 'normalised' form ready for use within a computer-based system. At this point the data descriptors constitute what is sometimes called the Logical Data Model (LDM) for the proposed system.

6.2 DATA STRUCTURE

For many of the processes to which data are submitted in a computer-based system, it is necessary to analyse items of data in greater detail than shown above, showing firstly the way that one item may be broken down into lower levels of sub-items, and secondly the rules which govern their appearance in the data entity. These analyses thus show the structure of data items. The descriptor items in the data description of the previous section were deliberately left in a form to illustrate data structures; NAME consisting of TITLE, INITIALS and SURNAME; and ADDRESS of various sub-items — an optional HOUSE-NAME, STREET, TOWN and COUNTY. We have already seen also that POSTCODE has a structure of its own. In the same way we may be interested in further sub-divisions of these sub-items, as shown in Fig. 6.3. Data items which are capable of division are known as group data items; those which are incapable of (further) sub-division as elementary data items.

Fig 6.3 *a data hierarchy*

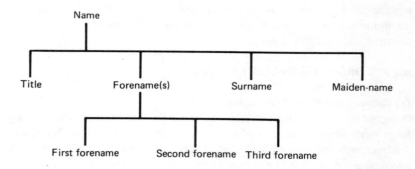

In addition it may be important to indicate on such a data structure diagram the different ways in which data items are related to other items. Fig. 6.4 shows three different elements of data relationships — sequence, selection, repetition, which can be illustrated as follows:
  (i) Sequence — Name consists of Title + Initials + Surname (at least in this LDM, which only caters for commoners).
 (ii) Selection — Title can only be 'Mr', 'Mrs' or 'Miss'.
(iii) Repetition — Initials consists of one or more characters.
This view of data structure is important because one of the main principles of program design (see next chapter) is that it should reflect the structure of data to be processed in the program, and therefore starts from the data structure diagrams of input and output data.

Fig 6.4 *data structure diagrams*

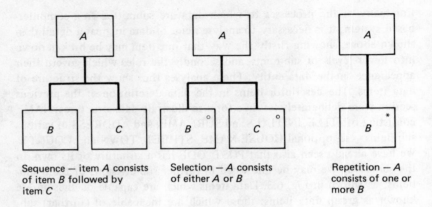

Sequence — item *A* consists of item *B* followed by item *C*

Selection — *A* consists of either *A* or *B*

Repetition — *A* consists of one or more *B*

Fig. 6.5 shows a very detailed data structure diagram for the Name and Address data items. Although the example may appear to be trivial in nature, in fact the keeping of Name and Address data on customers is very widespread in commercial computing, and shows itself in the numerous computer-printed labels and envelopes bearing both wanted and unwanted, solicited and unsolicited mail.

6.3 RECORDS AND RECORD ACCESS

(a) Records and Record Operations

A record is the term universally used for a collection of data items relating to an example or occurrence of an entity, so that Fig. 6.5 shows Name and Address as being part of a Customer Record. The term is also used in a physical sense, in that in a computer-based system a record is accessed and stored as a single unit of data, and is the basic fundamental element in data processing, in which data in record form is stored on permanent backing storage in a manner which permits the most efficient form of subsequent retrieval, or 'access'. The basic operations are:

- record creation and storage;
- record retrieval;
- record update = retrieval plus re-storage;
- record deletion = retrieval plus storage of blank record in place;
- record movement and copying from one form or device to another.

In programming and instruction contexts we use the terms READ and WRITE for retrieval and storage, although it is necessary to remember that not every record operation will in fact incur a physical operation — see below for an explanation. There are several alternative ways of storing and

Fig 6.5 *the structure of a name-and-address record*

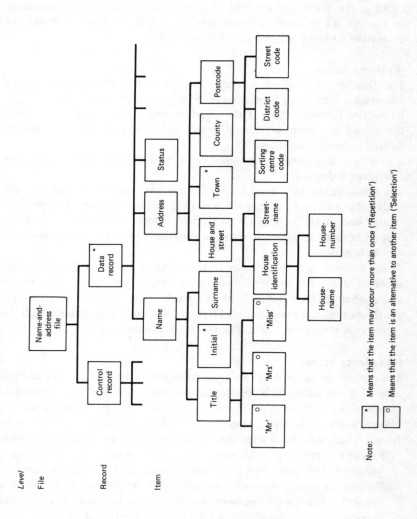

Note:

*	Means that the item may occur more than once ('Repetition')
°	Means that the item is an alternative to another item ('Selection')

subsequently retrieving records, the choice of which is likely to be the most important decision made in the design of a computer-based system which involves the permanent storage of data. The choice affects performance in two ways, firstly the ease and thus speed of record retrieval, and secondly the efficient use of the available storage devices. It should also be noted at this point that a record which is being sought may not be present at all, and an efficient retrieval method should be able to detect the absence of a sought record as quickly as possible.

(b) Direct Access

The first set of methods is only valid for storage devices that contain addressable locations ('Direct Access Storage Devices'), and all involve an immediate ('direct') start of the retrieval process at an address in which the record has been previously stored and which is known or can be derived in one of two ways:
- it is held in another data record (as a 'pointer') or in a specially constructed Index record;
- it is computed by a mathematical operation based on the value of the identifier or key data item (or 'key field') of that record. The operation (also known as 'hashing') is performed before the record is stored and again before the record is retrieved, obviously giving the same result on both occasions.

These methods are described as forms of Direct Access, although strictly speaking they take the read mechanism directly only to the start of the addressable location (sector, block, track, etc.), and the search then continues indirectly inside the addressed area, anywhere within which the record may have been stored. Fig. 6.6 illustrates direct access.

(c) Indirect Access

The second set of methods are used when either the device is not addressable, or if the addressable location of the required record is not known or computable. In these cases the retrieval operation can employ only two known points — the two limits between which the desired record can be found, which may be as wide apart as the beginning and end of the device.
 (i) serial access starts at the lower limit and continues until the record is found or the upper limit is reached, looking at each record in turn;
 (ii) sequential access operates similarly, but terminates in failure if a record is found with a value of the identifier or key item that is greater (numerically or alphabetically) than that of the record sought;
 (iii) binary search or binary chop proceeds by splitting the area of search into two at each stage, looking at the upper or lower half according to whether the sought record's identifier is lesser or greater than that of the record found at each mid-point.

Fig 6.6 *a flowchart of the process of direct access*

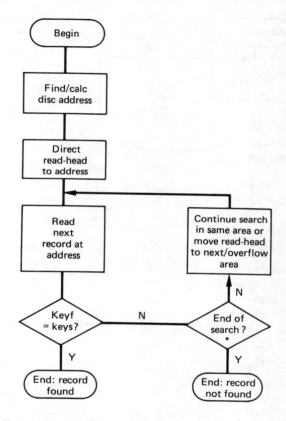

Key: Keyf = Key of record found
      Keys = Key of record sought

* There are various ways of deciding whether
  to continue or to stop searching

Clearly, sequential access and binary search can only be carried out on data which is arranged in alphabetic, numeric or chronological sequence. Figs 6.7 and 6.8 illustrate indirect access methods.

(d) Blocking and Buffering

When a single record is sought in a program, or in one iteration of a program, direct access is always faster, but when a number of records are sought, the advantage of direct access diminishes and ultimately disappears. When the proportion of records read in a program is in the area of 10–15

Fig 6.7 *flowchart of the processes of serial and sequential search*

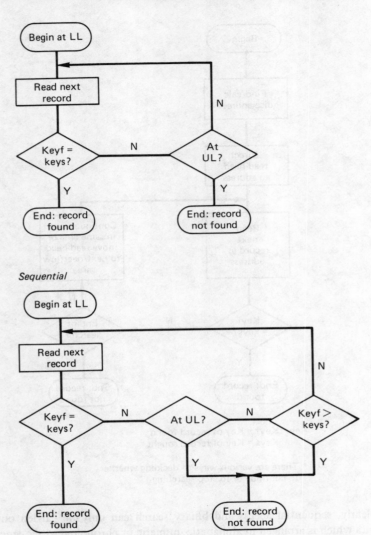

Key: Keyf = Key found
      Keys = Key sought
      LL   = Lower limit of search
      UL   = Upper limit of search

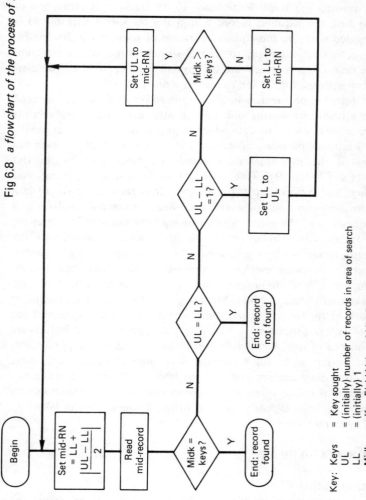

Fig 6.8 a flowchart of the process of binary search

Key: Keys = Key sought
UL = (initially) number of records in area of search
LL = (initially) 1
Midk = Key Field Value of Mid Record Number
Mid-RN = Mid record number
⎿ ⏌ = Integer portion of result of division

per cent or more (depending on a number of complex factors), then it is better overall to search for them sequentially or even serially, from the beginning of the file. However, even when records have been stored in a way that permits the fastest possible retrieval, the time taken in a program in record retrieval is very great, partly because the operation of physically moving the Read--Write heads to the track or cylinder, and of waiting to find the required record within the track (see Chapter 4) is large compared with the subsequent operation of transferring the record. The same considerations apply to records stored on magnetic tape, comparing the time taken to accelerate the tape to transfer speed and decelerating to stop with the time taken to read or write a record.

It is therefore good practice in computing to balance out the overhead of finding a record by storing and subsequently retrieving several records at a time, in one 'block' of data which is physically treated as an undifferentiated unit for purposes of storage and movement, within which the boundaries of the individual data records are determined by the I/O software (see Chapter 9). This operation is known as 'blocking' and 'unblocking', and means that if, for instance, four records are stored in a block, then only one out of every four Read commands will cause a physical data access, the other three incurring only an internal operation. Blocking factors (the number of records per block) or equivalently the block length, can be set by a programmer in most programming languages.

Another I/O software mechanism that has the same objective, that of minimising the effect on program run times of the movement of data to/from external devices, is double buffering. A buffer is an area of memory that is reserved for the use of incoming records or record blocks, and has to be filled before processing of that data can become. If two buffers are reserved instead of one, then while one buffer of data is being processed, the second buffer can be filled with the next block of data, and the next burst of processing can proceed without waiting. Double buffering can work because the operations of the processor and of peripherals can proceed almost independently of each other, a theme that is taken up again in Chapter 9.

6.4 RECORDS AND FILES

(a) Functions of files

The lower and upper limits within which records are stored define the 'extent' of a file — another concept taken over from manual data processing. A file is an organised collection of records relating to the same entity, occupying an area or areas of storage allocated to it by systems software; so a customer file will contain all the customer records. The concept has been extended to encompass any collection of data records:

- input and output files, including data output to a printer;
- transaction files, holding transactions such as invoices during their processing through a computer-based system;
- history files, used to hold old data and transactions for legal purposes or for subsequent comparisons with current data;
- security or dump files copied from current files in case of accident (see Section 6.6 below);
- work files, used temporarily during program runs or between successive programs.

Files containing permanent records are known as 'Master' files, and are of major importance in commercial computing. A master file will hold some data records, and usually one or more additional records containing information to ensure that the file is correct and correctly used — a header record or control record positioned at the start of the file holding data such as the date of creation, date of last use, number of records on the file, number of unused record spaces, and other control data. Checking that the right file, and the latest copy of the file, has been made available to a program by the I/O software is one of the tasks performed during the OPENing of a file, and updating control records and dates has to be done before the file is CLOSEd.

(b) File organisation

File processing is therefore the backbone of most commercial programs; files have to be declared and defined, by usage characteristics as well as record and data item content. File organisation is the term used to describe the way in which records are placed within the file when the records are created or updated, which then creates the environment within which records may be accessed. There are two basic forms of organising files:

(i) unordered or serial files, in which records are placed one after another from start of the file, in time order only;

(ii) ordered files, in which records are placed according to specific rules:
- sequential files, in which records are placed and maintained in sequential (usually ascending) order of the value of their identifier or key fields, and new records are added maintaining that sequence;
- random or direct files, in which the actual or relative position of the records are calculated by a hashing operation on the key field value (for DASDs only).

Serial or sequential files stored on DASDs may also have index records created for the data records, either one index record per data record or one index record per addressable area of data records. An index record contains a disc address and a record key value only, and the set of index records is usually stored as a separate (sequentially organised) index file. A data file that has an associated index file is known as an indexed sequen-

Fig 6.9 *the structure of an indexed file. (a) indexed random files — one index record per data record (b) indexed sequential — one index record per block or area of data records*

Data records | Index | Records

KEY-1		ADDRESS-1		ADDRESS-1	KEY-1
KEY-2		ADDRESS-2		ADDRESS-2	KEY-2
KEY-3		ADDRESS-3		ADDRESS-3	KEY-3
KEY-4		ADDRESS-4		ADDRESS-4	KEY-4
KEY-5		ADDRESS-5		ADDRESS-5	KEY-5

| KEY-N | | ADDRESS-N | | ADDRESS-N | KEY-N |

(a)

Data record blocks (i.e. 3 records per block illustrated) | Index | Records

HKEY-1	ADDRESS-1		ADDRESS-1	HKEY-1
HKEY-2	ADDRESS-2		ADDRESS-2	HKEY-2
HKEY-3	ADDRESS-3		ADDRESS-3	HKEY-3
HKEY-4	ADDRESS-4		ADDRESS-4	HKEY-4
HKEY-5	ADDRESS-5		ADDRESS-5	HKEY-5

| HKEY-N | ADDRESS-N | | ADDRESS-N | HKEY-N |

KEY: HKEY-1 is the highest key value in data block 1, etc.

(b)

tial file, although there are many variations of forms subsumed within this term. The I/O software looks after the index — all that is necessary is to request it. An indexed file permits direct access through the index (see previous section) as well as the appropriate form of access available from the data file itself, and thus is an all-purpose form of file organisation that is virtually standard. However, the storage space taken up by the index, and also other overhead space required by the so-called random files, means that sequential and serial files are more economical of storage space, a saving that has to be set against the advantages of direct record retrieval from either of these two forms of file organisation.

(c) Updating files

(i) Sequentially organised files need particular careful processing in two cases — firstly when records are added to a file and secondly when existing records are changed or deleted. In the first case, as a very minimum, records may be added at the end of the file and the entire file resorted into the correct sequence. More usually, however, for reasons which include efficiency, the records to be added are presorted into the same sequence as the records already on the file, and the two files (original or 'bring-forward' files and the additions file) are then merged in a single operation to form a merged output or 'carry-forward' file.

This principle is also used when changing or deleting records on sequential files stored on magnetic tape; since the reading of a block of data from magnetic tape causes the tape to be moved past the read–write head, the original copy of a record is subsequently unavailable for the changed contents. Thus it is necessary to sort all amendments to records and to apply these, as the 'changes' file, to the bring-forward file; deleting of a record is then performed by not rewriting the record to the carry-forward file. Fig. 6.10 shows a flowchart of the sequential update process.

(ii) Data records held on magnetic discs can be updated in different ways. Records added out of sequence may be left in the nearest empty space (sometimes special 'overflow' areas are left in a file for such purposes), and pointers put into the right places to tell the I/O software where the next record in logical sequence is to be found. Eventually it will be necessary to reorganise the entire file back into the correct physical sequence, because finding records out of sequence using pointers erodes efficiency. Records to be deleted are initially just marked, or 'tagged' as unavailable, and are physically removed during reorganisation. Finally, records that are changed can be rewritten back into the original copy of the record, in place or *in situ*, by waiting for the relevant portion of the track to appear under the read–write head. This means that the original copy of that record has been lost — which has other implications discussed in Section 6 below. Fig. 6.10 also shows how disc files may be updated.

Fig 6.10 *a flowchart of sequential and in situ updates (a) flowchart of the process of updating a record on a master file held on disc with data input from a terminal by direct access (note bi-directional arrows on line connecting program and file, showing update* in situ*); using the media-independent symbols of the NCC Standard. (b) Flowchart of the process of updating a master file held on magnetic tape with a file of data input on disc file by sequential access; using BSI standard symbols*

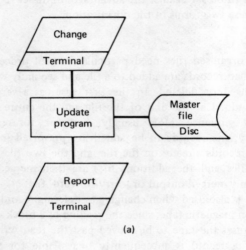

(a)

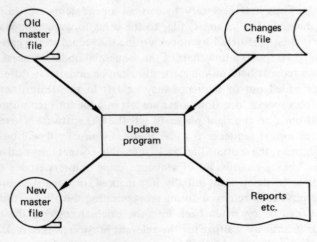

(b)

The greater flexibility of the magnetic disc in supporting all forms of file organisation and these less demanding forms of updating means that few master files are kept nowadays on magnetic tape; and equally the flexibility of indexed files, containing a sequential or randomly organised data file and an index file organised in special ways for quick access means that very few master files are organised in other ways. Fig. 6.11 summarises the features of file organisation discussed above.

6.5 RECORDS AND DATABASES

In some circumstances, storing data records in files starts causing serious difficulties; for instance, the same data item keeps appearing in different files, taking up unnecessary space, having to be updated separately for each file when its value changes, and often getting out of step in its several copies. Thus, product cost and description are data items likely to be found in a number of different files in a manufacturing or selling company, in computer-based systems developed separately, at different times and for the various departments in the company, each of whom has a legitimate and partially overlapping interest in the company's product range. In a hospital, it is likely to be a patient who may be treated in a number of different departments; in local government it will be a ratepayer who may appear on the files of the different departments — Rates, Housing, Social Services, Education.

The second disadvantage of separate 'entity'-based files is that the records in them are treated as independent of all other records, whereas in real life they are connected in various ways to other records, either in the same file or in other files. Thus a company may want to relate a product to the parts or components from which the product is made, or to customers who buy it or to suppliers who sell it or its parts/components to them, as an essential part of the process of organising its production. It is very difficult organising files and writing programs to manipulate such relationships.

The alternative approach to storing records in files is the database, which in this context (unlike some other uses of the word) has a strict meaning of an independent and application-free organisation of data, usually over a wide area of a company or other organisation's activities. This common pool of data is created and maintained separately, using software known as a DataBase Management System (DBMS) and supervised by a data administrator. The totality of data thus arranged is known as a schema, and is defined by programming-language commands in Data Definition Language (DDL). Other commands within or associated with the DBMS then make defined selections of the global data ('sub-schemas') available to any program which wishes to use it, with commands known

Fig 6.11   a summary of file organisation and record processing capabilities

File organisation	Access methods				Record additions and record update			
	Serial	Sequential	Direct	Binary chop	At end	Overflow	CF	In situ
Serial	✓				✓		✓	✓(Disc)
Sequential		✓		✓(Disc, RAM)	✓	✓(Disc)	✓	✓(Disc)
Direct			✓		✓			✓
Indexed sequential		✓	✓	✓(Index)				✓
Indexed random			✓	✓(Index)	✓			✓

collectively as Data Manipulation Language (DML). Fig. 6.12 gives a diagrammatic view of the data-base approach.

The second feature of a DBMS is that it provides facilities in both DDL
and DML for relationships between records other than common occurrence
of the same entity which the notion of the 'file' embraces. This feature is
mainly provided through the structure of a 'Set' in which one record has
a 'controlling' relationship to other records that is variously described as a
parent-child, owner–member or master-slave relationship; so that, for
instance, a product–part set has as owner the product and as members all
the parts which are used in its manufacture, and a product–customer set
has as owner a product and as members all the customers who buy that
product.

Fig 6.12 *database principles*

the CODASYL model

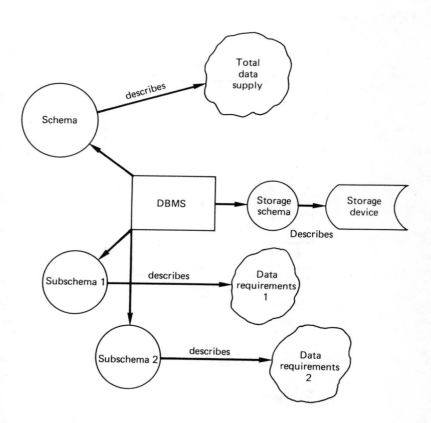

180

Finally, a DBMS also provides facilities for the physical storage and security of the data (the 'Storage Schema'), most importantly in automatically taking copies of the data and repairing damage to the data caused by failures in processing.

Technically we identify two main types of DBMS. The first and earliest type is known as a CODASYL DBMS, from the name of the committee which developed it (and the COBOL language – see Chapter 7). It is couched in COBOL-type commands, and its DML take the form of extra COBOL instructions. Data is defined as records and as sets (see Fig. 6.13). CODASYL DBMSs are very large and complex pieces of software, suitable only for large computers. By contrast, the other main type of DBMS, the relational database, represents a fresh start in computing. The basis of this approach is that the form of storage should permit a simple form of data manipulation facilities known as the relational algebra, which acts on data stored in two-dimensional tables which are very confusingly called relations (see Fig. 6.14). For the algebra to work, the data must be in fully norma-

Fig 6.13   *a set*

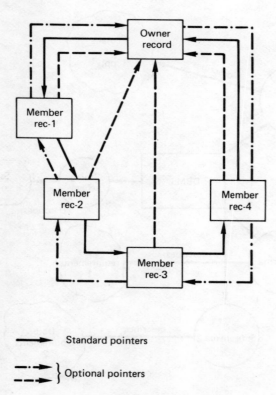

→ Standard pointers

—·→
—-→ } Optional pointers

Fig 6.14 *a relation, or table, from relational theory*

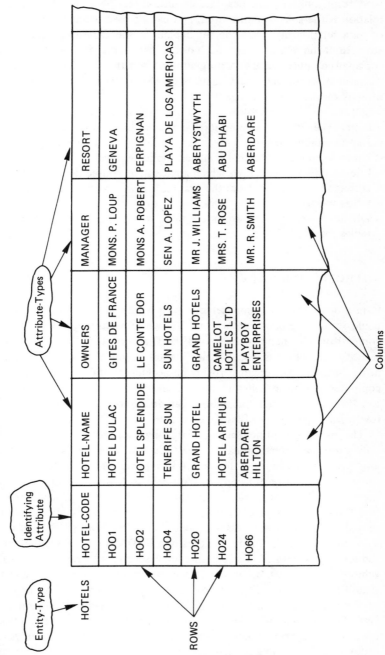

HOTELS	HOTEL-CODE	HOTEL-NAME	OWNERS	MANAGER	RESORT
	HOO1	HOTEL DULAC	GITES DE FRANCE	MONS. P. LOUP	GENEVA
	HOO2	HOTEL SPLENDIDE	LE CONTE DOR	MONS A. ROBERT	PERPIGNAN
	HOO4	TENERIFE SUN	SUN HOTELS	SEN A. LOPEZ	PLAYA DE LOS AMERICAS
	HO2O	GRAND HOTEL	GRAND HOTELS	MR J. WILLIAMS	ABERYSTWYTH
	HO24	HOTEL ARTHUR	CAMELOT HOTELS LTD	MRS. T. ROSE	ABU DHABI
	HO66	ABERDARE HILTON	PLAYBOY ENTERPRISES	MR. R. SMITH	ABERDARE

lised form, one relation per data definition (see Section 6.1 above). The relation is the sole structure used, and can be used to show the same type of data relationships that the set depicts in the CODASYL DBMS. The strength of the relational approach lies in low overheads, making it suitable for small computers, and easy programming, whether based on intermediate but still powerful languages such as dBASE II/III (see next chapter) or directly on the relational algebra:

- Select a row from a table
- Project (i.e. extract) a column from a table ⎫ on specified
- Join two tables together ⎬ conditions;
- Union — merges tables and removes duplicate rows;
- Intersection — selects rows which appear in all source tables;
- Difference — removes from the first table rows which appear in the other tables specified;
- Division — selects rows from one table which appear in all of the other tables specified;

6.6 PROTECTING DATA

Data stored within a computer system is a valuable asset, one whose loss could seriously embarrass the company who owned it, and a windfall to a competitor who happened to 'find' it. The important topic of computer security as a whole is discussed in Chapter 9, but at this point it must be made clear that the greatest risk from accidental or deliberate misuse of a computer system attaches to data. Lost or failed hardware and software can always be replaced, but nobody can do anything about lost data, which is why backup copies of files are essential.

The two major principles for protecting data are firstly to ensure that only authorised users can have access to it, and for authorised purposes (to give protection against deliberate misuse); and secondly to ensure that there is always a recent copy of data held somewhere secure, along with the means of starting again from that copy ('recovery procedures'). The first topic is discussed in Chapter 9, but the designer of computer systems should be aware of the assistance that is available from a DBMS or related software. One of the many facilities of a CODASYL DBMS is that when a sub-schema is defined, the designer may specify a Privacy Lock (a fixed value); when a program wishes to use that sub-schema, it must input the same fixed value as a Privacy Key, i.e. a form of password. A major piece of software often found within a DBMS but also available separately is a Data Dictionary (DD). This is more or less what the name implies — a register of all the data-names used in an installation, with meanings, definitions, etc. pertaining to them. A good DD will also, against the name of a file or program, hold the name of a program authorised to use that file and the files that a program is authorised to use. The I/O software will then check in the DD before accepting a request from a program to open a file, and will deny the request if that program is not on that file's list of authorised users.

The causes of loss of data are many and varied, particularly when we define loss as either actual or potential loss. For instance, a momentary dip in electrical power, of the type which causes the lights to flicker, may also affect the working of the currently loaded programs, which may at that instant have been changing data values; that mere possibility is as damaging to the integrity as a complete physical loss of the entire file (e.g. in a disc head crash). There is *no* completely effective way of preventing such mishaps (although some sensible precautions are discussed in Chapter 9), and it is therefore necessary to keep copies of all your data, to which you can return when a mishap occurs; in fact it is usual to keep two copies in case one copy itself is lost. A sequentially organised file, and especially one kept on magnetic tape, will automatically create a new version when it is updated (see Fig. 6.10), leaving the original as a copy; it is then always possible to recreate the new version, by re-updating the original with the retained changes, and it is customary also to keep the original and changes from the previous run, thus leaving three 'generations' of a file, known as grandfather, father and son, the latter being the current version.

Other collections of data have to be specially copied, or 'backed-up' as a separate exercise, and also changes effected have to be specially kept, on files known as logs or journals. Frequently or continuously used files would be copied once per day or once per shift as an absolute minimum. This copying may be done automatically by the DBMS or other I/O software, or it may have to be initiated by an operator, using one part of a type of software called 'utilities' — programs which perform media-to-media operations on files without changing their content. Such functions as:

- copying files ('dumping');
- recreating files from backups;
- printing out or displaying files;
- sorting and merging files;
- reorganising files

should all be performed from utility software provided with or in systems software.

Finally it is necessary, when a mishap occurs, not only to restore the latest backup as the current file, but also to get back up to date ('recover') as quickly as possible, usually by re-updating with the retained changes since the last backup in the log. Again, sometimes the DBMS or other software will do this automatically — if not, a program will have to be written specifically for the purpose. The more frequently a file is copied, the less work there will be to recover when a mishap occurs.

6.7 DATA IN A TRAVEL SYSTEM

(a) Data analysis

Data entities involved in a system can be initially identified by a succinct statement about what happens in that system, and in which the nouns represent the entities of the system. In a travel system we may try as follows:

A person or a travel agent acting on his behalf makes a booking with a tour operator, or separately with an airline company and a hotel, for a party of passengers to travel on a flight from a home airport to a foreign airport near to a resort/destination which contains a hotel or other accommodation in which the party will stay.

Words get a little awkward as the data analysis continues, but we may reasonably arrive at a data model as shown in the diagram opposite. From that starting point, a complete system (which of course may be only partly computerised), is likely to hold information about the following permanent data entities:

Tour operator
Tour
Travel agent
Flight
Flight operator
Airport
Hotel/accommodation
Hotel owner
Resort

and about the following significant transactions or semi-permanent entities:

Passenger
Booking
Invoice
Brochure

Finding a unique identifier for each of these entities is not easy. The organisations and people are self-identified by Name or Name-and-Address, which, as we have seen, is inadequate for computer purposes and will have to be replaced by some made-up code in each case. The created entities of flights, bookings and invoices may also be given artificial codes. Some attempt may be made to put 'meaning' into these identifiers, or to use existing codes, such as the ABTA code for travel agents, but unfortunately not all travel agents are members of that trade organisation. Passengers may be identified numerically within booking, hotel codes may contain a digit indicating type of accommodation, and flights may indicate the home airport or aircraft type. A tour is a specific combination of a departure

Fig 6.15   *an entity-relationship diagram of the holiday business*

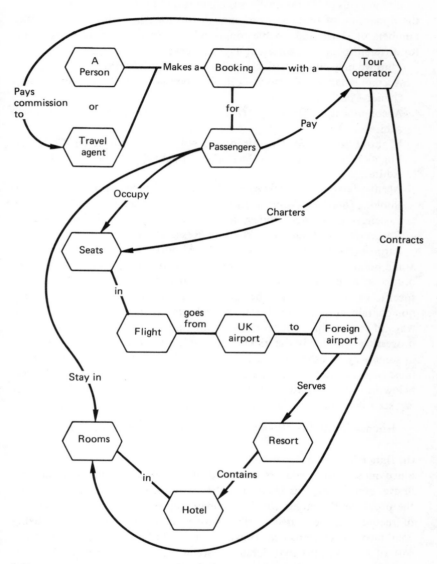

date, travel and accommodation (e.g. a coach tour or a shipborne cruise) and may be identified in several ways. Places (airports and resorts) may be left with alphabet codes abbreviated to a fixed length of say 5–10 characters as the likelihood of duplicates is very low. If you look in holiday brochures you will usually find the codes for hotels and flights, and sometimes you are asked to enter them yourself on the booking form (see Chapter 4).

Beyond this point the analysis is complicated by the need to encompass the dimension of time; it is not enough to show that a hotel has specific numbers of single and double rooms, when it is necessary to book them for different people on different days or weeks.

Thus we may end up with the following entity definitions:

Accommodation (*Accomm-Code*, Accomm-Name, Accomm-Address, Owner-Code. . .)

Accommodation-Owner (*Owner-Code*, Owner-Name, Owner-Address. . .)

Flight (*Flight-Code*, UK-Airport, Destn-Airport, Flight-Op-Code. . .)

Flight-Operator (*Flight-Op-Code*, Flight-Op-Name, Flight-Op-Address. . .)

Agent (*Agent-Code*, ABTA-Number, Agent-Name, Agent-Address. . .)

Booking (*Booking-Number*, Agent-Code, Lead-Name, Lead-Address. . .)

Passenger (*Booking-Number, Room-Number, Sequence-Number*, . . .)

Resort (*Resort-Code*, Airport-Code, Resort-Name. . .)

Airport (*Airport-Code*, Resort-Code, Airport-Name. . .)

Some points to note here – the frequency with which Name and Address occurs as a significant element of data, and thus the need to qualify a specific occurrence by the ownership of the name/address. The list does not contain an entry for Room-Availability, as there are many different ways of storing this vital data with a minimum cost in terms of storage and processing – probably the trickiest part of the whole data model. However, in some way or other, for each room available to the tour operator there must be a record that shows availability status and other data, as discussed below in Chapter 9, for each day, or perhaps for each week if all bookings can start only on the same day of the week, of the holiday season, e.g.:

Room-Availability (*Room-No, Room-Type, (Day*/Status $\times n$), . .).

(b) Data relationships

Since most tour operators are relatively small, single-function and 'cohesive' companies, it is likely that they will not yet have come up against the problems that argue for the database approach, and therefore the sets of records will be stored as files, with possibly some logical files being combined for convenience. However, it would be useful to illustrate the sort of relationships that databases are also set up to represent. We may easily identify owner--member relationships, or sets:

- one flight operator may operate several flights;
- one hotel owner may own several hotels;
- one resort may contain hotels;
- several flights may land at the same airport;
- several flight operators may operate the same route;

and many more. These data relationships are likely to be important in some programs, particularly when a prospective customer or a travel agent makes an enquiry and the first choice is unavailable, e.g.:

What other airlines fly the same route?
What other hotels do you have in the same resort?
What other flights on the same departure date?
What other flights use the same airport?

(c) Record content

It will be obvious that such systems require a lot of storage capacity, both because of the multiplicity of data entities and also because of the large number of passengers and bookings that may be taken and have to be held in the system from the time that a booking is made until the holiday is completed which, for reasons also discussed in Chapter 9, may be as long as a year. A full definition of each data entity plus all descriptors would take up a great deal of space in this book; however, it will be most helpful to include a typical record content for two data entities, Accommodation and Booking, using a data diagram and record layout form respectively.

Fig 6.16(a) *accommodation record*

```
Accommodation-Record  = Accomm-Code
                      + Accomm-Info
                      + Owner-Info
                      + Facilities-Table
                      + Price-Table
                      + (Supplements-Table)
                        etc.

Accomm - Info         = Accomm-Name
                      + Accomm-Address
                      + (Accomm-Tele)
                      + (Accomm-Telex)
                      + Grading
                      + Capacity
                      + Date-Last-Visited

Owner - Info          = Owner's-Name
                      + Owner's-Address
                      + (Owner's-Tele)
                      + (Owner's-Telex)
                      + Purchase-Ledger A/C-No
```

$$\text{Facilities - Table} = \{\text{Facility-Code} + \begin{bmatrix} Y \\ N \end{bmatrix} + \text{Facility-Cost}\}$$

$$\text{Price-Table} = \{\text{Date-Code} + \text{Adult-Price} + \text{Child-Price}\}$$

$$\text{Supplements-Table} = \{\text{Supplement-Code} + \begin{bmatrix} Y \\ N \end{bmatrix} + \text{Supplement-Cost}\}$$

Key [ ] = Alternatives; { } = Repetitive data, occurs once or more times.
    ( ) = Optional - may or may not occur

(b) record layout form for booking record (part only)

© 1969. The National Computing Centre Limited

Record description	System	Document	Name	Sheet
CUSTOMER-BOOKING	TOUR OPERATOR		BOOKING	S44 1/2

Record Specification NCC

Record length: Fixed / Variable — Record format: Fixed / Variable — Record size 340

File specification refs: BOOKINGS

Medium: Disc

Ref.	From	To	Level	Name (In system design)	In program	Data Type	Size	Algn ment	Picture	Occurrence	Value Range	Layout chart ref
1	1	5	5	Booking-number	BOOKNO	A/N			X(5)			
2	6	8	8	Agent's-number	AGENTN	N			9(3)			
3	9	33	33	Customer-name	CORNAM	A			X(25)			
4	34	58	58	Customer-address-line-1	CORAD 1	A/N			X(15)			
5	59	83	83	Customer-address-line-2	CORAD 2	A			X(15)			
6	84	103	103	Customer - town	CORTOWN	A			X(20)			
7	104	113	113	Customer - postcode	CORPST	A/N			X(10)			
8	114	128	128	Customer - telephone	CORTEL	N			9(15)			
11	144	147	147	Flight-code	CLTCDE	A/N			X(4)			
12	148	151	151	Hotel-code	HOTCDE	A/N			X(4)			
13	152	153	153	Number-of-adults	NOOFAD	N			9(2)			
14	154	155	155	Number-of-children	NOOFCH	N			9(2)			
15	156	159	159	Departure-date	DEPART	P			9(6)			
16	160	163	163	Holiday-cost	HOLCST	P			9(5).99			
17	164	167	167	Payment-made	PAYMNT	P			9(5).99			
18	168	170	170	Date-of-booking	DEPDAT	P			9(6)			
19	172	175	175	Cancellation-charge	BANCHG	P			9(5).99			
20	176	178	178	Date-of-cancellation	CANDAT	P			9(6)			
21	179	179	179	Tickets-sent-flag	TICKTF	N			9		0/1	

S 44
Author
Issue

The commentary will make it clear that the descriptors can be subdivided into four classes:
- fixed descriptors, which are not capable of change, e.g. Hotel/Villa/ Apartment Code;
- static data, which changes infrequently e.g. Hotel owner;
- processing variables, updated from transactions, e.g. Number-of-bookings-this year;
- processing flags (usually capable of only two values), e.g. Inspected–flag.

SPECIMEN QUESTIONS

1. (a) Explain the concept of a data base.
   (b) Explain each of the following methods of organising a disc file:
      (i) sequential, (ii) indexed sequential, (iii) direct or random.

2. Discuss (a) the popular and (b) the specific meaning of 'data base' and give examples.

3. What is 'data analysis' and why is it important?

CHAPTER 7

PROGRAMMING A COMPUTER

After reading the description of computer program instructions in Chapter 3, the reader may well be approaching this chapter with trepidation, not without justification, since programming a computer at that level, in instructions drawn directly from a machine's basic instruction set, is both tedious and very detailed. In fact, for most computer users, including perhaps 95 per cent of all computer programmers, writing computer programs is a much less difficult, if still demanding, task and one that is within the grasp of a large number of people, at a certain level, who are not professional programmers.

7.1 THE PROGRAMMING TASK

The task of computer programming is in fact much wider than that of merely writing programs. It includes;
- (i) defining the function of the program (or having it defined in a program specification);
- (ii) designing the program – determining how it is to be organised (its *structure*), and what it is to perform (its *logic*);
- (iii) coding the program in a programming language;
- (iv) testing and debugging the program, to ensure that it is free from errors *and* does what is wanted of it;
- (v) documenting it for subsequent use by operators and modification by other programmers (and oneself).

By using the analogies referred to in Chapter 1 for computer programs – recipes or crochet patterns – the relevance of these subdivisions will become clear. Developing these analogies, one may also say that, just as few meals or few garments require only one recipe or crochet operation, few computer applications require only one computer program. The number may well be 50 or even greater, subdivided into linked programs known as *program runs*, for the reason that they are a sequence of programs run at one time. A typical system will have runs that are performed at different times of the system cycle — daily, weekly, monthly, quarterly, yearly, on demand — and runs to perform significantly different functions, most of them concerned with file processing such as an update run or a reporting run. The whole collection is known as a *program suite*. A number of the programs will be similar to the same types of programs occurring in most other program suites, including some which merely change the order, media, or format of data, and are known as 'utilities' or 'housekeeping' routines, usually provided as part of systems software (see Chapter 9).

As an example, the payroll system mentioned in Section 4.2 might contain about 50 programs, of which about 10 might be Sort programs, divided into 12 Runs as follows:

Run 1   Input to and update of the employee file and statistics summary file with adjustments to the previous week's/month's payroll.

Run 2   Input to and update of the employee file with all amendments and transfers.

Run 3   Input to and update of the employee file with details from time sheets and returns of overtime, standby, etc., and compute net pay.

Run 4   Produce all main payroll output from the employee file.

Run 5   Produce payroll statistics from the employee file.

Run 6   Print lists of Save As You Earn deductions, and clear down employee file cumulations.

Run 7   Produce month end reports from employee file and statistics summary file, and clear down the cumulative totals within these files.

Run 8   Produce the quarterly National Savings data from the employee file.

Run 9   Produce the end of quarter National Insurance card change schedule.

Run 10   Produce year end statements of data extracted from the employee file, and clear down the employee file annual cumulations.

Run 11   Compute back-dated pay rise details.

Run 12   Employee file enquires.

Computer programming is therefore not an individual task at professional level. Programmers usually work in small teams on parts of, or related, programs, often with the support of senior technical assistance known as a *chief programmer team* (CPT). The CPT provides the technical environment, support, advice and quality control for a programming team, as part of the wider program production (sometimes called 'software engineering') task.

7.2 **THE PROGRAM SPECIFICATION**

Whoever is responsible for this part of the programming task, there are some essential items of information that must be determined or agreed at the outset, and collectively they form the *program specification*:

   (i) title;
   (ii) function within larger system;
   (iii) detailed description with appropriate documentation;
   (iv) files used, with reference to other documents if appropriate;
   (v) input and output, with reference to other documents if appropriate;
   (vi) controls and error messages required;
   (vii) program structure method to be used;
   (viii) hardware and software environment, including language to be used (see Section 7.4);
   (ix) implementation schedule;
   (x) test/acceptance data (see Section 7.5).

The accompanying documentary evidence may include:

   (xi) extract from the systems flowchart showing this program as one activity;
   (xii) file/code library references, and data dictionary (list of approved data-names).

The detailed description may itself be written in a formal *program definition or design language* (PDL), a pseudo-programming language which is capable of precisely defining procedural functions (or 'schematic logic') of a program's procedural activities, and from which may be launched the subsequent design and coding or, in the longer term, possibly even automated coding — there are several such approaches under serious development and in trial use at the moment.

7.3 **PROGRAM DESIGN**

The objective of program design is to map out the detailed work of the program (the 'program logic') and the form that it will take ('program structure') in a way that will help to ensure the subsequent production of programs that:

   (i) meet the user's requirements;
   (ii) are error free;
   (iii) require less maintenance and are easy to modify when necessary;
   (iv) can be produced on time with minimum effort.

The difficulty of meeting these objectives without specifically planning for them lies in the very nature of a computer program.

A program when written down appears as a linear list of instructions; in fact, because of the JUMP/BRANCH instructions in every computer's basic instruction set, instructions are executed out of sequence, and because of the conditional BRANCH (IF ... THEN) a program will contain alternative subsequences. This can be shown in a *program flowchart*. There are British, American and international standards for flowchart symbols. The principal symbols in a program flowchart are: an operations box, for unconditional instructions of all types, and a decision box for conditional instructions from which, as shown in Fig. 7.1, there can be two outcomes, or 'exits'. There will thus be a number of unique ways of following the flow of control between the beginning and end of a program; each one is known as a 'path', and is treated as a distinct entity in testing, even though there will be common sections. In theory there are 2^n separate paths in a program with n decisions.

A further element of complexity to programming is added by the length of many programs, which the growing cheapness and volume of internal (and 'virtual') storage are encouraging. In these circumstances it is only too easy for a program to present a bewildering picture of paths and flows of control (the typical plate of spaghetti). The first step in more methodical programming is to use only a subset of all the permissible combinations of program instructions. Under this principle, known as structured programming, all programs can, with some rearrangement, be composed from three basic forms:

- Sequence (one unconditional instruction or one block of instructions followed by another);
- Selection (one conditional instruction followed by two or more alternative unconditional instructions or blocks of instructions);
- Repetition (one instruction or block of instructions repeated a number of times depending on a condition).

Fig 7.1 *principal program flowchart symbols*

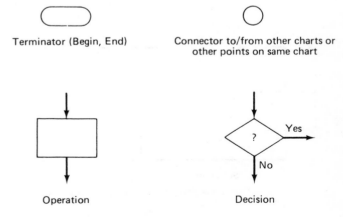

Terminator (Begin, End)

Connector to/from other charts or other points on same chart

Operation

Decision

These forms and some equivalent coding conventions are shown in Fig. 7.2 below. Reference back to Fig. 6.4 will reveal an equivalent set of basic data structures. It should be noted that there is strictly no place in structured programming for the GOTO instruction, and it is sometimes known as GOTO-less programming; it is the careless and wholesale use of GOTO which can cause so much messiness in programs, and it may be easier to avoid them altogether than to use them sparingly and with care. Note that in all of the three basic forms an instruction can be replaced by a named 'block' of instructions — see below for a discussion on block-structured languages and subprograms. The use of structured programming can provide a much cleaner internal differentiation and 'structure' of paths in a program, leading to easier testing and understanding.

Fig 7.2 *basic constructs of a program*

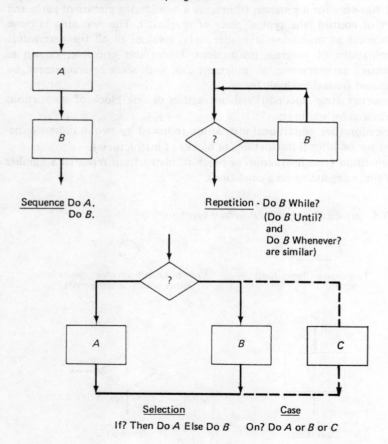

Sequence Do *A*.
           Do *B*.

Repetition - Do *B* While?
         (Do *B* Until?
         and
         Do *B* Whenever?
         are similar)

Selection
If? Then Do *A* Else Do *B*

Case
On? Do *A* or *B* or *C*

Modular and structured programs

In order to avoid the difficulties which surround the writing of large and complex programs in an undifferentiated, or 'monolithic' structure, it is now standard practice that program design starts from the 'top down', using the program description as a starting point. It is then the (senior) programmer's task to map out the way that a program will work, and then progressively to split up the program into either short understandable sections (or modules), or, where the environment allows it, into a series of levels or hierarchy, so as to define a 'modular' or 'structured' program.

A *modular program* is one which in effect consists of a number of smaller subprograms, each subprogram being initiated by a program instruction. A *structured program* extends this by constructing modules using as components only the three basic program constructions of structured programming. The advantages of defining a program as a controlled structure of modules, of a size of no more than 50 to 100 instructions, are that the units of code can be tested thoroughly in themselves, and also that the whole program can be progressively assembled to guarantee reliability. A modular program should also be easier to understand and easier to modify. It may also be possible to identify and use common modules and so reduce the total volume of coding.

There are two methods that can be used in the process of splitting up a monolithic program into modules and fitting them into an appropriate structure: 'functional decomposition' and 'data-driven design'. *Functional decomposition* is a common-sense process of partitioning a list of program activities into separate functions, particularly by identifying them by phase and frequency of execution, and by the nature of input, output and processor function. Small programs may be subdivided into modules on one level — a simple 'functional decomposition' of most programs would produce the simple structure shown in Fig. 7.3. Larger programs will require subdivision of the inner loop, in such a way that a single level structure is turned into a tree structure, and the program structure can be illustrated as a modular hierarchy or module dependency chart (Fig. 7.4); various other names are used for basically the same diagram. The chart may also be used to show the flow of control between the modules and the data passed between them, if any, and is then sometimes called a structure chart. Another way of showing a program's structure that is closer to the list of instructions that makes up a program listing is to rotate the tree structure sideways and show the successive breakdown of functions from left to right, using curly brackets to show inclusion, as in Fig. 7.5. This is known as a Warnier diagram, after the French inventor. In this way the diagram can be made to look very similar to a program listing indented to show blocks and subprograms.

'*Data-driven design*' methods are based on an axiom that program

Fig 7.3 *a first-level program structure for a typical program*

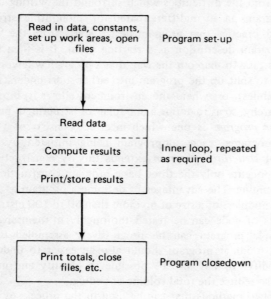

Fig 7.4 *a modular hierarchy or module dependency chart*

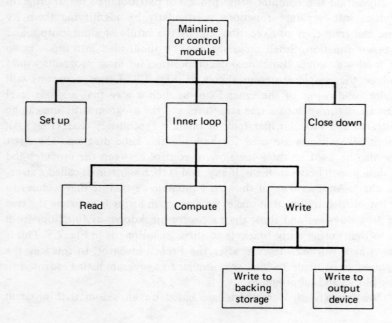

Fig 7.5 *a Warnier diagram*

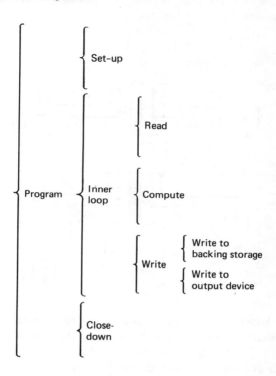

structure should be governed by the data which it processes, either on the data structures of a program or the data flow. The data structures method starts from the data structure diagrams (see Fig. 6.4) of each data stream input to and output from the program. These data structures are combined, by using the correspondences between them, into a single structure, since the same diagrams are used both to describe data structure and the logic flow of a structured program. For example, assume that we wish to produce a program which will:

(i) read a Name-and-Address file which contains a header record and a number of data records;

(ii) test each record to see if it is of interest according to a code;

(iii) for each record of interest print a label and increment a running total;

(iv) at the end print out a total of labels printed.

The data structure diagrams for the input and output data streams would be as shown in Fig. 7.7 (p. 199), and they would be combined as shown in Fig. 7.8 (p. 200).

Fig 7.6 *a data structure chart, showing the flow of control and data from one module to another*

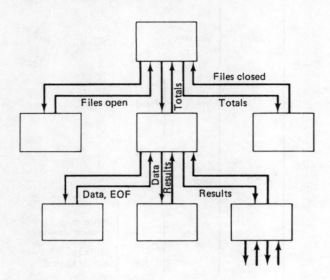

The operations required to convert the input to the output are listed (in any appropriate formal language or 'pseudo-code') and allocated to the relevant part of the program structure. Finally the diagram can be turned onto its side and converted into textual form, indenting the operations to show the original tree-like structure.

The dataflow method similarly starts with a data flow diagram of the problem which is massaged and transformed into a structure diagram under a set of rules to give the initial version of, or 'first cut', program structure.

7.4 EFFECTIVE PROGRAMMING

However, the potential diversity of forms that a program can take is relatively unimportant provided that any version meets the following criteria:
  (i) it should solve the problem or provide the correct output;
 (ii) it should stop faulty data getting into it;
(iii) it should have a structure that permits understanding and modifications;
(iv) it should always work regardless of what data is given to it;
 (v) it should be easy to use.

A program's speed of performance is almost always determined by accesses to data stored on discs rather than on instructions executed in the pro-

Fig 7.7 *JSP data structure diagram*

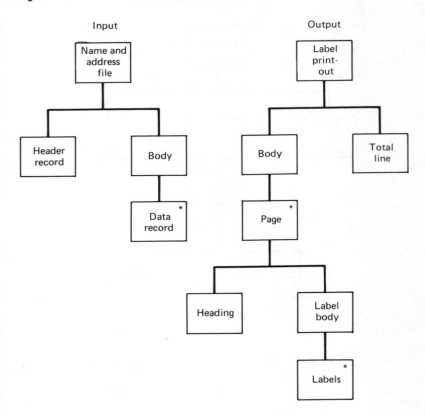

cessor, and trying to save a few instructions here and there or striving for the acme of elegance is usually a waste of a programmer's time.

7.5 CODING

Coding is the writing of the program text as a set of program instructions, usually by direct input from a keyboard using a WP package or a simpler Editor. The code is written in one of (very) many *programming languages*, and constitutes the 'source' program. Programming languages are categorised by level. A Low-Level language is close to and usually a mnemonic form of machine code (the instruction set of a computer in machine-readable form); a High-Level language is more powerful in that one instruction is equivalent to maybe six to ten Low-Level language forms. HLLs have

Fig 7.8 *JSP program structure diagram*

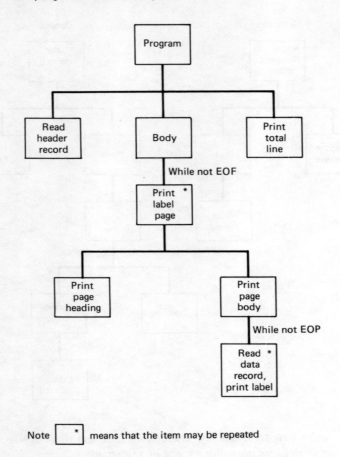

Note [*] means that the item may be repeated

been invented for the convenience of programmers for different types of task, and have to be converted into a form acceptable to a computer. A Very High-Level language is more powerful than a High-Level language by about the same factor of six to ten, and is mainly intended for users who can only instruct the computer what he or she wants out of the computer and not how the computer should do it.

Only the machine code, in bit patterns, is directly executable (or via microprograms) on a computer; all other languages require translation into machine code, by software specially written for the purpose. If the translation and execution are immediate, the software is known as an 'interpreter'; if it is a distinct two- (or more) stage process, it is known as a 'compiler' (for HLLs) or 'assembler', and an 'object' program is produced which can be stored and run independently in that form. If the process of translation is performed on one machine and the object program run on another machine (usually a small computer) then it is known as 'cross-assembly' or 'cross-compiling' respectively. Fig. 7.9 shows a flowchart of

Fig 7.9 *the process of program testing through compilation and interpretation*

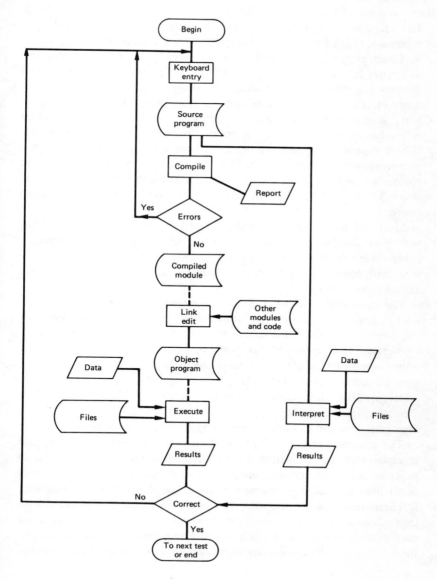

these processes. The advantages of using an interpretive language is that you avoid one stage of the process, which makes it quicker to get going and to correct errors; correspondingly, an interpreter cannot hope to do in one stage all that the compiler does in two, and thus interpreted programs are generally less efficient than compiled programs — slower, larger and more prone to errors.

An *assembly language*, or *assembler* for short, is essentially a one-for-one version of the machine code used by the computer — see Chapter 3. The operation code (opcode) of the machine language is replaced by a mnemonic (LDA for 'load the accumulator') and the operands are replaced by *labels* or *symbolic addresses* which are usually letters of the alphabet or a letter followed by a digit (Y2, G9, etc.). The assembler program then decodes the mnemonics and allocates storage locations to the operands. Assemblers are unique to particular machines except where, for compatibility within or to other machine ranges, a semi-standardised assembler is produced, in spite of architectural differences, via microprograms. Microcomputers, however, are nearly all built using one of a very short list of microprocessors, so that quite different machines which all use, say, the Motorola 68000 processor will have the same assembler. Assembly language is also known as *symbolic code* and *mnemonic code*, for the reasons given above.

Most high-level languages, on the contrary, are not machine-specific but have been designed to be industry-wide machine-independent languages. (There were intermediate languages known as autocodes which were machine-specific, several-for-one, versions of assemblers, but these have almost disappeared.)

The arguments in favour of a number of *standard HLLs* are:
- languages can be written in forms related to users' environments (for example, scientific, commercial, real-time, process control, beginners);
- programs can be (hopefully) portable from one machine to another, thus permitting transfer of products and skills;
- programming can be made a less demanding task, and one that is therefore available to a wider cross-section of society (thus permitting the greater expansion of the industry);
- programming can be easier, therefore faster and less expensive.

The disadvantages are firstly that they require extra software, and secondly that the translation process very often produces machine code programs which are less efficient (in terms of storage space and execution time) than equivalent programs written in assembler. Now that hardware is cheaper and more powerful, the latter disadvantage has faded into insignificance and the productivity benefits of high-level languages are even more significant; as a result of which very high-level languages, sometimes called Fourth Generation Languages (4GLs) have sprung into prominence. They arise from various sources and there is no *de facto* or *de jure* standard, just a Tower of Babel similar to the old days before the pressure of consumerism forced the creation of standard languages.

(a) Some standard languages

BASIC (most HLLs are known by acronyms) is the *b*eginner's *a*ll-purpose *s*ymbolic *i*nstruction *c*ode, and is the easiest generally available language to learn. As such, most 'Beginning Programming' texts rely on BASIC (and the companion volume in this Mastering Series is no exception). More than this however, the size of the BASIC interpreter makes it the standard or only HLL for many micro and small computers, for which it has been extended well beyond its original objectives into a reasonably effective all-purpose programming language. It is also cost-effective for throw-away programs, and can be used to write the demonstration and mock-up programs used in the system design stages.

FORTRAN (*for*mula *tran*slation language) and ALGOL (*algo*rithmetic *l*anguage) are 'scientific' languages, which means that they have powerful mathematical and computational features suitable for use by scientists and engineers. They differ, however, in that ALGOL is a *block-structured* language, which means that it has facilities for building up a program in blocks, each block forming part of a higher level and initiated by it. Block-structured languages are therefore more suitable for 'structured' programming.

COBOL (COmmon Business-Orientated Language) is described as a 'commercial' language, which in this context means that it is directed towards computer applications of all businesses whether operating on strictly commercial criteria or on other criteria of public service. The characteristic of business procedures was discussed in Chapter 2, and thus COBOL is high in data and file manipulation and in report generation but low in computational or graphical facilities. It is not a block-structured language, but a COBOL program is highly structured into four divisions — Identification, Environment, Data and Procedure — and can be made to support structured programming. It is by far the most widely used professional programming language (at the time of writing about 65 per cent of programming on mainframe computers and 35 per cent on minicomputers; and since about half of all programming is concerned with changes to existing programs it is likely to remain so for the foreseeable future. There are also some excellent and semi-portable COBOL compilers (such as Microcobol and RM Cobol) available on a wide range of microcomputers, with which a large proportion of the available packaged software has been written.

Other well-known languages have been created for more specific uses. PL/1 (Programming Language 1) was designed by IBM using the best features of both COBOL and FORTRAN so that it would be possible to write both commercial and scientific programs in the same language. Unfortunately it did not spread outside IBM and has failed to replace COBOL inside it. Pascal (not an acronym but named after the famous French mathematician of the eighteenth century) was created by an eminent computer scientist with great care to incorporate the best of structured programming constructs and with some elegant additions such as the CASE instructions for multiple choices. It is, by general agreement, the best vehicle for learning and demonstrating the art and skills of computer programming, and there are some excellent 'learning' compilers such as UCSD Pascal and TurboPascal, but it has not spread into 'production' programming because of weaknesses in I/O and sub-programming facilities. Ada (again not an acronym but named after Ada Lady Lovelace, Charles Babbage's patron) was designed and produced on a US Department of Defense contract for use in large and highly structured real-time systems. The first compilers are already available and American and NATO defence systems will be programmed in it in the near future.

Ada is a heavy tool for a heavy job, a professional's tool. Many other recent developments in programming languages have taken the opposite approach — simpler and cleaner languages, even DIY languages for the non-professional end-user. There are many examples of languages based on or associated with Data Base Management Systems; some closely following the forms of the Relational Algebra with its seven commands for retrieving data stored in tabular form (see Chapter 6.5), and known collectively as 'Query Languages'. The most notable of the languages less closely modelled is dBase II and III, probably the most widely used purposeful language on microcomputers and with a host of imitators. The power and simplicity of dBase can be illustrated by the single command to CREATE a file which prompts the user to respond to repeated definitions of fields:

NAME

TYPE

WIDTH

DECIMAL PLACES

from which point records can be entered in to the file so defined via a formatted screen display (see Chapter 8). Finally, and to remind us of perhaps the main theme in programming for the future, the Transputer (see Chapter 1) has its own language named Occam after the medieval philosopher who is best remembered for his razor (an archaic word meaning motto) 'Entia non sunt multiplicanda praeter necessitatem' or very roughly 'keep things as simple as possible', and even more crudely as the acronym KISS — Keep It Simple, Stupid.

Whatever programming language is used must be capable of expressing the specified or desired structure, logic and manipulation. Ideally the appropriate language should be used for the task in hand, but choice is restricted (mostly by the availability of the compiler, but also by installation standards: most well-organised computer departments like or require their programmers to use only one HLL).

(b) Common features of programming languages

Faced with such diversity in type and number of programming languages, what can be done to make the whole field comprehensible? Most texts on programming deal with one language (either BASIC by default, as in Mastering Computer Programming) or a named language, as in Mastering COBOL Programming. Extensive experience in different languages will reveal certain similarities. Firstly, nearly all are based on a small subset of the natural (English) language, in combination with arithmetic and other symbols. Designers of languages have used their selected English words, however, just like Humpty Dumpty, to mean just what they choose it to mean, neither more nor less – and you just have to learn and remember just what that meaning is.

Secondly, they use these words within the constraints laid down by the underlying and fundamental characteristics of the computer; in retrospect, how pleasant it would, and will, be to design a language that will allow us to say what we want to say and then design a computer to follow the language! Nevertheless, we can therefore identify that most programming languages possess the following features in common.

(i) Input/output instructions

All languages need statements which cause data to be transferred from one part of the computer system to another. This could be to or from a terminal in the case of an interactive computer system, using words such as INPUT/ACCEPT or PRINT/DISPLAY which will cause data to be transferred between the terminal and main memory. The words READ and WRITE are usually associated with the transfer of data between files and main memory.

(ii) Jump instructions (transfer of control)

A jump instruction is an instruction which causes not the next instruction in sequence of the program to be executed but an instruction situated in some other part of the program. Such instructions are said to be either unconditional, a peremptory GOTO a part of the program identified by a unique label, or a conditional jump which depends on the truth or otherwise of an assertion.

A conditional jump will always involve a logical test of the form IF (some assertion) THEN (a directive). Logical assertions usually contain one of six relational operators. These are:

=   Equal to

≠   Not equal to

>   Greater than

<   Less than

> =   Greater than or equal to

< =   Less than or equal to

For example a conditional jump would be of the form:

$$\text{IF PAY} \geq 5000 \text{ THEN GOTO INCREASE-PAY}$$

This means that the part of the program labelled INCREASE-PAY is the next to be executed if PAY is greater than or equal to 5000. If the test of the value of PAY fails (that is, it is less than 5000) the next instruction in sequence is executed and the jump to INCREASE-PAY is not made. In some languages the form is:

$$\text{IF} \ldots \text{THEN} \ldots \text{ELSE} \ldots$$

Conditions may also be expressed in other forms, such as:

$$\text{PERFORM} \ldots \text{UNTIL}$$

(iii) Arithmetic instructions

All HLLs allow for the performance of arithmetic on pieces of data by statements such as:

$$\text{(LET) AVERAGE} = \text{TOTAL/NUMBER}$$

but beware of the use of the = sign which has a very special meaning in this context. It is actually used here as an assignment instruction, saying that the result of the calculation performed on the right hand side is assigned to the variable on the left hand side, and in some languages is replaced by ← for this purpose. The use of the word LET is used in some versions of the BASIC HLL as a reminder of the assignment role played by the = sign. Symbols for addition and subtraction are used as normal in arithmetic but / is used for *divide* and * for *multiply*.

The up-arrow, ↑, is used for *raise to the power* (sometimes ** is used) and together with a liberal use of brackets these enable complicated formulae to be evaluated, at least in languages designed for that purpose. Any book on programming in a specific language will detail the way it performs its arithmetic functions.

(iv) Looping instructions

These allow a section of code to be repeated either a fixed number of times or until a pre-determined condition is reached. Some mechanism is provided in HLLs to define the start and finish of a loop — words such as DO, REPEAT, FOR for the start and UNDO, CONTINUE, NEXT for the end.

(v) Labels
In order to permit the change of sequence in the Jump Instructions it must be possible to uniquely identify instructions within a program. The descriptors of instructions are known as labels, and can take numeric or alphabetic form. In some languages they can be given only to certain types of instructions and not generally, and there may also be a special non-functional instruction whose sole meaning is to signal a label.

(vi) Variables
Variables are objects that can change their value, operated on by instructions ('operands') in a program, and must be properly named within the rules of a language, usually starting with an alphabetic character and subject to a maximum length. Words that are otherwise used as structural parts of a programming language are known as Reserved Words and may not be used as variables or labels, so that in BASIC it is illegal to say:

$$PRINT = TOTAL/NUMBER$$

or

$$IF\ PAY > = 5000\ THEN\ GOTO\ PRINT.$$

(vii) Data definitions
These are usually statements about certain variables to be used within a program and state at the outset whether certain variables are to be treated as integers, complex numbers, lists of numbers or strings of characters, for example. The nature and extent of data definitions in a program depend entirely on the HLL. For example, the data definitions available in a language such as BASIC are very restricted but in PASCAL they are very varied to the extent that the user can define his own data types.

(viii) Comments and remarks
See Section 7.6.

(ix) Subroutine and subprogram facilities
If a program is structured so that different parts can be executed independently of the main logical flow of the program then two mechanisms are required: a *naming mechanism* so that sections of the program can be uniquely identified and defined, and a *calling mechanism* so that one section of program can control another, known as a *subprogram*.

Subroutines are strictly separately compiled and stored programs which can be 'called' by another program and executed at that point, with a subroutine CALL statement. There may be a library of subroutines for such tasks as the calculation of square roots, evaluation of logarithms, and so on, provided by the manufacturer as part of the compiler for each language, but the programmer may also define and produce his own subroutines. An advantage is that a subroutine does not have to be written in the same language as the main program, and so, for example, a program written in a commercial language may CALL a FORTRAN subroutine for a special piece of mathematical work. The most important set of subroutines provided (in systems software, see Chapter 9) for use by application programs are subroutine packages (called 'access methods' or 'housekeeping packages') which perform (or rather initiate) READ/WRITE operations required by an I/O instruction, by a call to the system software (supervisor call). There may be separate packages to perform the different types of record access described in Chapter 6.

A similarly organised 'library' of *source code* routines is known as a *'macro' library*. Macros are consolidated into a program, either by using the macro-name as a pseudo-instruction (as for functions) or with a separate instruction such as COPY or INCLUDE. Several programming languages provide both short pre-written sections of code for common *'functions'* such as square root, and also allow the programmer to define his own functions. They are then usable just like program instructions: LET Y = SQR(X). Fig. 7.10 shows the essential difference between these forms.

(c) Other forms of instruction

Programming languages are used to construct programs that are executed by and within the main processor of a computer system. As indicated in various places in Chapter 4, other devices may also contain true microprocessors or other control mechanisms which can be 'instructed' or set with different values. Physical control mechanisms include DIP and other types of switches and dials, but more generally VDUs and printers operate under microprogram control. Most VDUs contain a set-up program requestable by a special key on the keyboard, giving a series of menus for different aspects of the VDU — line speed, character size and set, etc., and a choice of alternatives for each parameter. For VDU settings that the user may wish to change frequently, or to use within a program, the keyboard processor will accept key combinations usually consisting of the Escape key plus one or two other keys, sent either direct from the keyboard or from a program in a character string. For example, to sound the Bell, which is something that you might want to draw attention to a specific event, such as an input error (see Section 7.6 below), you can either press the Control and G keys together, or issue a 'PRINT CHR$(7)'; command in BASIC. Similarly, to clear the screen, on an ASCII terminal the key-

Fig 7.10 *subroutine and subprogram facilities*

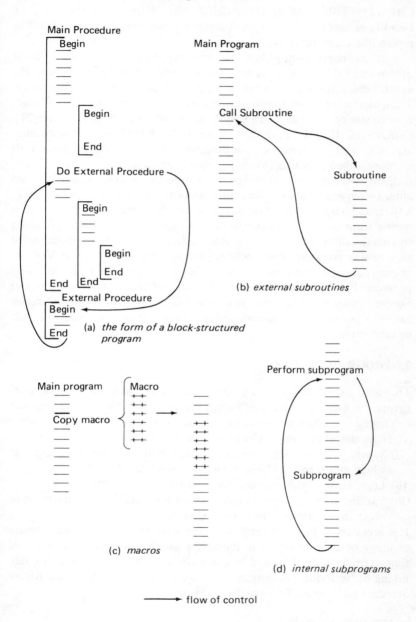

(a) *the form of a block-structured program*

(b) *external subroutines*

(c) *macros*

(d) *internal subprograms*

→ flow of control

board sequence is Escape,[,2,J; and the BASIC equivalent is 'PRINT CHR$(27);CHR$(91);CHR$(50)+CHR$(74);'. Very occasionally a High Level Language will contain an equivalent command, e.g. Clear or Bell to replace the character string.

Printers are programmable in the same way, except that the direct input option from the keyboard is not available, and it is necessary to send the control character strings before sending the data characters to be printed. Thus, on the matrix printer, shown in Fig. 4.17, to print in Enlarged Mode, it is necessary to issue an Escape/W command or its 'PRINT CHR$(27); CHR$(87);CHR$(1);' equivalent command in BASIC. Printer commands are more likely to need a special program resident in the main processor's memory, called a 'Printer Driver' for their execution.

Unfortunately, control character strings for printers and VDUs are almost unique to individual manufacturers and models, except for ASCII VDUs, and you cannot avoid changing the characters when a program is moved from one device to another. Some packages have been programmed to contain alternative VDU or printer code files, selected by model name in a set-up program; others will require specific codes for the VDU or printer functions used in the programs to be fed direct to the set-up program. If you are writing programs yourself that directly use VDU or printer functions in this way, you should similarly treat control character values as potentially changeable and put their values in a separate module or subroutine.

7.6 PROGRAM TESTING

The only useful programs are those that work, and work every time. Errors, or bugs, prevent this happening and the object of testing and debugging is to eliminate errors in computer programs.

Three classes of error can be identified:
(i) Syntax errors — illegal use of a feature of the programming language which means that the program will not work at all;
(ii) Logic errors — the program will work but not as intended;
(iii) Execution errors — the program works as intended but illegal input or other circumstance at run-time makes the program stop.

It is necessary to plan and carry through a series of trials or tests to remove as many of these errors as is humanly possible in a reasonable period of time. The term 'test' is used to cover any activity concerned with establishing or 'verifying' the correctness of a program, as defined in the British Standard on Program Testing (BS 5515).

(a) Inspecting the code

Every programmer looks at his or her code during and after it has been written down or entered through a keyboard. It is not very easy looking at a program on a screen, so that a print-out or hard copy is highly desirable at this stage. If any of the diagrammatic methods of program design described above have been followed, the program should look the same sort of shape. Trying to follow the way that the program will work is known as desk checking or dry running. It is very helpful to ask a friend or colleague to check your program for you; as a programmer your code is likely to be inspected more formally, either by an organised group of colleagues, when it is known as a 'structured walkthrough' or by an independent Code Inspector.

(b) Removing syntax errors

The first part of the operation of a compiler or interpreter or any other source code translation program is detecting and reporting on errors in the source code — 'syntax errors'. These errors are often called 'bugs', and the activity of removing syntax errors, with the help of the compiler's error reports, or 'diagnostics', as debugging, which sounds less culpable than 'removing errors'. Compilers vary enormously in the way in which they report errors, and some are biased towards it. The marks of good diagnostics are:

 (i) the instruction in which the error occurs should be clearly identified, either by printing the error message immediately after the instruction, or by referring to a line number in the source program;

(ii) the nature of the error should be made clear ("SYNTAX ERROR IN LINE N" is not very helpful);

(iii) the compiler should attempt to categorise the error by its seriousness (e.g. Fatal/Warning/Suspect);

(iv) the compiler should attempt to suggest corrections for or alternatives to the code in error (e.g. "ILLEGAL OPERAND FOR ARITHMETIC INSTRUCTION _ REDEFINE OPERAND".)

The programmer then has to correct the source code, usually in the same way as the source code was originally entered, noting at the same time whether the compiler has automatically changed minor errors to a fixed and safe 'default' value. And then try to compile the program again . . .

(c) Program testing

A program test is a trial execution of a program or program module with specially prepared input data — 'test data'.

Testing is the most time-consuming part of programming, which is probably why it is most often neglected. Since the object of writing a program is to make it work, it is essential that every path through the program is explored so that as near 100 per cent reliability as possible is obtained for the program. Without it, all the effort put into writing the program will go to waste.

It is therefore necessary to plan a series of tests, firstly by identifying all the separate paths through the program (i.e. different ways to pass through the program between BEGIN and END); and secondly to prepare suitable test data for each identified path. Once again, if your program has been carefully designed it will be easier to identify all the paths. The total set of paths can be drawn in a diagram called a test schema or control graph and a list of tests derived from the diagram. Each test then requires a set of test data to be prepared and passed through the program and a comparison of the output produced with the output expected . . . and then back to the drawing-board if the two do not coincide.

Testing also has to be a planned process, particularly for a structured/ hierarchical program. Although top-down design (working from the specification towards the code) is an accepted strategy, there are two alternative testing strategies − top-down and bottom-up. Top-down testing means writing and testing the highest levels of modules first, which means making 'dummy' entries for the lower level of code 'called' by them. *Bottom-up* testing is the coding and testing of the lowest level modules first, which means testing part-programs. Special software is required to compile and test (part-program) modules − known as *module test harnesses*, or *drivers* − in the absence of the high-level modules which control them.

A programming language that provides for subroutine or function libraries, or for separate procedures to be compiled into 'load modules', will require a phase of development known as *link-editing* or *consolidation*, which is exactly as the name implies, a formal consolidation of all the object code into one named object program.

It is this object program that is the one that is finally executed by the computer and it has to contain every piece of code necessary for the implementation of the original specification. The job of the final link-editing phase is therefore to tie up all the subroutine calls to library subroutines, all the I/O routines which are handled by the systems software and all the separately written subroutines, which form part of the suite of programs, into a complete 'run-time' packet. This is then stored away on a disc file so that at the appropriate command this complete packet of machine code can be loaded into storage and immediately executed.

It is now recognised that the production of error-free software is immensely aided if the programmer has a properly organised set of software to assist in this arduous and tedious part of the work. This software is known by various terms − programmers work bench and programming support environment among them. The use of software aids is part of a methodical attack on the problems of producing software known as software engineering.

(d) Making the program secure

It is not enough merely to ensure that the program works as the user intended; it must also be secured against execution errors caused by faults in input data or in the computer in which it is being run. A large part of a professionally produced program will be devoted to keeping faulty data from passing the initial checks, and one form of program testing is known as 'destructive testing', in which somebody attempts to make the program stop ('crash') by inputting data at random into the program. Another large part of a program should be devoted to detecting other untoward events, and most programming languages have error-trapping instructions such as BASIC's ON ERROR for this purpose, and a list of error conditions which can be identified uniquely by an error code or status bits. Finally, it may be necessary for the programmer to include code to enable a program to be restarted from a known point if circumstances totally outside the programmer's control (such as a power failure) cause the program to stop in the middle of a critical task such as updating a data file or printing a long report.

7.7 PROGRAM DOCUMENTATION

Given that about 50 per cent of the total programming effort and costs are attributable to program maintenance, it is common sense to write programs for easy maintenance. Part of this objective is reached by documenting programs to make their structure and operation understandable. We have already seen some formal documentation relating to a program — its specification and design diagrams. Formal operational documentation that is, ideally, producing during the testing stage, consists of two forms: program comments and external write-ups.

Programming languages all allow the programmer to insert *comments* into the program text — lines introduced by an identifying symbol or pseudo-opcode which are bypassed by the compiler. These should be used to identify the program and sections, and to provide instructions on how to use them. In the case of interactive programs, operational instructions should be contained in the program's dialogue at the terminal, or assistance should be available if required by requesting 'HELP', which should throw up a detailed narrative on to the screen. Beyond this, the way that a programmer names his variables and his code sections should make their function clear by mnemonic names wherever possible, while indentation and layout of code should also help to clarify structure.

The programmer should also produce some additional documentation to accompany the program specification, his working documents and the program listing:

- flowcharts and other diagrams;
- operating instructions;
- test data and results.

These should all be put together as a formal program file with index contents list and amendment list. This is the basis for further program maintenance, and must be kept up to date when changes are made to the program. There is also a British Standard on Program Documentation (BS 5887) which should be used as a professional guide to what is necessary.

7.8 PROGRAMMING A TRAVEL SYSTEM

(a) Programming requirements

The task of writing programs to implement the contents of travel trade systems is determined initially by the nature of the processing involved in them. From the relevant sections of the previous two chapters (5.5 and 6.7) it will be evident that most of the programs will involve:

- file and record handling;
- document and report printing;
- evaluation of alternative rules.

The performance required of the programs will add 'fast response' to the list, and the need to change the rules frequently will add 'ease of maintenance'.

This list puts travel trade programs fair and square in the category of data processing, with little or no need for scientific or algorithmic capabilities. As such, you would expect to find the programs written in one of the conventional DP-oriented programming languages that contain extensive facilities for data handling and reporting, permit self-documentation, and deliver good performance (i.e. probably compiled rather than interpreted at run time); thus COBOL, PL/1 or RPG among the older languages, and a 'good' BASIC or dBASE among the microcomputer-oriented languages.

A prior demand is for well-designed programs that identify and implement as modules or subroutines those sections which are subject to change in processing rules, e.g. the routine which calculates child, date or other discounts and extras on the basic holiday price, and thus makes them easier to change between brochures or even in mid-season.

(b) Additional aids

The productivity of programmers working on these programs will be aided by additional features in languages; for instance, the Report Generator feature of large COBOL compilers, which enables reports to be specified in an easier way that in the normal processor of defining print lines and moving data values into them before issuing a Print or Write command. An even higher level aid towards generating reports is to allow users to specify their own, one-off reports, in a Report Generating program specially designed and written for that purpose, without coming to a programmer with a request to write a separate program.

One particularly demanding aspect of travel trade programs is the evaluation of rules for pricing holidays. Any glance at a holiday brochure will show that tour operators seek to fill their holidays throughout the year with pricing rules which are different for almost every month throughout the year, and carefully calculated to stimulate demand — peak prices during school and public holidays, lower prices during the rest of summer, lowest prices about November and February. There are also rules for child discounts and hotel extras, along with special offers ('three weeks for the price of two'), bonuses for early booking, different flight and airport supplements designed to attract customers to fly in the dead of night from outlandish airports, and so many more that it is often very difficult for the customer and even the agent to know exactly what the holiday should cost. It is not unknown for the computer programs of even the largest tour operator to get it wrong, with the result that such programs often need to accept manual adjustment.

A new area of computing may help things out in the next few years — that of 'expert systems', which are computer-based systems designed to incorporate the accumulated knowledge of human experts — typically that of a doctor, prospector, tax specialist, computer designer, etc. They work mostly by setting down all the rules which apply (another name for this type of work being 'rule-based' systems), and then letting an evaluation routine known as an Inference Engine work out the relevant outcome of these rules for a given set of circumstances. I am confident that rule-based approach would be worth investigating for the purposes of calculating prices, and particularly because a change of rules could be effected very simply by adding a new rule at the end, which has the effect of superseding all previous rules under the principle of 'the last word'. The same advantages are also likely to apply in enquiry programs — 'Find me somewhere to go that isn't too hot in August and will take young children and flying from my local airport but without . . .' There are programming languages designed for expert systems, such as Prolog, and higher-level aids known as Expert System shells.

The structure of an expert system is described in Fig. 7.11, and the significance of expert systems in general is further discussed in Chapter 11.

Finally, there are some features of travel trade programs where programmers would seek assistance from software aids, either supplied separately or developed especially for a company; in particular, software to assist the computer to handle requests and data coming in from remote terminals (data communication software), and software to present data

Fig 7.11 *the structure of an expert system*

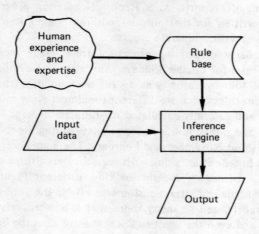

and limited graphics on the TV screen in Viewdata mode. Systems programmers would be expected to organise this software for application programs, leaving the application programmers to use the software unseen (e.g. by reading from a remote terminal just as if it were a fixed local terminal), or by a subroutine call.

SPECIMEN QUESTIONS

1. (a) Describe the operation of key-to-disc devices. Give an example of the use of this form of data input and comment on the benefits of its introduction.
   (b) What is meant by an Optical Character Reader? Briefly discuss the benefits of an OCR device, with the aid of a relevant example.

2. Describe (i) magnetic disc and (ii) magnetic tape storage devices. In each case name two different types of device, and give one typical application for each case. Name two advantages of disc storage and two of tape storage. *

3. What is a Local Area Network? Describe how it can be of use in organising the use of microcomputers in schools.

4. What is meant by an 'application package'? Give two examples of such packages and comment on their content. Assess why packages are bought for (a) mainframe computers, (b) microcomputers. *

5. The feasibility study is one of the main stages in Systems Analysis. Name the other main stages and indicate the logical order in which they

would be performed, and why. Describe what is involved in one of these stages. *

6. State and explain the fundamental steps involved between the definition of a problem and the execution of a computer program to solve that problem. Briefly describe how the correctness of a program may be established, and name other characteristics of a successful program. *

7. State the main purposes of program documentation. Discuss how it may be produced, and assess the potential consequences of using a program without the corresponding documentation.

8. What is meant by the term 'structured programming'?
Why are sub-programs needed in the development of structured programs, and what are the benefits of producing programs in this way? *

CHAPTER 8

ACQUIRING COMPUTER HARDWARE

Whether for an individual or an organisation, buying a computer is a serious matter; it represents a sizeable financial outlay, even with consistently falling prices, and decisions are complicated by the current and foreseeable state of the computer market-place, particularly the following factors:

(i) there are more types of computer, more alternative models from different suppliers, and a greater range of performance between the largest and smallest than in any other area of technology;

(ii) the high rate of technological progress means that most models are lucky if they survive for two years before their manufacturer brings out a better machine for the same price or a cheaper machine with the same performance; as a result many models and some suppliers will not survive;

(iii) in an expanding marketplace, many newly-arrived outlets have little experience of the business and even less credibility;

(iv) the industry has a tradition of aggressive marketing and vigorous competition.

As a result, *caveat emptor* applies very strongly, as getting it wrong and having to start again can be very expensive.

8.1 SOURCES OF HARDWARE

The intending purchaser today is in a much stronger position than his predecessor of fifteen years ago, in that he can select from a wide variety of machines offered for sale by a range of different types of organisations:
- computer manufacturers;
- dealers;
- add-on suppliers;
- systems builders;
- brokers;

- leasing companies;
- retail shops.

(a) Computer manufacturers

The mainframe computer manufacturers and some of the larger mini-computer manufacturers maintain national and regional marketing organisations (and in some cases agents), and their marketing costs are reputed to be a high proportion of their selling prices. However, computer marketing traditionally requires a high degree of pre- and post-sales support, without which the spread of computing would have been very much slower. Computing has grown on the backs of these manufacturers, and the assurance of their support is still one of the main reasons why companies choose one machine rather than another.

No potential user is likely to be unaware of these companies; their marketing database is usually very thorough on current and potential customers, and their approach is both personal and direct.

The smaller minicomputer manufacturers, and some of the specialist mainframe manufacturers operate with national sales forces only, often operating in specialist areas. For instance, there is a sub-sector of the industry, in both computer and terminal/mainframe sales, which specialises in making equipment identical to IBM, and supporting IBM software, but with a better cost–performance ratio; this is known as the plug-compatible market.

The term 'manufacturer' is somewhat misleading, as very few companies make their own components even at the level of disc drives, printers or terminals, and even fewer make their own processor and memory chips. It is often very useful to know the true sources of supply of the bought-in units in a computer system, without underestimating the role of the 'manufacturer' in assembling the units and integrating them along with the systems software into a working system.

(b) Dealers

Smaller manufacturers and virtually all manufacturers of microcomputers sell mainly through a geographically organised network of distributors and dealers. Dealers are independent commercial companies licensed to sell the products of a small number of manufacturers (sometimes only one), usually from a central premise that provides demonstration facilities but little else, but often with mobile salesmen in support. They will deal in equipment and software that requires little after-sales support. Dealers are mostly single-site companies, but with a small number of nationally distributed chains. As a very recent phenomenon, dealers have come into the computer market from office equipment, from electronics, and as start-up companies founded by people with some previous experience in computing and by pure entrepreneurs. Standards are extremely variable, and most dealers are unable, because of their limited selling range, to give impartial advice over a wide range of machines. Assistance from and supervision by the manufacturers themselves also varies greatly, as does the process of approving an initial request for a dealership; a recent innovation is the 'franchising' of dealers, a business practice that has made, for example, MacDonalds a famous name the world over. Although using dealers is almost inevitable in the microcomputer market, it will pay prospective purchasers even more than elsewhere to make independent enquiries about product comparability and customer satisfaction.

(c) Add-on suppliers

A long-standing market that has recently been augmented by new entrants is the business of manufacturing terminal and peripheral equipment for direct sale to existing computer users – terminals, hard disc drives, joysticks, light pens, printers, and the like. Many sell from catalogues and by mail order, others from local agents who also deal in computers. Many of the best products in computing arise from this source, particularly Japanese products which have set high standards of reliability as in other consumer products.

(d) System builders

Systems builders or systems houses are a source of complete systems of hardware plus software (sometimes referred to as turnkey systems). They obtain their hardware from a computer manufacturer, usually under favourable terms, and add their own packaged or bespoke software to provide a complete working solution to a customer's problem. Such companies are also known as OEMs (they treat their supplier as an original equipment manufacturer). The practice of badge engineering (changing the name on the hardware) was quite common at one time, and many small business systems were built around DEC and Texas Instruments' hardware, but most systems houses are closely identified with their hardware supplier and are often better value for money than their supplier.

(e) Brokers

The explosion of the computer market, and the selling hype of the major suppliers, has further cultivated the cult of newness to which all technologists are congenitally prone. Most mainframe computers appear to have a working life of about five years before being replaced, other machines somewhat less, but careful use and regular maintenance can extend useful life well beyond this point. There is, at the moment, only a very small market for second-hand computers, conducted by independent computer brokers, who act very much as brokers do in any other line of business, and it is something of a mystery as to where all of the displaced computers go. In fact a second-hand and older computer can be a bargain, since the electronics do not wear out in the same way as moving parts, when used with new terminals and printers. The major difficulty, as with outdated cars and washing machines, is the availability of spare parts and maintenance support.

(f) Leasing companies
Leasing of computers was a phenomenon that first appeared in the late 1960s, although leasing of other capital equipment such as aircraft is widespread. Leasing companies are financial organisations who will buy computers directly from manufacturers and then lease them to customers, and in general represent the only way of acquiring a new mainframe computer other than directly from the manufacturer. At the end of the lease of course, the machine reverts to the leasing company who then has to dispose of it as a second-hand machine. Many computer manufacturers operate leasing themselves, and most independent leasing works with IBM equipment.

(g) Retail shops
The very smallest computers are now sold 'over the counter' in retail shops, chain stores and even supermarkets, aimed almost totally at the home and hobbyist market, along with suitable computer games and adventure software. Computer shops suffer from a highly seasonal trade and from disappearing/changing fashions, and the survival rate is not high, leaving many customers in the lurch. Chain stores have the capacity to vary their space between their many products ranges according to trade fluctuations, and have taken over the major role in supplying the home market; and you can moreover expect to see and try most of the contending machines for starters under one roof. In some of the major electrical and electronic chain stores the level of expertise and support is pleasingly high, and this source can be recommended.

8.2 FINANCING HARDWARE – PURCHASE, RENTAL AND LEASING

This is one of the major controversial areas in computing at the moment, and the potential purchaser is warned to beware of entrenched positions. Straightforward *direct purchase* is, in principle, the cheapest way to pay for equipment: all the rights of ownership, including tax allowances and investment grants go with it. The disadvantages of purchasing are both the need to dispose of second-hand equipment, and the cost of financing your own purchase, either by tying up cash instead of using it productively in your business, or by borrowing it from banks or elsewhere, in which case you are at the mercy of fluctuating interest rates and overdraft recalls. Originally, also, the very high cost of computers, in an area of a company not used to capital investment, meant that financial directors were unwilling to authorise outright purchase.

The first alternative to purchase was *rental*. Rental gives usage rights, but not tax advantages (though some companies will pass on special regional investment grants in lower rentals), and rental charges can be disguised as revenue operating costs. Manufacturers have traditionally fixed their monthly rental charges in a way which brought large profits to them; currently mainframe rentals are about 1/36 of purchase price, and terminal/peripheral rentals about 1/30. Rental is an advantage therefore for usage periods of up to three years, and is flexible in that rental agreements work on one or three month's notice.

Most companies will plan to keep their equipment for much longer periods than this, even though manufacturers are tending to bring out new models at about this frequency, and the introduction of *leasing* was an enterprising bid to break the grip which the large companies exerted on their customers. The economics of leasing are based on a fixed-term legal agreement under which most of the benefits of ownership and usage pass to the lessee, in return for fixed annual or monthly leasing charges, though the lessee can usually re-lease at very low rates. At the end of the fixed period the equipment reverts to the lessor. Tenancies of up to seven years are normally available. As the principal owner, the lessor can claim the full capital allowances, but the lessee can also claim leasing charges as operating expenses deductible against tax.

Two forms of lease are currently available: an *operating lease*, in which the lessor does not cover his initial outlay over the period of the lease, and has to consider the residual value of the equipment at the end of the lease, and the *financial lease*, in which the full outlay, plus profit, is recovered. Operating leases are more risky but offer better financial terms to the lessee, and it is this form which has gained wide support from computer managers and their financial directors. More recently, however, customers have become more wary of signing fixed-term leases which would not enable them to take advantage of new products in the meantime, and some of the leasing companies have introduced what is known as *flexible leasing*. This allows a lessee to escape from a leasing agreement at certain points, provided that he takes out a new lease for replacement equipment with the same company, and also recompenses the lessor for any shortfall between his original leasing revenue and his revenue from a re-lease of the replaced equipment.

Hire Purchase is not widely used at the moment, partly because of restrictions on the length of the HP period, which result in relatively higher payments, and also because HP controls are a favourite weapon of governments in our stop/go economy. Most personal computers, particularly for home and hobbyist use, now fall below the limit for purchase by credit card or mail order/store account extended credit.

In conclusion, the financing of hardware acquisition is altogether a complex subject, and one in which an intending purchaser should seek local, independent, expert and up-to-date advice.

8.3 SELECTING A COMPUTER

The selection of a computer system, whether for the first time in a company or as a replacement for an existing system, can be both lengthy and very complex. As the effect of the use of a computer system can be far-reaching, especially on a company which has previously existed without one, much time, expertise and just plain common sense needs to be expended. The selection procedure shown in Fig. 8.1 is strongly recommended, although in principle it differs very little from that which most companies and individuals would follow for any significant purchase except in its formality.

(a) Stage 1 — decide what you want it to do

The need for a computer is, in the first case, usually triggered off by an operational problem, or a dissatisfaction with current methods and the wish to do better or to compete successfully — a basic business drive, in fact. A *first-time user* is faced with two pitfalls: either he does not know what a computer is capable of, or he thinks it can solve everything. The first can be overcome by informed advice from organisations such as:

- trade associations;
- other computer users;
- your nearest branch of the Federation of Microsystems Centres, usually to be found in the regional Polytechnic;
- the National Computing Centre;
- computer consultants;
- management consultants.

The golden rule at this stage is *not* to approach any organisation which has a commercial interest in selling you a computer or any computer. The UK Government has recognised the difficulty of getting impartial advice by setting up over the least few years several schemes in which firstly such advice can be provided without fear of commercial interest and which secondly offer financial grants for companies to seek such advice. These schemes are variously administered by government departments or on their behalf by trade agencies, and there are separate schemes for small businesses, for microprocessor applications and for manufacturing companies.

224

Fig 8.1 *the process of acquiring hardware*

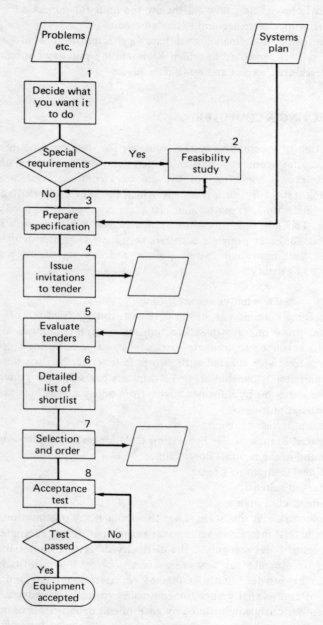

The spearhead of these schemes are the Microsystems Centres, a co-ordinated federation of about 25 centres established originally by the Department of Trade and Industry to assist businesses to make effective use of microcomputer technology. These centres are to be found in most large towns and cities in the UK, usually with a regional identification (e.g. the South Wales Microsystems Centre) and situated in the regional polytechnic (so the South Wales centre is to be found in the Polytechnic of Wales). Each centre provides workshops containing a representative sample of current systems, offers advice and training courses, and under-takes more detailed evaluation and consultancy assignments — all impartial and free from commercial pressure, since no hardware or software is sold from them. In addition each centre specialises in one particular aspect of microcomputers or their application, and this expertise is shared using an electronic mail system to effect transfer of information. Nobody is far from such a centre and without a source of independent and impartial advice.

An *existing computer user*, on the other hand, will probably have an on-going systems or computerisation plan, and will need to acquire new equipment either to replace existing machinery or to provide extra power to support a new application.

(b) Stage 2 — the feasibility study
In most cases a would-be computer user can be confident that a computer can do the work required of it, in principle at least. There are very few computer applications that have not been tried successfully, somewhere, and although the fine details are always unique, generally a computer application qualifies for a 're-inventing the wheel' label. (This is one reason therefore, for buying-in that experience by using packaged software; see next section). There are, however, always pioneers: there was a first holiday company to use a computerised reservation system, a first traffic authority to install a traffic light control system, a first washing machine manufacturer to replace a relay timer with a chip. In such rare cases, it is advisable to perform a detailed technical study to ensure (i) that it is technically possible and (ii) that it is economically worth while to do it. Feasibility studies are tasks for skilled systems analysts or other experts.

(c) Stage 3 — writing a specification
You are more likely to end up, after the exercise, with a computer that will meet your needs, if you produce a detailed and accurate specification of what you want. Such a specification performs several other functions in addition to providing information to tenderers: it acts as a blueprint for further systems analysis and design work, and can also form the basis of

acceptance tests. You will find specification guidelines and checklists in various publications, including Standards guides, but at a minimum you should include:

(i) the system's objectives and functions;

(ii) the work load to be executed (volumes of transactions to be input, processed, output, stored);

(iii) performance targets, expressed in units per hour of batched processing throughput, or response time for terminal input and output;

(iv) special requirements in hardware, software and support services;

(v) operational requirements (availability targets, etc.).

At this point you should consider the necessary arrangements which will have to be made to accommodate, man and service the computer system you are envisaging. The installation of a computer, depending on its size, can include such things as special power supplies, air conditioning and structural alterations to existing premises. It should be made clear that tenders should include a precise account of any special features which need to be supplied by you. A clear indication of the cost of maintenance outside the warranty period must be obtained and remember that this often will include maintenance of hardware and software alike.

A specification of this type does force you to undertake some elementary business systems analysis, of a type which calls for business understanding rather than technical knowledge, but this is preferable to giving potential suppliers something of a blank cheque (for example 'Please supply a system to run my payroll') which provides a basis neither for comparative evaluation nor objective measurement. Beware of giving an indication of the expected cost on the specification. If you do, the quotations will always be at or slightly below the price you have suggested and you will give yourself an additional task in deciding what is put into the tenders as padding and the quotes will not be truly competitive.

(d) Stage 4 – invitations to tender

Because of the enormous diversity of the computer market it is usually beneficial to undertake some preliminary analysis before deciding on the list of tenderers to whom you will issue invitations to tender. Companies wishing to extend or add to ('enhance') an existing computer system will clearly wish to consider only those companies (including their current or original supplier) who can supply compatible hardware, i.e. that will immediately work together with their existing equipment, and it may be easier to find this out by prior enquiry than by merely making it a condition of tender. Because of the drive towards Open Systems (see Chapter 4) this is now a less restricting condition, but you should make a convincing demonstration a prerequisite for further consideration.

For first-time computer users there will usually be no shortage of contenders. Valid factors to be used in preselection can include:
- nationality of machine (not always very easy to identify, even when you know the source);
- reputation of supplier, particularly in your line of business;
- locality of supplier (you want service from a local base, and you may well wish to favour local companies particularly in development areas).

The specification is ussued along with tender documents and instructions, and in order to get back what you want, it is useful to send a pre-printed questionnaire as well. Most suppliers will subsequently want to discuss your needs and clarify obscurities in your specification before delivering to you a formal quotation and presenting a formal briefing.

(e) Stages 5/6/7 — evaluation, test and selection
Your difficulties begin when the tender documents from each invited supplier are delivered to your door. The task of selecting one only of these calls for some extensive and tedious work, which is best approached in three stages: reduction to a short-list, detailed testing of the short-listed alternatives, and the final selection.

Short-listing is based on the tender documents and the mandatory briefing session, and candidates can be assessed by a number of subjective factors; mostly hinging on the global credibility of their proposals and their sales effort:
- are you impressed by their salesmen?
- do you believe that the system can do what it claims?
- have they included everything that was asked?
- does the proposal meet your cost target and delivery dates?
- what (free) support and guarantees will they offer?

This judgemental process should leave you with a short list of, say, 3 to 5 proposals, which are outwardly satisfactory, in that they appear to meet the specification, from companies with whom you would be happy to enjoy the intimate relationship which computer usage engenders.

Detailed evaluation relies on some analytical investigation of comparative performance to be weighted against comparative costs of the contenders. Performance assessment or performance evaluation techniques broadly fall into the following calsses:
- comparison of machine characteristics, such as instruction timings or weighted combinations of them, known as mixes;
- power measurement *vis-à-vis* certain 'scalar' machines (usually a comparable IBM computer);
- actual, artificial or simulated tests on each system of representative work loads, by the time taken or response achieved.

There really is nothing better than a full test on each machine configuration offered, of an actual work load (known as benchmarking) but this is not always possible, and is certainly never easy, particularly in terminal-based systems, and some form of artificial or simulated test may be all that can be achieved. There are, however, some useful professional aids — the Auerbach Corporation test every new machine announced on a series of typical computer routines ('kernels') and offer their results, on which reliance can be placed, to subscribers to their service. Many large computer users with purchasing muscle, such as the government agencies, will at a minimum insist on a set of standard representative programs ('synthetics') being run on as near a working configuration as possible. For microcomputers, several of the better magazines run their own benchmark programs on newly-announced machines and publish the results along with those of other comparable machines — see Fig. 8.2 for a typical but hypothetical example.

The *final selection* has to be a weighting of test results against cost, and finally moderated by one personal or collective judgement both of the equipment offered and the company itself.

It is arguably only the most experienced, or most foolhardy, who will consider a model which they cannot test in any way, which has not been produced even as a prototype. It is, however, a fact of life that when IBM announce a new model, with new deliveries a year or more away, it immediately attracts massive orders merely on the basis of the manufacturer's own estimates of cost and performance, and one *may* take this as a measure of that company's reputation for delivering the goods.

Fig 8.2 *a microcomputer benchmark report*

BENCHMARK TIMINGS (in seconds)			
PRODUCT			
	COMPUTER 'A'	COMPUTER 'B'	COMPUTER 'C'	COMPUTER 'D'
TEST 1	1.1	1.5	2.0	1.8
TEST 2	3.7	5.2	7.4	8.6
TEST 3	9.9	12.1	17.0	15.2
TEST 4	9.8	12.6	17.5	10.4
TEST 5	10.5	13.6	19.8	20.5
TEST 6	18.7	23.5	35.4	25.5
TEST 7	29.6	37.4	55.9	44.0
TEST 8	5.1	3.5	4.3	4.7

Consultants are widely used during this stage, but it would be a mistake for a company to rely entirely on outside technical advice and ignore the expertise which exists in their own organisation.

(f) Stage 8 — acceptance tests

It is essential that you lay down acceptance tests as part of the conditions of purchase, and that you strictly adhere to them when the time comes. This is the final opportunity to ensure that you are getting what you asked for, but unfortunately the normal circumstances in which they can take place (at the final test stage in the factory, and after installation on your premises) put pressure on both sides to cut corners. You will need patience to hold the supplier to demonstrating formally that his machine can meet the performance targets and operational requirements which you laid down in your specification. Only when you are convinced that these are all met should you sign for the machine.

8.4 ACQUIRING OTHER EQUIPMENT

The same type of procedure should also be followed when selecting additional peripheral or terminal units, or when enhancing or replacing an existing computer. In these cases, however, you need to specify the computer currently in use, to ensure compatibility of physical and logical connection or ease of replacement and conversion. In addition support for the conversion process ought to be specifically requested and should form a major criterion of choice. It is also advisable to specify trial usage of any terminals put on the short-list, for full-scale operational and user trials with your existing machine.

The purchase of *personal computers* ought to be approached with particular care, the selling and systems companies still being in something of an unsettled state and the market bedevilled by rapid change and badge engineering, giving all the appearance of an Oriental bazaar.

Inevitably, many buyers are going to find themselves with machines which they cannot get serviced, whose manufacturer has gone out of business or has abandoned the model, or that the rapid rate of obsolescence has condemned to a premature disuse.

You should give particular attention to the following precautions:
- ensure that the machine of your choice can receive local maintenance;
- beware of short-life and obsolescent products with no development prospects;
- avoid manufacturers and retailers whose survival is in doubt;
- examine and avoid potential weak points in the machine (for example the keyboard, which is often the weakest part of a machine, and messy connections in the form of trailing wires, loose sockets, etc.);

- look closely at the frame of your machine if you intend it to be moved about frequently, since flimsy plastics packaging may fracture connections;
- don't pay excessive prices for brand-name peripherals such as videos or cassette equipment which you can buy more cheaply as ordinary domestic TV sets or audio-cassette equipment from a High Street store;
- make sure that you are able to add more storage and devices when you can afford to (Parkinson's law of computing – see Section 5.1 (f) – applies strongly to personal computers).

Particularly at this level, the purchase of hardware and application software packages is likely to proceed in tandem. While the contents of the software are of paramount importance, they should not influence the purchaser into acquiring unsatisfactory hardware in contravention of the suggestions above. Many of the better packages will be available on different machines, and indeed the lack of this choice is of itself a cause of suspicion; if not, it is preferable to compromise slightly on software in order to acquire reliable hardware to run it on.

In addition, the purchaser should also consider the potential availability of additional software for which a need may arise subsequently. Purchasing a microcomputer powered by an Intel or Motorola microprocessor, or running under a widely-used operating system such as MSDOS or UNIX is more likely to guarantee that a wide range of suitable software will be available at that time.

8.5 USING SOMEONE ELSE'S COMPUTER

The drawback of the exercise of selecting your own computer is not usually one of the reasons for deciding to use somebody else's computer in preference to obtaining your own. If you fall into one or more of the following categories, however, you should be seriously interested in one of the various forms of proposition that are itemised below:

- your computer usage is occasional or sporadic or one-off;
- your computer usage is regular but very small;
- your computer usage is regular but has extreme and infrequent peaks;
- you wish to keep your computer costs as low as possible;
- you don't want to bother with the hassle of obtaining and running your own computer;
- you are approaching your first experience with a computer;
- you wish to use some specialised software which you haven't got on your machine;
- you wish to arrange standby facilities in case of accidental or deliberate failure of your machine.

(a) Computer bureaux

The most widespread method of obtaining the services of a computer, without directly or indirectly owning it, is to become a customer of a computer bureau. This is a commercial organisation whose sole function is to sell its computer services at a profit – punching and verifying (data preparation), systems and programming, and computer operations.

Typical customers of a computer bureau can include first-time users, who may soon develop the need and confidence to acquire their own machine; existing computer users with excessive peak loads or abnormal one-off requirements (such as file conversion or program conversion); computer users with infrequent needs; and, finally, large and sophisticated customers who have decided as a matter of policy to leave the whole business in the hands of experts.

Computer bureaux cover the whole spectrum of computer work, from batch to interactive mode (which needs a terminal on customer premises), and from general-purpose to specialised application areas. Most computer bureaux are well-established companies of substance, and you will probably want the additional safeguard of choosing one that is a member of the appropriate trade association such as the CSA in the United Kingdom or ADAPSO in the United States. Fees are generally work-content (x pence per sheet of printer output) or time-related (y pence per kilobyte of disc storage used per week), but you may get a fixed-price quotation for systems and programming work.

(b) Time-selling

Most computer departments will sell time on their machines to outside users: usually spare time on an evening, night or weekend shift, with or without operators in support. Contractual arrangements can take various forms, and in some cases can be permanent agreements, such as exist in a number of places in the United Kingdom between a county council and its constituent district councils, or in the University Regional Computer Centres.

(c) Consortia

A consortium is a permanent agreement by two or more organisations jointly to purchase and operate one computer. The objectives of a consortium are two-fold: firstly to concentrate scarce manpower resources, and secondly to achieve the benefits of scale that larger machines are thought to deliver (see Grosch's law in Chapter 1). It has to be admitted that experience in computer consortia and co-operatives is not uniformly favourable, and you need to be convinced that you can work in harmony with another organisation in matters that intimately concern your own organisation, over a period of years, before considering such a proposition.

(d) Facilities management

This term is used to describe an activity which very many companies support in their catering or transport operations; you provide the equipment and accommodation, and contract an outside specialist organisation to run it for you, at a fee, under your broad directions. Most large computer service companies will offer an FM contract, and there is usually an added benefit that an FM outfit will use spare time either for time-selling or for their other activities, passing on a contribution of the income to the contracted company.

8.6 ACQUIRING SOFTWARE AND SERVICES

(a) Systems software

With even the smallest computer you are also buying systems software, without the basic part of which you will not be able to use the computer. Systems software is a collection of software which can be divided into two groups — systems control and systems service — and it is the first which controls the 'bare' machine on receipt of commands from operators or programs. Systems service software includes all the aids to programming which have already been discussed in Chapter 7 in particular — compilers, editors, etc. Organised collections of systems software are known also as operating systems, but only the essential systems control functions are necessarily included with the hardware, and much of the systems service software may be acquired separately and subsequently. There is usually very little choice of operating system with a specific computer, except in the microcomputer market, where, for instance, MSDOS and CP/M may be available as alternatives for single-user machines and Concurrent DOS and UNIX for multi-user micros; and also, and somewhat idiosyncratically on the smaller minicomputers manufactured by Digital Equipment Corporation. The system control functions of system software are discussed in the next chapter; as far as selecting an operating system is concerned, there is one major issue which may exercise the intending purchaser of a microcomputer. The most troublesome forward option, but one which occurs in many situations, is the move from a single-user system to a multi-user system. The simplest way is to buy another single-user machine and run it completely independently, but this is expensive and does not allow the shared use of a facility that either must be shared for proper processing, e.g. a central customer file, or that would be prohibitively expensive to provide on both machines, e.g. a hard disc, letter quality printer, or expensive software. There are three main solutions, each of which poses more problems for the systems software than for the hardware dimension:

(i) turn your single-processor machine into a multi-processor machine by adding extra processor boards into spare slots ('expansion slots') inside your machine, or by using multitasking software;

(ii) buy another single-user system containing the minimum separate facilities (usually keyboard, screen and processor) and connect it to the original system by a Local Area Network;

(iii) add extra terminals to your existing machine to turn it into a multi-user shared-processor system.

Fig. 8.3 shows these alternatives. For all three cases, the hardware requirements are relatively easy to organise, but to become effective they also require an operating system that can share central resources in a controlled way. The minimum facilities needed are firstly to control access to a printer with a routine that queues up printer output and initiates physical printing from the queue ('spooling'); secondly to allow more than one program to open a file at the same time; ('file-sharing'); and thirdly to stop more than one program from updating the same information at the same time ('record locking'). Not every operating system can do this, and not

Fig 8.3 *alternative multi-user configurations*

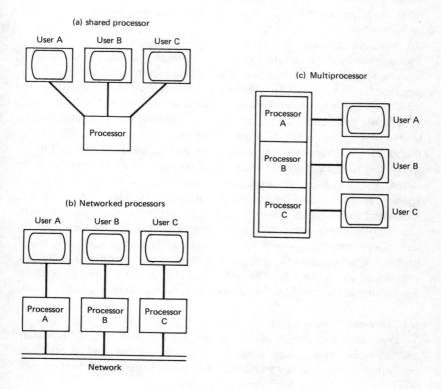

every operating system has a higher version that can do this (nor indeed can every small-system application package), and it is very painful to have to explain to someone caught in this trap that, in addition to the cost of the hardware, it is necessary to change to a new operating system and a new application package as well.

Another implication of this choice is that moving from a single-user micro to several stand-alone micros or to a network of single-user micros may also entail the additional purchase of an extra copy of each of the software packages used for each of the additional processors, since a program licence is valid for one computer only. With a shared-processor (or 'shared-logic') multi-user computer, different users of a multiple-use program merely have their own 'internal' copy of the original program, which is licensed to the one processor regardless of how many copies may be in use at any one time. This distinction becomes very difficult to justify in a network in which all the programs are permanently kept in a shared hard disc, and also becomes very expensive. This is one reason why there is so much illicit copying of software, either by users themselves or by other software houses. This commercial nonsense is at last being faced by the bigger producers, who are now beginning to offer 'Site Licences' which allow unlimited use within a site of a single purchased program.

(b) Data communications

To use data communications to link your computer to another you need a modem or other interface; a line; and software. None of these have to be purchased at the time you purchase your computer, unless, mainly for reasons of convenience and tidiness, you want an 'integral' modem (one built inside the frame of your computer). However, there are two pitfalls here — firstly you cannot do anything without the software, and secondly the modem/interface, the line and the software at both ends have all to be set to the same operating characteristics (speed, transmission mode, data format, etc.). You can get good advice from British Telecom or Cable and Wireless about external interfaces and lines, but for the software you are dependent upon your computer supplier or upon other independent sources of software. If you have reasons to think that you may want to link your computer to another computer, particularly one much larger or from another manufacturer, it would be a wise insurance policy to ensure that this software exists and works before you commit yourself to buying that computer, however closely it may suit your immediate purpose.

(c) Other computer services

Your procurement needs, of course, are not satisfied only by hardware and software. You will need various materials and services to run your computer installation, for which you will find no shortage of willing suppliers. Stationery is the most essential consumable item, and from time to time shortages and long lead-times appear, so that it is essential to keep a high level of stock in hand. Running out of computer stationery would be an operational disaster, the sort of nightmare that haunts DP managers.

By far the most critical operational source is *hardware maintenance*, a service until recently exclusively provided by computer manufacturers, at an annual charge of about 10 per cent of the capital cost or its equivalent. It is already possible, however, to obtain servicing from one of several independent computer maintenance companies. These companies have a less extensive repair network, and you will also need to check that they have the requisite machine knowledge and spares availability.

A maintenance contract should cover the following points:
  (i) scope of cover: for example, weekdays, morning and afternoon shifts only, continuous;
 (ii) callout response on machine faults: for example, within two hours of call;
(iii) availability of spares: for example, on-site or at nearest maintenance centre;
 (iv) back-up facilities to local service: particularly for faults diagnosed as software-generated;
  (v) preventive maintenance: frequency, time and length;
 (vi) availability of your company's facilities: engineer's room/work desk storage.

The overall level of service from your maintenance engineer is critical to the level of availability of the computer to its users, and the preventive maintenance session is often a bone of contention. The engineer will need to run diagnostic tests to detect actual or incipient faults, and then remedy them. He will thus require the system for this period, which will be unavailable to the user. This poses some difficulties if you are running a computer application of a real-time or continuous service nature, and in this situation you will in any case probably afford a duplicate/standby machine to provide cover in case of scheduled *or* unscheduled breakdown.

In general the reliability of computing equipment is high, and with the move towards electronics inside the electro-mechanical media-handling peripherals, we may expect further improvements. We are at the point where it is no longer economic to take out a preventive maintenance contract on low-cost VDUs, for instance, but merely to repair on call. Your computer manufacturer may also offer an on-line diagnostic service, in which the diagnostic program and other tests are run remotely without requiring the engineer to be present or the machine to be taken out of service.

It is also advisable to take out a similar maintenance contract for any application software which is purchased. In this case, however, the nature of the risks is different — unlike hardware, software does not wear out with use or with age — instead it comes with errors already inside it which may come to the surface when in use, and it becomes unusable because of changes in the environment which invalidate the existing processing rules. Software maintenance can cost from 7.5 to 12.5 per cent of the purchase price, and the same type of arrangements need to be made as for hardware maintenance.

There is one extra precaution that may be worth considering at this point — the possibility of your software supplier going out of business through insolvency. When this happens, all the property of the supplier passes into the control of the Receiver, Official or otherwise, whose sole responsibility is to sell these assets for as high a price as possible, without any other consideration such as the fate of customers dependent on the supplier for the ongoing health of their software. This has happened often enough for a little known but longstanding legal arrangement known as 'escrow' to be imported into computing. Under this arrangement, the company can arrange for important assets to be held in trust by a third party, under terms whereby they are released from that trust only on the bankruptcy of the supplier and in which case they do not fall into the hands of the receiver. This remedy is only necessary because software houses have no legal protection for their products and therefore protect their investment by total non-disclosure of source code etc., whereas computer manufacturers are more likely to release copies of logic and wiring diagrams confident in the protection of trade copyright and patent laws.

8.7 ACQUIRING COMPUTERS FOR TRAVEL SYSTEMS

(a) The choice
For a company intending to acquire a computer for use in the travel business, there is potentially as wide a choice as in any other application area — you can acquire your own computer or use a bureau service, you can buy a small, medium or large computer. In fact, choice is somewhat constrained by the following factors:
- the competitive nature of the business, at least among tour organisers, means that you must have the computer working in a hurry;
- competition and the 'regulatory' role of the trade organisations means that most companies tend to follow the same procedures in their market sector;
- the relatively large and integrated set of activities involved in these pro- cedures takes a long time to set up and validate as software.

The consequences of these factors are:
- this is an ideal area for packaged software, and few companies would or

should be brave enough to consider a DIY approach (virtually all the large airlines in the world use a Seat Reservation System containing packaged software and hardware from either Sperry or IBM);
- most of the reputable packages operate on minicomputers or mainframe computers, since most of the professional microcomputers have not been in existence long enough for the establishment or transfer of the software;
- a large-scale operator, such as an airline company, seeking a larger computer is not likely to have survived at all without some form of computer assistance, so that his need is for exansion or change rather than a start from scratch.

For new companies, therefore, the choice of hardware will be secondary to the choice of packaged software, while the choice of hardware by larger companies is likely to be one of expanding or replacing their existing system while retaining their investment in software or otherwise avoiding a major disruption in their operations.

(b) The availability

The British travel trade has a strong and semi-regulatory trade organisation, the Association of British Travel Agents (ABTA), which also acts for tour operators, although there are smaller organisations which also act for the latter. Among its services is technological advice, and it has recently published two surveys of computer systems, one for travel agents and the other for tour operators, based on investigations performed on its behalf by the National Computing Centre. In addition, articles on computer applications appear regularly in its weekly publication the *Travel Trade Gazette*. There is no better starting point than this, since the surveys not only contain an analytical description of each of the available systems themselves (see Fig. 8.4 for an example) but also a list of its, presumably, satisfied users (among whom are to be found most of the well-established companies). It is intended that these publications will be updated with addenda, particularly in respect of microcomputer packages, where advice is particularly strongly needed; however, most new sytems emerging will be advertised in travel trade publications.

In fact, for reasons described in Chapter 2, the retail sector, the travel agents, tend to be (a) users of the tour operators' systems, and (ii) much smaller, typically one-shop, companies; so that as a whole they are much less penetrated by computers, and ABTA did recently actively participate in the specification and development of a system for travel agents.

As described in Chapter 4, an essential feature of systems in the travel trade is access via Viewdata terminals, which can be achieved in three ways:
- using the public Viewdata system (Prestel) for both access and processing;

Fig 8.4 *describing tour operator systems (courtesy of ABTA)*

COMPANY	Name
	Address
	Telephone No.
	Contacts
SUITABILITY	Tour operator sectors catered for
	Market strategy
STANDARD FACILITIES	Inventory Management
	Price/Cost Management
	Agent/Customer Management
	Holiday information
	Holiday reservations/administration
	Component sales
	Enquiries and alternatives
	Transfers/Consolidations
	Client/Agent Documentation
	Principal Documentation
	Statistics
	Accounting Ledgers
	Viewdata/Prestel
	Telecommunication networks
	Office services/other
	Security and Controls
INSTALLATION SUPPORT	Contractual terms
AND TRAINING	Development/Testing
	Training
	Installation
	Support/User Group
	Enhancements/User modifications
	Documentation
	Typical time to implementation
EQUIPMENT	Computer
	Bureau services
	Terminal configuration
	Environmental considerations
	Recovery procedures
COSTS	Typical hardware costs
	Typical software costs
	Installation and support costs
	Maintenance and warranties
CONSTRAINTS/LIMITATIONS	Passengers
	Computer processing
	Storage
	Typical run times
CURRENT POSITION	State of development
	Existing users

- using Prestel for access to another computer for processing via a 'gateway';
- using a Viewdata terminal to a private Viewdata system.

To the user of a Viewdata terminal there is little evident difference between these alternatives, except that Prestel processing is currently limited in scope by the nature of its data organisation and in speed by the characteristics of the standard modem (1200 bits per second from Prestel to the terminal, 75 bits per second return). The availability of all forms of Viewdata services for the travel trade is also well tabulated in the *ABC Videotex Travel Directory*, which is printed quarterly.

(c) Selection

For tour operators, packaged software is expensive, costing thousands rather than hundreds of pounds, for two reasons: firstly it is expensive to produce (my estimate for a full package as described in Fig. 5.10 would be about £100 000), and secondly there is a limited market from which the software company could recover its costs (and there seems to be little evidence of companies with good bespoke software selling it to their competitors).

Limitations on the performance of the entire package of hardware and software seem to be set mostly by the hardware on which and for which the software was written, and principally consist of upper limits on how many terminals can be used at the same time and how many data records can be held. As discussed above, the first point is critical for the microcomputer user, and the second very much depends on how many bookings are sold. These two factors of high prices and uncertainty about requirements argue in favour of avoiding purchase altogether and using a bureau service, at least until the pattern of sales settles and hopefully generates enough profit to cover the costs of purchase; and a number of companies have followed this route with at least two excellent bureaux offering a service which is indistinguishable, at least to the public customer, from that given by an in-house system, at a cost of about £1.50 per passenger booked.

For the intending purchaser, the upper limits of a system's capacity is a starting point in selection, followed by the list of users of the system which will not only give some reassurance but also an indication of the sub-sector of the market for which it is suitable, e.g. villa or hotel accommodation, coach or flight travel. This should give a tractable short-list of systems in a capacity and capability range for more detailed examination, and also a broad indication of cost.

In addition to the normal process of evaluation discussed above, some specific checks also ought to be made about a potential systems capability for data communications, not only at the moment but in the future when different forms of communication will become available. At the moment, the standard entry point is via the public Prestel network, and it would be foolhardy to lock oneself out of this capability.

SPECIMEN QUESTIONS

1. 'The advent of mini and microcomputers represents a threat to both the business of computer bureaux and to the sales of larger computers.' Discuss this statement and compare the relative advantages and disadvantages for the smaller company of owning a small computer or of using a computer bueau.
2. Draw up a specification/invitation to tender for (a) your next personal computer; (b) a multi-user system for a large school.
3. Why do (a) many computer dealers fail to survive, (b) IBM computers continue to dominate world markets?
4. 'The best time to buy is always tomorrow.' How can you make sure that the machine which you buy is a good purchase?

ORGANISING AND RUNNING A COMPUTER SYSTEM

Having obtained a computer with the necessary software and programs to run on it, the would-be user must then proceed to organise its use and operation so that he may enjoy dependable and satisfying service from it. For the user, correct operation of a computer means that (a) it delivers the correct output at the required time; (b) it does not lose data or corrupt it; and (c) it does not allow data to be read by those unauthorised to do so. Putting general principles of management into the particular context of computers, there are in addition some particular provisions to be made and activities to be performed. Thus a computer has to be set up with suitable accommodation and services, and with the people to use and work with it; work has to be arranged for the computer and its raw material (data) brought to it for input and its product (information) distributed to its users; and people have to learn how to drive the computer, which they do through the significant feature of systems software. Finally the whole set-up has to work towards some critical operational targets of reliability and security.

The need for these arrangements varies with the size of the computer system, and this chapter talks about a computer department or section which thus implies a significant part of a company responsible for a computer. However, exactly the same principles apply to a personal computer on somebody's desk at work, in school or at home; they will apply in different measure, but they will certainly apply.

9.1 THE COMPUTER DEPARTMENT

The most important factor in organising a computer for use is, paradoxically, people. They are required:
- to operate it;
- to develop/maintain programs and systems for it;

– to maintain and service it;
– to manage it.

(a) Computer operations

(i) Computer operators

These are the people who physically control a computer, by starting it up, feeding it with input, removing output and responding to messages from the operating system with commands. That description does not, and cannot, convey the full nature of the job. The computer is not a simple machine, and the speed and complexity of its operation, particularly with large mainframes operating under multi-programming and with telecommunication links, make heavy demands on the operator's speed of reaction and technical understanding. It is thus a technician's job and requires a technician's skills and education.

Most organised computers work either round the clock (particularly embedded or real-time systems) or over two shifts, and most operators at some time will work on shifts, in shift teams.

(ii) Data entry

This is the operation of data preparation or data entry equipment on data provided to them by the users via data control. Still essentially a keyboard task, it requires bright clerical staff with keyboard training, as do the related tasks of specialist terminal operator and word processor operator.

Increasingly, however, a computer terminal or workstation or personal computer is becoming a standard piece of office furniture, so that data entry is not only done within, say, the accounts department, but is also done by accounts staff as one part of their job responsibility. We are all computer operators and data entry keyboarders now; and the advent of cash-card terminals and Prestel puts the general public at large in this situation. How to ensure easy but correct data input under these conditions is discussed later in this chapter.

(iii) Data control

This is the interface between the user and the computer department, often a very busy registry. Data control may also be responsible for operating any of the post-printer ancillary machines still in use — collators, folders, envelope stuffers, franking machines — in computer departments with a direct-mail output role. Data controllers play an important role in scheduling the work of an operations section, and may also be increasingly involved in data administration for database systems.

(iv) Media library

In any large data-handling computer department, the circulation and use of disc and tape volumes are under the care of a media librarian. These volumes will contain master files, transaction files, history files, program libraries, etc., and there will be separate rules covering their security (see Section 9.4) and retention.

(b) Computer development

(i) Systems analysts

Systems analysis (see Chapter 5) is the most important function in making a computer work effectively for the organisation, and a job requiring both business knowledge and technical knowledge. There have been moves to split the role into two — with a Problem Analyst and a Systems Designer — and to vary the location in which they are organisationally placed, in order to improve their effectiveness as the liaison and interpreting function on the boundary between the computer department and the user.

(ii) Systems programmers

These are concerned with systems software, as defined in Section 9.3 below, and also with other delivered software and packages, such as database management systems (Section 6.5) and data transmission software (Section 4.4). They also perform some work directly concerned with computer operations — the maintenance of stored procedures and computer performance studies — and some or all may be responsible to the operations manager.

(iii) Applications programmers

They may also have a split role, in that about a half of their work, on average, is taken up, not in developing new work, but maintaining existing programs. Commentators have been predicting their gradual disappearance, as the industry finds less labour-intensive and more productive ways of producing programs, and there is now just a little evidence to suggest that this may be happening.

(iv) Project teams

Because of the project nature of systems development, most analysts and programmers will work together in mixed project teams under a (temporary) project leader who may be either a senior systems analyst or senior programmer. Project teams may be assisted by support teams of specialists, either a chief programmer team (see Section 6.1) or a technical support section containing, for instance, database and/or telecommunications specialists.

(c) Maintenance

Hardware maintenance is almost always performed under contract by engineers working either for the equipment manufacturer or retailers, or from specialist maintenance companies. Their function is divided between breakdown repairs, for which they must be on call, and preventive maintenance carried out on a regular monthly basis.

(d) Computer management

It goes without saying that any organised activity requires co-ordination, control and responsibility for it, vested in management. There is some justification for an opinion that computer management is an undervalued activity, perhaps arising from the early days of organised computing when a computer manager was often the senior technical person in post rather than a true manager, and when a company treated its computer as it treated, say, its transport department. Computer management also includes the arrangements made for board-level reporting; originally many computer managers themselves reported to the finance director because of their original preoccupation with financial systems, but it is now more common for them to report to a board member with sole responsibility for computing (and perhaps management services), reflecting the dependence which many companies have on their computer systems. It is also common for the computer manager to report to a computer steering committee consisting of other senior staff whose work also depends on the efficiency of the computer department.

There are several different models on which the formal organisation of these groups of people are based. In the first, as shown in Fig. 9.1, all groups of staff are responsible to one person and organised in one department called, usually, the data processing department. Such a department is an active and executive part of a company, an organisational 'empire' in its own right and very much part of the *status quo*. At the moment it is under attack because it tends to be mainframe-oriented, and thus antipathetic, and even resistant, to the recent technological trends in computing, most of which refer to smaller computers and decentralised operations.

The second model separates responsibility for the day-to-day operations of the computer from that of developing new work for it. The dividing line varies: the systems analysts are always on the other side from computer operations, but the systems and application programmers may be on either side. In the extreme, systems analysts will be found in user departments only.

Under pressure from the new technological trends and the maturity of the computer industry, there is some evidence that the central organisation of computers and computing staff may be changing. There is a strong

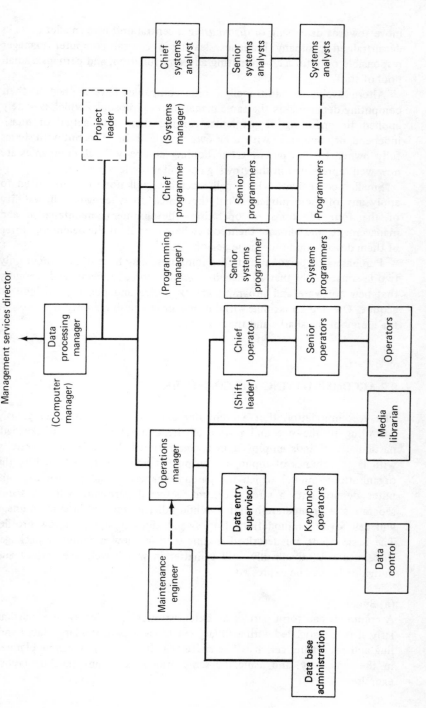

Fig 9.1 *the organisation of a typical data processing department (common alternative titles are shown in parentheses)*

move towards dispersing or *distributing* a central unit into smaller units in decentralised company branches, leaving a central computer manager responsible only for a co-ordinating/advisory function, and perhaps a small pool of staff.

Alternatively, or additionally, some companies have applied to their computing departments the same management philosophy which is widely applied to operating departments, turning them into actual or quasi-independent companies with their own boards of directors but with shares fully owned by the parent group/holding company. Such companies are now well represented in the growing computer services market.

Smaller companies, with small machines, will not of course need to apply any of these models. What they must do is recognise the validity of the four functions of operations, development, maintenance and management, and allocate them somewhere even if, at the beginning, three of them devolve upon the same person.

Purchasers of personal or home computers may have to remember only two lessons: firstly that all machines require some servicing, and secondly that new software and programs are expensive and possibly difficult to acquire. Owning a machine without any programming ability puts you at the mercy of the sharks and the cowboys.

9.2 ACCOMMODATING THE COMPUTER

The accommodation that a computer and its staff needs varies greatly according to the size and power of the computer and its work load, particularly if it is employed in a conventional data processing activity with large volumes of input and output. It will also be affected by the organisational model which the parent organisation adopts for its computer department: a strong, central, active department will call for a separate site or separate building, while a distributed and integrated image will call for accommodation of a less ambitious type, with a low profile. The basic needs are described in this section: how a company packages these needs is, thankfully, still a matter in which welcome variety and individuality can be expressed.

(a) Space
A computer can form part of an extensive man–machine system, particularly if it is associated with ancillary machines as part of a large data handling and processing activity. The space that it is to occupy can be planned in the same way, and using the same principles, as any machine-layout exercise.

(i) The total space has to be sufficient for all the requisite functions and services, with some prudent allowance for likely enhancements:
- data control and data preparation;
- computer room;
- terminal room(s);
- media library and storage;
- work rooms for programmers and analysts;
- offices for management and secretarial staff;
- work room/bench for maintenance engineers;
- storage for paper and other consumables.

(ii) In many cases, for reasons of security, privacy and environmental controls, these functions will be housed in separate rooms, and in some cases must be (see section (b) below); what is more important is that their spatial relationship should follow the basic principles of following the work flow and of minimising physical movement. Thus data control, data preparation and the computer room and media library need to be physically adjacent either horizontally or vertically. For development staff, the physical proximity to the computer room is not so urgent, particularly if program development is via terminals, but the spatial organisation of work-rooms to facilitate supervision is more important.

(iii) Within each room the space and layout are defined by operational criteria: for *equipment*, to permit easy access for normal use and for maintenance; and for *staff*, to meet work requirements and at least any minimum legal stipulations. There is no typical or preferred layout, except that in a computer room it is usual to have the processor and operator's console in the middle of the room, and the I/O and backing storage devices arranged around it in a circle or half-circle, or around the walls, both to minimise cable runs and to permit easy observation and monitoring by the console operator. This may also be true in a data preparation room, particularly one equipped with key-to-disc equipment in which there is again a control console. Fig. 1.6 showed a large computer arranged in this way.

(b) Special requirements

Of these rooms or sections, it is only the machine rooms which call for special facilities, and then only in the case of large computers. For smaller computers it is often a matter of policy to make them as unobtrusive a part of the office furniture as possible (see Fig. 1.10).

(i) Power requirements

Large computers (mainframes and some minicomputers) require a high-voltage power supply and a transformer to boost the voltage from the normal power supply. Computer systems with demanding operational reliability criteria will also justify standby generating equipment, both as a precaution against total power failure and against temporary fluctuations in the public power supply which can cause brief but potentially serious failures in processing.

(ii) Floor requirements

Most large computers with stand-alone units will require either a false floor or special ducting to carry the connecting cables between them and the processor. Trailing cables may well be illegal under safety regulations. Large computers and storage devices may also need specially strengthened floors to support their weight.

(iii) Environmental requirements

Many large computers require an operating environment in which ambient temperature, humidity and dust are controlled by air conditioning equipment. Processors still generate considerable heat, and some large processors are water-cooled, which calls for special plumbing. Others are fan-cooled, blowing heat into the room for disposal by air-conditioning. Dust particularly affects storage media, discs and tape drives where the precision of the gaps between read/write heads and the recording media is critical — one reason for the move towards sealed Winchester discs.

Most smaller computers are intended to work in normal business environments — but be careful because in some countries 'normal' implies some air-conditioning in any case (for staff comfort). The need for full air-conditioning, in sealed computer rooms is, in my opinion, one of the factors fostering the mystique of the all-powerful and unapproachable machine, and the sooner they are dispensed with the better for user–computer understanding.

(iv) Access requirements

It is surprising how many times large and heavy equipment has to be delivered by crane, or hoisted through the roof, because the necessary access via doors and corridors has not been available. Access to rooms for stationery supplies is also advisable.

(v) Data transmission lines

Terminal-oriented computer systems will require the installation of cables for internal use, and Datel-type external services. Restrictions, for example on the maximum length of local cable lengths, may affect room-layouts, and it will also be necessary to avoid potential sources of 'noise'. There are further constraints on using external data transmission services; for instance there are restrictions on the layout of some terminal networks in which multiple terminals are connected to one line. The availability of some services, for example wideband or packet-switched services, are also geographically limited and, at an international level, the whole range of services and costs applicable in any one country may influence the choice of location for a supra-national centre.

(vi) Sound insulation

Teletypes, impact printers, some card/tape readers and some ancillary equipment (card and cheque sorters) create excessive noise and even vibration. It is advisable to install sound insulation or buffering to minimise nuisance to adjoining rooms. There may well be legal requirements which have to be satisfied.

(vii) Rubbish disposal

Another problem, often overlooked, is that a large-scale data processing computer department creates a lot of waste paper for disposal or burning. Waste listing-paper is, however, often of value either as scrap paper for recycling or for use in schools.

(viii) Fire precautions

Part of physical security, see Section 9.5.

(ix) VDU accommodation

There is now reliable evidence that particular care has to be taken in the provision of the working environment for VDU operators who, more than any other working group in computing, will be sitting down and working in a fairly static manner throughout a working day. The normal ergonomic problems of seating and operating a keyboard are in this case intensified by the effects on the eyes of staring at a screen, and the room lighting and screen quality are particularly important in minimising the effects of glare. In fact working conditions for VDU operators often include regular (two-hourly) breaks for this purpose.

9.3 ORGANISING THE WORK

A computer department is in the position, similar to some other functions but unique in its intensity, of being both a service company in that its work is the workload of other operating departments, and an operating company in that it is directly in the line of execution of other operating departments' work. Those departments depend very largely, if not entirely, for the volume, timing and quality of their own performance, on the computer department – a factor accounting for some ambivalent feelings inside such a company. The organisation of workloads is therefore a particularly important aspect of computer operations management.

(a) Authorisation of use

Because it is an operational department on whose services people depend, and for which they have effectively subcontracted, it is necessary for both regular and *ad hoc* use of a computer to be authorised, either by the computer management or by the computer steering committee, one of whose functions must be to determine priorities if the machine's capacity is potentially over-committed. Routine work is authorised by its incorporation into a work schedule, and takes priority. *Ad hoc* work, including terminal users (except full-time terminal operators) therefore need authorisation up to the level at which the total capacity will meet demand, but no more. Authorisation in some accounting methods will also entail allocation of the appropriate costs to other budgets, so that a computer department's running costs may be recovered from the other company functions who make use of it. Finally, authorisation of use is one method of fostering security (see Section 9.5).

(b) Work scheduling

(i) Most routine *batch* work performed by a computer has a target deadline or response time largely dictated by the wider company system: for example, salary cheques to be ready by Wednesday midday, monthly accounts to be produced by the end of the first working week of the next month. To meet all the different targets it is necessary to have a work schedule showing the jobs to be run, their promised delivery time and a loading time that will make some allowance for fluctuations in the volume of input data. The preparation of this schedule, and the organisation of routine and one-off jobs on the computer as required by it, is still largely a human operation task, using work boards or lists in liaison with data control and data preparation to ensure that the data is ready for the time that the job has to be loaded into the appropriate queue. Some operating systems, however, can accept a DEADLINE command as a qualification for an EXECUTE command, and adjust priorities according to the relative differences between the deadlines of loaded jobs and the current clock time. Gaps in a work schedule will show if and when other time-critical work can be fitted in.

(ii) A computer system running a *mixed work load* of terminal and scheduled batch work will have to adjust the amount of time available for terminals according to the state of the work schedule. This may permit some program testing to be performed during the working day, but most large-scale systems testing will have to be performed out of the normal working day. Most systems analysts and programmers will have to work occasional irregular hours for this reason, and flexitime is now common in data processing departments.

(iii) Computer systems entirely devoted to *terminal users* will of course not have a work schedule, and should in any case have been designed to accommodate all predictable levels of demand. It is in the nature of many types of terminal-oriented systems that they are subject to occasional peak demands, at which time either a degraded service has to be accepted or the level of demand artificially reduced by either automatically logging out some connected terminals on some order of priority, or by refusing to accept any further LOGINs. Most operating systems designed for such applications will have facilities for monitoring performance levels and taking such action.

(c) Preparing data for processing

Since the function of a computer program is to process data and produce results, it follows that either before or at the very start of a program execution, it is necessary to have prepared or have available the data required; or alternatively to ensure that the program can be run whenever, or as soon as, the data is available. Which of these two alternatives will be followed, *routine-dominated execution* or *event-dominated execution*, will depend upon the nature of the task, and the choice is also affected by the timescale and distance between the data arising and its processing.

Many business and non-business activities are performed according to a regular routine, as is the nature of organised life, and since computing assists in such work, many computer program suites are run regularly according to an operational schedule which reflects normal business patterns — weekly salaries, monthly salaries, daily warehouse dispatches, etc. For these regular runs, all the data that has occurred since the previous run will be accumulated, regardless of volume, into one or more batches, and then processed as a batch. *Batch processing* is both a continuation of previous data processing practice, and a contribution to operational efficiency, in that the delay between the data occurring and its processing provides time for carefully planned preparation for processing; it also, incidentally, makes best use of a processor in that a program is only loaded and started once for a large number of iterations of the inner loop (see Section 7.3). The time-scale will also, in most cases, allow for transportation of data from branches and other locations to a centralised computing function. The computer industry has well-developed procedures for data preparation in these circumstances (sub-section (b) below).

Other business activities, like other aspects of real life, require that as soon as an event occurs and data originates, it should be processed without the delay inherent in batch processing. *Transaction processing* implies the immediacy of event-dominated computing, whether real-time, in that a reply has to be given within the time-scale of the wider activity, or pseudo-real-time, in that the immediacy is one of convenience rather than necessity. Most of the transactions of this type, such as requests, bookings and enquiries, occur at the point of sale or point of customer contact, and thus too far away to permit the direct use of centralised computing equipment except by *data transmission* (see Section 4.4) and by input and output at a *terminal* (see Section 4.3).

(d) Batched data preparation

The objectives of data preparation are to ensure that:
- all the data that the user has is submitted and processed;
- it is as error free as possible.

(i) Data control

Control over data is a joint exercise. In the department(s) where the data originates or arrives, transactions are recorded, checked and accumulated into batches. For each batch, a batch control sheet or card is produced, containing a sequentially allocated batch number, the transaction total and a check total (either a summation of a variable, such as order quantity, or a total of document numbers). Completeness may also be aided by giving each transaction a sequentially numbered identification — for internally raised documents these can be pre-printed. The data will then be recorded into the computer department by a data control clerk, and will remain as a batch through data preparation and some if not all stages of processing. The completeness of the batch by transaction counts or sequence number will be checked during processing.

(ii) Error control

Errors in input data are the bane of computing (GIGO — garbage in, garbage out — applies). As in most matters, prevention is less expensive than cure. The prevention of errors is to be achieved in two ways — firstly minimising the quantity of data created manually in the first place, and secondly by improving the clarity and legibility of data that has to be copied or transcribed from the original source of the data, which is usually a document of some type. The first objective can be attained by preprinting as much as possible of the data to be entered, either in good clear print for the data entry operator, or in direct machine readable form using OCR font or Barcodes (see examples in Figs 4.11 and 4.12). A particularly useful technique is for the computer itself to pre-prepare a printed data collection form in which the variable data can itself be entered with marks for direct document entry — a form known as a 'turnaround' document (see Fig. 4.10).

Fig 9.2 *a computer input document*

If this is not possible, then attention must be given to the source document from which data will be entered into the computer. If the document originally comes from within the same organisation (e.g. it is sent out to be completed and returned), then it should be specifically designed as a punching document, from which the data preparation operator will punch either on to a medium or directly into a computer file. Such documents, with boxes for characters and internal column number, will be familiar to many people who belong to consumer organisations; an example is shown in Fig. 9.2. If this is not achievable, then it may still be necessary to copy data from the original document on to a punching sheet to give the data preparation operator a clean data source. The completion of original or punching documents needs to be guided by formal instructions, the preparation of which is one of the responsibilities of the systems analyst during implementation.

The *detection* of errors starts with a repeat performance of input punching on the same cards, etc., or a visual check by the same operator before the record is released, known as *verification*. It continues in the first processing run on the batch of data along with the batch control header, in which a number of checks are performed, known as *data vet* or *data validation*:

- records read against input transaction total and computed check total against input check total;
- check digit verification — many key numbers have an extra digit attached which is produced by the result of a mathematical operation on the original digits (usually a modulus 11 operation — sum the weighted digits, divide by 11 and take remainder). The ISBN book number is one such code. Recalculating the check digit and comparing the result with the original will detect an error in that field;
- programmed checks for data type, value range and key field value on file.

Errors detected are then corrected, and re-input until the entire batch is clean before full processing begins.

The same process, up to data validation, applies to any type of input device used for batched data preparation, whether off-line on to cards or magnetic media, or on-line by direct data entry into internal storage (the terms 'off-line' and 'on-line' were discussed in detail in Section 2.2). It is also possible to input data directly for batch processing, from a remote terminal, though in most cases a batch would be created locally and then transmitted as a batch.

(e) Data input at a terminal
It is difficult to over-emphasise the importance of terminals in computing today. They are more than just an input device, more than just a remote

device — they are, to very many people, the embodiment of the computer and, if present trends continue, they will constitute, with built-in processors, the vast majority of the world's population of computers. Terminals can be classified according to their mode of usage, into fully interactive and semi-interactive.

By *interactive* we mean a pattern of computer use in which there is frequent interaction between the system and the user in the form of question and answer or input and response, item by item, line by line, or record by record. *Conversational* is also used with the same meaning. Interactive programming means computer programming in a language which gives a response after each instruction, interactive I/O means a program in which each piece of data is requested from the terminal user and checked item by item. The form that this interaction takes, between the system or program output on a screen or printer, and the user input on keyboard, is known as a *terminal* or *man–machine dialogue*, and is one of the most important parts of program design for terminal input.

Semi-interactive means, in the same way, a process in which there is less interaction. Output from the system only at the end of an execution, or a stream of data input at a terminal for subsequent delayed batch processing, would qualify as semi-interactive. A particularly common form of terminal use with local storage media (see data collection terminals in Section 4.3) is collecting data (interactively or not) and then submitting it to the processor at the end of a shift or day. This is known as:

- *remote job entry* (RJE) if accompanied by commands to initiate the processing;
- *remote batch entry* (RBE) if purely data;
- *conversational* RJE/RBE if there is an interaction in inputting the data only.

Data input at a terminal needs particular care because in some cases (that is, real-time or pseudo-real-time) the source of the data is lost immediately after the transaction is processed, and also because there is no time for the careful preparation of data, starting with data input instructions and through to data validation, as in the case of batched input. The same principles, however, have to be followed, and have to be built into the form of interactive dialogue between the terminal user at his keyboard and the system, via the display screen or printer.

The first objective of a *terminal dialogue* is to prompt, invite and guide the terminal user/operator to input the correct data and complete data. The terminal user will particularly need guidance if he is only an occasional user, or if the structure of the data is complex, guidance which in batch data input can be provided by instruction manuals. There are a number of different methods for providing this guidance, of which the most important are *menus* and *forms control*.

Menus are lists of options displayed or printed out from which the user has to select by typing in the appropriate number or keyword. The act of selection inputs a particular value, or causes a further menu list to be printed out, or causes output to be displayed at the terminal. A very good example of a menu-driven terminal (although primarily for output selection) is provided by the Prestel service, which at the beginning of an enquiry provides an option list covering *all* the information available. Entering a number from 1 to 9 then provides a further list of options, and so on, depending on the information required, until the bottom level of classification is reached and the full data page is displayed. Fig. 9.3 shows such a menu-driven search for information about cinema shows in Cardiff.

Menu-driven input is particularly important in some sales/order input systems in which different materials or products have significantly different characteristics, options or alternatives. Not all data, however, can be selected from lists of alternatives, and the prompting for such data can best be performed by either a straight printed *request/instruction*:

ENTER SURNAME

or a straight *keyword* prompt:

SURNAME?

perhaps with format or dimension instruction:

SURNAME (UP TO 20 CHARACTERS)?

Forms control is the displaying on to the screen of the blank outline of a form (of the type which could be used if the information were being input on a form of convenient batch data preparation). The cursor is then moved, by program control, into the first data field position to await input, and from there to the next, again guiding the terminal user to provide all the data necessary. Fig. 9.4 shows an example of a form-driven input procedure for sales order input.

The latest fashion in ways to initiate input from the terminal user uses a combination of display techniques that the latest microprocessor power makes possible in intelligent workstations and microcomputers. *Windows* are described as a feature of screens in Chapter 4 – under program or mouse control you can create display areas within the dimensions of the screen and even overlapping, in each of which a separate activity can be proceeding concurrently. *Icons* are pictures representing functions available within the system and displayed on the screen usually for selection by a mouse; for instance, a diary function would be shown as a picture of a diary or an electronic mailing facility by a picture of a post-box. A *'mouse'* is a device for moving a cursor around a screen and inputting a request

Fig 9.3 *a menu driven terminal dialogue: X indicates user selection by pressing the appropriate key on a Prestel keypad (see Fig. 4.9). In the Prestel service it is also possible to look up the detailed page numbers directly in the manual classified directory or to use an alphabetical index*

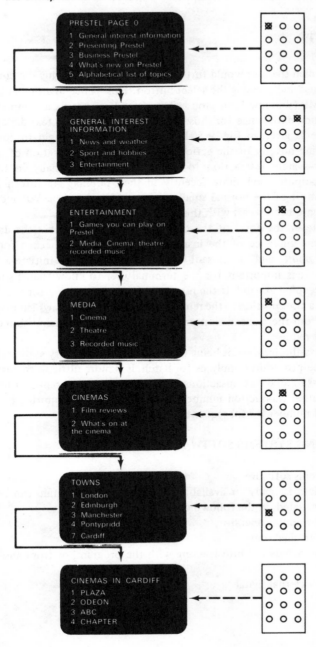

for the facility currently being pointed to by the cursor. A *'pop-up menu'* is a menu (see above) that suddently appears when a facility is requested by pointing to an icon, e.g. if you selected a Mail icon using a mouse a small menu would suddenly appear ('pop up'):

Send
Receive
Quit

from which the user would further select at will by moving the cursor with the mouse and pressing the select button. This whole environment is called the WIMP (Window Icon Mouse Popup) and represents a completely new computing experience for those brought up with simple text dialogues. An example is given in Fig. 9.5, but a picture cannot begin to convey the entrancing novelty of the action. We owe the popularisation of this form of user–system interaction to Apple Computers, initially in their Lisa microcomputer and more recently in their popular MacIntosh micro in which most of the normal small-system software such as WP and Spreadsheets have been recast with this form of interface.

Whatever the form of the dialogue, it is essential that the data input under the guidance of the instructions is rigorously checked for validity *at that point*, and errors sent back to the terminal to initiate a re-input. Equally it is important for the terminal user to know that his input has been accepted as valid. If the terminal is not intelligent, error checking will require a transmission to the remote computer, a process which may induce errors from the transmission process and cause a re-transmission or even a re-input request.

Unless the terminal is being used as a direct data entry station, in which the same procedures apply as for batch, it is more difficult to ensure completeness of all data transactions, but it is usual for the computer to allocate a sequential transaction number to each set of data submitted to it and to use that number for subsequent throughput checking.

9.4 USING SYSTEMS SOFTWARE

(a) Systems software
When data is ready or available for processing, a program can be started up, or initiated, in the following ways:
- by a computer operator;
- by a terminal user;
- by commands fed into it along with the program, or from another program;
- by an external signal.

Fig 9.4 *forms control display* — *cursor;* [ ] — *data input fields*

```
OUR ORDER NO.      000022        CUSTOMER      FOR AMENDMENTS :-

CUSTOMER ORDER NO [█       ]     ORDER FORM    TYPE '1' = CANCEL

ACCOUNT NO.       [       ]      -- PAGE 1. -- TYPE '2' = NEW QUANTITY

                                --------------- TYPE '3' = NEW DELIVERY

        DESCRIPTION   STOCK NO. QUANTITY REQUIRED  TYPE OF AMEND.   NEW WEEK NO.

DEVON TOFFEES         ABC1      [       ]           [ ]              [ ]

BARLEY SUGAR          ABC2      [       ]           [ ]              [ ]

WINE GUMS             ABC3      [       ]           [ ]              [ ]

BUTTER SCOTCH         ABC4      [       ]           [ ]              [ ]

JELLY BABIES          ABC5      [       ]           [ ]              [ ]

LIQUORICE ALLSORTS    ABC6      [       ]           [ ]              [ ]

SYSTEM MESSAGE AREA [FI]                            LAST ORDER NO. 000021
```

The process of initiating a program does not involve only the data source, the program and the computer, it primarily requires interaction with, and through, some aspect of 'systems software'. Systems software is an organised collection of programs, provided along with the 'naked' processor, which collectively make it possible for programs to be developed, stored, changed, loaded and run. It is the systems software which handles all the I/O routines and organises the access of data within disc or tape files. In fact a programming language is locked into an operating system, except in the most simple of computer systems, so that when an instruction causes a READ to be made from a disc file it is the systems software which handles this. The systems software acts as an interface between the programming language and the 'naked' computer.

Systems software can be divided into two types: *systems service* and *systems control*. The term 'operating system' is also widely used, sometimes to include both types of function, sometimes restricted to the second, and will be used in this book in the *latter* sense.

Fig 9.5 *a typical WIMP display (courtesy of Research Machines Ltd)*

Systems service routines are those which have already been mentioned earlier in this book: compilers/assemblers, libraries, editors, testers and utility programs. Their function is to provide service and support for programmers and other users. They need not necessarily be provided by the computer manufacturer, and are often available from software houses and other software sources (see Chapter 8).

Systems control routines, usually called a monitor or supervisor, are concerned with program initiation and execution, and with system management in the context of most computers today which run more than one program concurrently ('multi-programming' — see below). There is a wide range in the scale and type of functions included, and no commonly agreed terms or structure. One common way of looking at systems software is to consider it as a hierarchical structure, each 'layer' moving progressively further away from the naked machine. The lower-level routines are as much a part of the machine as the hardware, and are almost always provided with it. Fig. 9.6 illustrates this view of systems software. There is an increasing trend to implement systems software in firmware, that is, permanently 'blown' on to some form of ROM.

(b) Systems commands — job control and operator commands

The facilities of systems software are used in two ways: firstly by *systems commands* which are explicitly issued by operators, by terminal users and by programmers, and secondly by involuntary *controls* on, and *calls* made by, programs during execution, which the operators, terminal user or programmer cannot see, and of which they may not be aware.

Systems commands are equivalent, at a higher (systems) level, to instructions in an applications programming language, except that their execution, by a systems software routine variously known as the reader/interpreter, or command handler affects either individual (sets of) programs or the whole set of programs currently active in the processor. *Job control commands* relate to jobs, a job being a set of programs (or program-steps) run as one task at one time; *systems control commands* refer to the complete working system and therefore to any or all active jobs. On microcomputers, where only one job is active at a time, normally, the distinction disappears.

(i) Job control commands

These are written in *job control language* (JCL) and effectively form a higher-level program in which the names of application programs and datafiles appear as the operands, as will become clear from the examples which follow. Since there is no standard form of JCL, except in one significant case (those supplied with the BASIC programming language), the examples given are merely representative forms.

Fig 9.6 *systems software — the bare machine and its software superstructure*

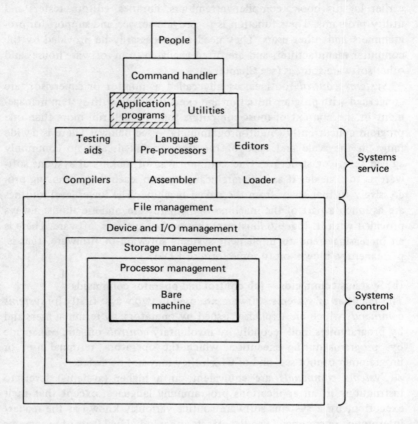

(i) To compile a source program

COMPILE	prog-name WITH COBOL
EXECUTE	COBOL with prog-name
RUN BASIC	
COBOL	

(ii) To store a program on a library, and remove

SAVE ⎱	
STORE ⎰	prog-name
COMPILE	prog-name TO LIBRARY
DELETE ⎱	
REMOVE ⎰	prog-name or file-name

(iii) To load and run program

GET LOAD }	prog-name
START GO }	prog-name
EXECUTE RUN }	prog-name (equivalent to LOAD and START)
CHAIN	prog-name from another program
PROG-NAME	(gets and starts program)

(iv) To use utility programs

SORT	file-name on sort-key
LIST TYPE }	file-name or prog-name
MAIL	file-name to user-name
DUMP	file-name to device-name
DIR, LIB	display files in Library or Directory

(v) To create/change a file

EDIT CREATE }	file-name

(vi) To identify input data in files and assign to devices

DATA	file-name (or symbol indicating data in card reader)
ASSIGN	file-name to device-name
FILE	file-name

(vii) To identify a job and password (see below)

JOBNAME . . . PASSWORD . . . ACCOUNT-NO . . .

(viii) To start and end a terminal session

LOGIN, LOGOUT

(ix) To delimit the operation of a previous command

ENDJOB, EOD
(a standard symbol may also be used for END)

The stand-alone commands, for example EXECUTE, may also be qualified, for instance giving a priority to a job, giving a program a time-limit or stating its resource requirements. Also, very important, either as a qualification or as a separate command, conditions may be stated, for example:

EX prog-name-1 BEFORE prog-name-2
IF FAIL ...

Job control commands issued by terminal users, *terminal commands*, are usually simple and clear, influenced by the commands which, uniquely in BASIC, are supplied with the programming language itself, distinguished from program statements only in that you do not require a statement number. In other cases commands are issued whenever the system software prints an invitation symbol on the screen such as @ or *. Terminal commands are normally issued at the time they are needed, and it is in the nature of terminal use that these needs are relatively unpredictable. It is part of the dialogue between a terminal user and the system that a response will be given by the system after each command. The following example shows a typical sequence of commands and responses for a terminal session in which a program is loaded, run and then changed and re-run (the operator input is underlined).

```
@LOGIN GGL-WRIGHT
 Job 20 on TTY52 23-Sep-80 10:26:26

@RUN BASIC

READY, FOR HELP TYPE HELP.
OLD NADADD

READY
RUN

NADADD          10:27          23-SEP-80


                         NAME-AND-ADDRESS FILE ADDITIONS
ENTER YOUR CODE WORD                                    ?MACSDH4

ENTER YOUR DATA RECORD ITEM BY ITEM AS REQUESTED

CODE NUMBER        ?45632
SURNAME            ?EVANS
INITIALS           ?NH
TITLE              ?MR
HOUSE AND STREET   ?THE MANSE
TOWN               ?TREHARRIS
COUNTY             ?MID-GLAM
POSTCODE           ?CF469ZZ


RECORD 45632 ACCEPTED ON FILE

ANY MORE RECORDS? ENTER 1 FOR YES, 2 FOR NO    ?2
SIGNING OFF 34 RECORDS ON FILE


TIME:  0.61 SECS.

READY
LIST


NADADD          10:30          23-SEP-80
```

For batch processing, job control commands are prepared in advance, and submitted to a computer either along with a source program or object program, and data, or stored away in a library as a command file ('stored procedure'). Job control commands are prefixed with a special symbol such as // or ?, to distinguish them from program instructions. A typical set of job control commands submitted, along with a source program and test data, to compile and test a COBOL program, could be:

£JOB ... ACCOUNT-NO ... PASSWORD ... (Defines a specific job and references it to a particular programmer)

£COBOL

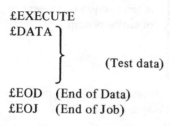

source program (Enters program in HLL and compiles it)

£IF FAIL THEN EOJ (Terminate run if program does not work.

£EXECUTE
£DATA

(Test data)

£EOD (End of Data)
£EOJ (End of Job)

Job control for routine work would normally operate from stored procedures, with references to a command-file and to data also, usually, stored as a data-file, for example:

£JOB ...
£EXECUTE   £proc-name
£DATA   data-file name
£EOJ

Such stored procedures would normally be very much more complicated than simple commands that application programmers would generate themselves, particularly on large mainframe computers. Their preparation would be the responsibility of a 'systems programmer' whose role is to maintain and use systems software. In such cases the job control language may well be more similar in form to an assembler language, rather than to the high-level language forms illustrated above.

(ii) System control commands
In batch-processing operations jobs are prepared in advance and fed continuously to the system by the operator. System control commands enable the operator to maintain control over the system and *all* the jobs

running on it at any one time. They will be typed in at the operator console, and will elicit responses from the system, and may well be prompted by initial error messages or warnings on requests from the system itself. In this case the dialogue is between the system and the operator.

System control commands, for ease of use, are usually simple and clear, and may well be abbreviated as the operator can quickly become accustomed to them. Their use is, however, a key part of the operator's job which, as will be discussed in the next chapter, is concerned with the efficient running of the entire system. System control commands will therefore mostly not be available to a programmer or terminal user except in small business systems where the system is not so complex and where there may be no full-time specialist operator. Typical operator commands will be:

```
START
STOP
HALT
CONTINUE          individual job or streams of jobs,
DISCONTINUE       or entire system
CANCEL
SET or CHANGE PRIORITIES
```

SET TIME and DATE and other options
START the system and CLOSE it down

DISPLAY various items and status
ASSIGN and REMOVE on-line devices
process the system LOG

(c) Operating system functions

One of the operator's first functions at system start-up is to start up the operating system by what is known as a 'bootstrap', usually now automatically from a ROM when power is switched on. The operating system then runs all the time, intermittently between, and in the middle of, application programs. It performs certain functions as the result of job control or system control commands input when a job is loaded or terminated, or whenever the command is received, and other functions according to 'calls' made to it as the result of events occurring during the course of programs' running. These functions can be classified as:

- *processor management* — deciding which jobs are to run and in what way ('scheduling');
- *storage management* — allocating internal storage to programs;
- *I/O management* — controlling the use of devices;

– *file management* – controlling files on backing storage and supporting I/O operations on those files.

The scope and complexity of these functions, and the volume of the software provided to perform them, vary according to the degree of multiple activity in a computer. The task of internal management is one created by specialisation and co-ordination, so that the greater the level of activity inside the computer, the greater is the requirement for it to be centrally controlled. The smallest monitors are those required by single-program computers, and by embedded or dedicated real-time systems; in the first case because the sequence of activities is relatively straightforward, and in the second case because the alternatives are restricted by the environment.

(i) Processor management and multi-programming

The major complexity is introduced into computers when it is necessary for the computer to run more than one program at a time. The older and somewhat misleading term for this regime is 'multi-programming', but more recently the term 'multi-user' has come into use; also 'multi-tasking' and 'concurrent processing', both of which permit the notion of different parts of one program being executed at the same time. Multi-programming means multiple program operations on one computer, in which there will be more than one applications program resident in internal storage (along with storage reserved for the use of the operating system). This gives the impression that the computer is executing more than one program at a time. Its prime objective is to ensure that the processor is as continuously in use as possible, by enabling another program to use it when one program has (temporarily) to discontinue using it. (In a single-processor computer, only one program can actually be in control of the processor at any one time.) A secondary, and in terminal-based systems usually the main objective, is to serve a number of users apparently simultaneously in a situation where it is necessary for them to use the same processor or a resource controlled by the processor.

Reasons why a program may be unable to use the processor continuously and/or have to relinquish control of it, include:

– it has come to the end of its current allocation of time ('time-slice');
– it issues a READ/WRITE request to a peripheral which operates independently of the processor, thus causing a call to I/O software;
– another program's READ/WRITE request is completed and that program is ready to continue;
– a hardware or software fault;
– a normal halt or termination;
– a higher priority program, or a previously suspended program, is ready to (re-) use it.

(ii) The interrupt

When more than one program resides in storage at any one time the switching of control is by a simple but extremely powerful mechanism known as the 'interrupt'. It is primarily a hardware feature which:

- recognises the occurrence of certain events;
- stops the processor from continuing with a program after the current instructions have been completed;
- stores away information related to that program, mainly the contents of the IAR (that is, the address of the next instruction to be performed) in the status register or a specially reserved area in internal storage;
- causes a branch to a systems software routine which determines the cause of the interrupt and the next action to be taken − usually the passing of control to another program whose status information is reloaded in the IAR, etc., from the stored area.

Originally the interrupt was provided to enable a high-priority program to be initiated when required by an external signal (an *external* interrupt) indicating that data is incoming and has to be processed immediately. This is how a program is loaded and run in an interactive system. The interrupt is caused by the person at a terminal typing a command such as RUN.

The combination of internal and external interrupts allows for the highest priority to be given to real-time programs, normal priority to I/O-intensive programs, and low priority to compute-bound programs. Interrupts can also be generated deliberately, for instance to cause a timer to interrupt a program if it has been running without a break for longer than a fixed time-slice of a few milliseconds. This permits the sharing of a processor among multi-access users. Fig. 9.7 shows how interrupts operate to effect multi-programming.

(iii) Distributed computing

Multi-programming also requires the other resources of the computer either to be shared among the concurrently active or to be allocated to one (group) of them. It is common practice to segregate common programs by their resource requirements and load them for execution in streams or queues accordingly. In fact, the demands of storage, device and file management are very much more demanding than those of processor switching and allocation, and collectively contribute to the situation that the time and space on the machine taken up by operating systems routines almost wipe out the gains in machine efficiency which multi-programming contributes. The inescapable size and complexity of large machine software are reasons why systems designers are deliberately exploiting the lower costs of hardware by moving away from central mainframes into linked groups of smaller machines with simpler software − a process known as 'distributed computing'.

Fig 9.7 *multi-programming and interrupts*

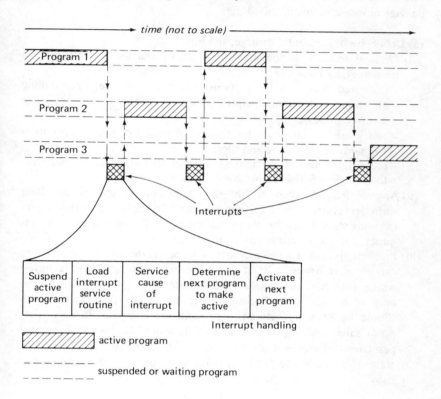

Interrupt handling

| Suspend active program | Load interrupt service routine | Service cause of interrupt | Determine next program to make active | Activate next program |

active program

suspended or waiting program

The related process of putting processing power into terminals and other devices also contributes to the simplification of the work of 'proper' processors. *Distributed* systems, incorporating both distributed computers linked by data transmission, and distributed intelligence, finally enable computing power to be provided at the user's elbow, in keeping with the organisational trend of decentralised company operations. There are now very few reasons for retaining centralised computing systems with their vast and complex operating systems, other than the support of a central company-wide database.

9.5 SECURITY AND RELIABILITY

A computer department is the custodian of two valuable, rare and strategic properties: the computer equipment and its processing capabilities, and the information contained on its files. The security of these properties is one of the most important responsibilities of a computer manager, against damage or loss, and unauthorised use.

(a) Deliberate or accidental damage, and loss

(i) *Physical security* is the prevent of access and use to unauthorised personnel, by means of:
- restricted access: locking rooms when not in use, or installing electronic badge-card operated locks for continuous use, or using security guards;
- restricted use: use only by authorised names or under supervision for hardware, software and files;
- precautions against theft or sabotage with burglar and other anti-theft devices fitted to portable devices.

(ii) *Natural hazards* such as fire should be anticipated by installing sprinkler systems or inert gas emitters. In certain situations, precautions should also be taken against flooding, subsidence or earthquake, and power surges due to lightning.

(iii) Precautions against *accidental loss* or *deliberate destruction* of *software* can be taken by using ROM, and involving operating system facilities, where available, to make software inaccessible (by password), read only or execute only. Security copies of all key files and software should be kept, and stored away from the computer room in fireproof safes, and log or journal records should be taken whenever a permanent change is made to a master file record, so that the current state of a master file can be speedily restored from the previous full copy.

(b) Unauthorised use of information and programs

There are three identifiable risks:
- access to files containing either company-confidential (for example, production costs) or personal-confidential (for example, employee details) information;
- use of, or tampering with, programs for fraudulent purposes ('computer fraud');
- stealing or unauthorised copying of programs or files that have a commercial or competitive value.

These risks constitute 'computer crime' which exercises a continued fascination similar to that exercised by sophisticated bank robbery, which it resembles in several ways; firstly it is usually an 'insider' job, secondly it is perpetrated by professional 'middle-class' criminals and thirdly the victims will rarely admit to it for fear of losing business. There is also the fringe activity known as 'hacking' in which the motive is not financial gain but merely the satisfaction of 'beating the system', a form of vandalism which, like most other forms, may have roots in the social environment (see Chapter 10).

Protecting confidential data in data bases and files is now, in most countries, additionally sanctioned by Data Protection Acts relating to the storage and use of personal data. This is one aspect of the Privacy issue which is also discussed in the next chapter.

Precautions against computer crime are mostly controls over access to data and operational programs, restricting access to computer rooms only to operators, and to programmers only for specific and authorised purposes, and strict controls over company transactions input to the computer. These precautions are very much more difficult when a computer system is, by its nature, established to provide access to users outside a controllable site, that is from remote terminals and even terminals open to the general public in the street. The following methods are available for identifying legitimate users or denying illegitimate users:

- restricting the knowledge of the system's modem numbers;
- using dial-up modems with the remote modem number stored in it;
- authenticating users by passwords, account codes and by other personal data and unique identifying information known both to the system and the owner of the data;
- using terminals with built-in 'addresses' or that are 'lockable' with electronic keys, cards and other electronic gadgets known as 'dongles';
- identifying users by unique physical characteristics which can be stored in digital form and checked on re-input by techniques of pattern recognition – voice, signature, fingerprint and even the pattern of blood-vessels in the eye.

Data is also at risk during transmission along data communication media which are outside the physical control exercisable over other parts of a computer system. There is no doubt that sophisticated electronic listening devices exist to pick up any electronic signals, ironically developed by our security and police services. There are two forms of protection – firstly the data can be 'scrambled' in such a way that it is unintelligible to the unauthorised eavesdropper, and secondly through the use of optical fibre cable in which the signals are much harder to detect. Scrambling is now mostly performed by 'encrypting' data before transmission – that is, applying a mathematical operation on the pure binary data using one or two large numbers ('keys') which are known only to the sender or receiver and which are unlikely to be discovered by chance or by systematic iteration by eavesdroppers. The data is then decrypted in reverse by the receiver, or may be stored in encrypted form for further security.

Another, and perhaps unsuspected, source for eavesdropping are the electronic signals from the electron gun inside our VDUs, which are not all trapped by the phosphor coating on the screen. Protection mostly involves distorting the signals outside the VDU with metal or magnetic strips.

The fail-safe mechanism, finally, is to 'police' a system with current monitoring of activities, system logs and reports, and by providing what are known as 'audit trails' for use by internal or external auditors; these are complete records of what happens to a business transaction from when it is received to when it is finally passed through all the stages of processing.

Even supposing these measures failed, it is still necessary to decode the bit signals into data or instructions, and get through the layers of software protection to execute programs. In real life the undramatic truth is that confidentiality, integrity and security of software and files are most at risk from bored, unscrupulous or disgruntled employees, ex-employees and contractors, using regular but unauthorised means of access allied to their insiders' knowledge of how the software and programs work. Perhaps the most reliable precaution against such abuse is proper personnel management, and a totally 'professional' computer industry.

(c) System failure

Reliability is freedom from failure. Unfortunately every man-made object is subject to failure in operation, either as a result of a component failing or as a consequence of something else happening outside the system. Things suddenly fail at random, and things eventually wear out. Continued operations without failure are of interest to every computer user and totally essential to real-time and life-support systems. Thus reliability has to be sought and engineered into computer systems both in their original manufacture and during their use.

(i) Reliability engineering

Reliable hardware can be sought in the following ways:

- using good-quality and well-tested components;
- good design that eliminates potential areas of failure, e.g. moving parts, friction, stress, heat, etc.;
- providing extra capacity ('redundancy') that can be used to check the correctness of an operation;
- providing spare units which can continue in use if the first unit fails ('replication');

Software has different failure characteristics, in that it does not wear out with use, but is very difficult to produce without leaving errors in it. Thus reliability can be achieved by good design that makes it possible to detect as high a proportion of errors as is realistic at the time of production. On the positive side, however, it is possible, and necessary, to use software to be constantly looking for errors and to effecting means of recovering from them, usually by taking copies of data and transactions and going back to the last 'clean' state before an error occurred to restart the system.

It is through a combination of these methods that a small group of highly specialised computer manufacturers are able to offer 'non-stop' computer systems which they can confidently guarantee will not fail. In fact, non-stop systems will experience failures internally, but failure of components will not stop the system working, and for this reason they are also called 'fault-tolerant' systems.

(ii) Operational precautions

Since most hardware wears out with use and age, the most essential precaution is testing hardware regularly either in time or by use, and replacing defective parts. This is known as preventive maintenance, and should reduce random or wear-out failures to a minimum, the effect of which can be further controlled by holding spares and by arranging a rapid and guaranteeable repair service. With modern electronic solid-state technology, the greater number of failures are likely to be caused by errors in software, so that reliable software and similar software maintenenance procedures are equally essential, both for application software and for systems software.

Ultimately, and perhaps unfortunately, all computer systems rely on electrical power. The power supply to your home or work or school is, from time to time, affected by situations outside your control – total failure, a planned shut-off for repairs, other users taking a lot of power at once, a surge of power caused by lightning, or even power cuts caused by industrial action. A reasonable precaution for most companies is a power line conditioner – a black box which 'cleans up' your power supply from the mains and delivers a constant supply free from small but critical disturbances. Companies which cannot tolerate a complete power failure must provide their own back-up power supply – either a battery which provides enough life to enable a computer system to close down in an orderly fashion (in order to be able to start-up as easily as possible); or, in the extreme, a standby generator which is immediately switched into use when a failure of the mains supply is detected.

(d) Disaster Centres

The ultimate precaution against the loss of a computer system is one which indicates the way that large companies totally and absolutely depend on their computers. In several locations in the USA and at least two in the UK there are to be found secure and often underground centres containing complete operational computers, with all necessary services and communications, but doing nothing. They are, however, at instant readiness for any eventuality which could cause the computer systems of any of the paid-up clients to become totally unusable, at which time the whole computer operation could be transferred to this secure centre and restarted immediately. They are known as 'Disaster Centres', since the loss of a computer system could be regarded as nothing less than a disaster by, say, the large banks and other financial institutions, who are willing to pay about a million pounds a year for this insurance policy.

A lower scale of precaution of this type is one well within the scope of most companies, in the form of independent Data Security Centres which will keep copies of your data, usually on magnetic tapes, in fire-protected premises secured by all the latest electronic devices. For any company, loss of data is the biggest operational disaster.

9.6 RUNNING A COMPUTER SYSTEM IN THE TRAVEL TRADE

(a) Starting off

The travel trade is a very seasonal business, apart from business travel which tends to be fairly constant throughout the year, and in particular holiday travel operators in two half-yearly cycles — the summer season for holidays between April and September, and the winter season for the rest of the year. Except for the specialist winter holiday companies, the summer season is by far the busiest and most critical, the starting point of which is the issue to the retail trade of the summer season brochures containing details of all the holidays on offer. The issue date for the next summer season's brochures used to be aimed for the depth of winter, so that people could make their choice in a relaxed and mellow mood during the Christmas holiday; but more recently the date has been brought forward in order to tempt people to re-book while still full of euphoria from this year's holiday. This means, therefore, that a brochure has to be ready for the printers at the end of summer; negotiations with hoteliers and flight operators take place during mid-year, and plans have to be finalised by the companies for submission to them even earlier in the year, thus compounding the uncertainties.

Assistance from computers is vital in keeping the time down to a minimum — in producing drafts of the brochure, in reconciling demands from different operators and scheduling aircraft to flights, and in forecasting traffic levels and prices. The timing of the issue itself is a matter of fine judgement — the earlier it comes out, the sooner the operator receives and banks deposits and pre-empts the competition, but the greater the risk of getting it wrong or of giving the competition the chance to undercut on price. As it is, it is becoming more common to reissue brochures in mid-campaign, usually around Christmas, to correct earlier mis-estimates. It is also necessary to ensure that all the holiday details are entered into the master files, and that all program changes are completed and tested, so

Fig 9.8 *extracts from a typical holiday brochure (courtesy of Intasun)*

that business can be transacted the very same day that the brochures are available.

(b) Enquiries and options

Most tour operators provide immediate access to travel and to the public by telephone and, in most cases, through Viewdata terminals. Telephone operators are usually equipped with telephone headpieces to leave both hands free to use their terminals. As Fig. 9.9 shows, the first stage of arranging a holiday is an enquiry about the availability of a holiday selected from the brochure, usually involving a separate choice of flight/coach and hotel/other forms of accommodation. If the selected choices can be met, then the customer or travel agent is offered a temporary reservation of flight and rooms, or 'option', which will be held for the customer for a short period, usually three days, before the end of which it is necessary for the temporary reservation to be converted into a confirmed booking; and the customer is given a reference number for the option, which usually becomes the reference for the confirmed booking.

For the computer system, this is really the 'sharp end'. The demand on the system is heavy for both data storage and processing. For each seat and room allocated on or between two dates, the system has to record:

- status (free/temporarily reserved/permanently taken);
- option number/booking number;
- date of expiry of temporary reservation.

The computer has to perform these tasks quickly, in 'real-time' while the computer is waiting, in order to assist the customer to make up his or her mind on the spot. This may not be too difficult if the first request can be accepted, but much harder in the more usual case that the first choice of date or holiday is full and the computer seeks, as a sensible enquiry program will ask it to find, the next date when the flight and hotel can

Fig 9.9 *a typical holiday enquiry display*

```
Bargain Holidays                                    1828618c          Op
CARDIFF OFFICE
*****************************************************************
           L     A   TTTTT EEE     DD  EEE    A   L
           L    AAA    T    E       D D E     AAA  L
           LLL A   A   T    EEE     DD  EEE A   A LLL
*****************************************************************
              DEPARTURES FROM CARDIFF-RHOOSE AIRPORT

Crete
5280       14 Nts    25 Aug    Pension Eleni      2B      SQE     £323
           14 Nts    28 Aug    Hotel Atlantic 3BBx4       SQS     £208
           14 Nts    01 Sep    Hambos Studios     3B      SQD     £295

Rhodes
5345       10 Nts    18 Aug    Georges Tav TAV/BBx2       LQT     £275

Greek Mainland and Saronic Islands
5155       14 Nts    17 Aug    Taverna Socrat TAVx2       GQA     £211
           14 Nts    24 Aug    Hotel Hydra        3B      GQD     £244
           21 Nts    26 Aug    Poros Rooms        2B      GQT     £312

***************** BOOK THROUGH LATE DEAL NOW ********************
   Key 0 for LATE DEAL INDEX        Key 1 for FLIGHTS ONLY LIST
*****************************************************************
```

accommodate the request, or another hotel or flight for the same date. This demonstrates the need for the data model to encompass the data relationships described in Chapter 6.

(c) Confirming the booking
In order to convert an option into a firm booking, two things are necessary — firstly a potentially non-returnable deposit on the cost of the holiday has to 'change hands' — in cash, cheque or by credit card — and secondly full details of all passengers have to be conveyed to the tour operator's computer. These actions can be performed remotely via a Viewdata terminal (if the Viewdata software will accept input as compared with merely displaying answers to enquiries), but more generally by the customer filling in a booking form found in every brochure, of the type shown in Fig. 9.10 and sending it to the tour operator by post.

As soon as the booking form is received by the tour operator, these details are entered by a data entry operator into the computer, causing the temporary reservation to be confirmed, all relevant files to be updated, and an acknowledgement or confirmation document to be output for printing and despatch to the agent or customer. At the same time, the balance is computed and a request for payment by a specified date appended to the document, and the deposit is formally entered into the accounting sub-system. At this point the contract is struck.

Confirmation is again a demanding load on the computer, but of a different type, in that a booking request must be entered immediately it is received in order to avoid the option expiring inadvertently — which means same day processing, regardless of how many forms are received in the post that day. In fact the bottle-neck at this stage may well be the printer, but most good operating systems have a feature called the Spooler which takes care of the output of printer requests to the printer independently of processing, so that, for instance, the printer can be left to print out the Acknowledgements overnight when the data entry operators have gone home. The efficiency of the 'man-machine interface' — the forms and the screen dialogues — is critical in ensuring that as many transactions of all types (not just the bookings, as described below), can be input during the working day.

(d) Processing and progressing the booking
From the point of data entry, the booking record (see Chapter 6) is the focus of further processing and progressing. At any point, the booking may be subjected to changes requested by the customer, some of which may pose severe difficulties for the original; e.g. 'can Granny come along as well, we'll put her in a three-bedded room with the children and we'll go into a double room on our own, but she will want full board and . . .'.

Fig 9.10 *a holiday booking form (courtesy of Intasun)*

intasun booking form summer '87

DO NOT WRITE IN THE SHADED AREAS

BOOKING REFERENCE	OPTION DATE	CONF. DATE

FLIGHT/COACH CODE	DEPARTURE POINT OR AIRPORT	RESORT	DEPARTURE DATE	NIGHTS	HOTEL/APARTMENT (NAME & CODE)

TO BE RETAINED BY TRAVEL AGENT

	Title	Initials	(BLOCK CAPITALS PLEASE) SURNAME	Enter age & date of birth if under 18 or over 60 on day of departure AGE	DATE OF BIRTH
1st ROOM					
2nd ROOM					
3rd ROOM					
4th ROOM					

PLEASE COMPLETE THIS FORM CAREFULLY AND ACCURATELY. MISTAKES MAY LEAD TO ADMINISTRATION CHARGES

MEAL REQUIREMENTS – If the hotel offers a choice of meal requirements, please tick the correct box.

FULL BOARD FB	HALF BOARD HB	BED & B'FAST BB	ROOM ONLY RO

ROOM FACILITIES – If you have confirmed private bath shower & toilet, please tick here.

SPECIAL REQUESTS (Not guaranteed & subject to availability)

CAR HIRE Driver's Name (See page 286)
Resort / Car Category
From / To
Number of days (inc. first & last day).

Please state here, in block capitals, name and address of person to whom all correspondence should be sent
Name
Address
Postcode
Tel. day / Evening
Out of office hours phone contact for first named

ESSENTIAL INSURANCE **YES**
All persons named on this booking form will be automatically covered by our insurance unless you delete YES here. The appropriate premium will be considered included in your deposits and will be added to your final invoice. If you do not require our insurance, you must complete the following:
My insurers, providing comparable or greater cover than Intasun holiday insurance, under all sections, are:

DEPOSIT The deposit payable is £50 per person for all holidays. No deposit is payable for infants under 2 years of age on the day of departure or for children qualifying for a free holiday; if applicable, insurance premiums will be considered included in the deposits paid by accompanying adults.

AMOUNT ENCLOSED £
Cheques, etc must be crossed "a/c payee only".

CLIENT'S DECLARATION
I certify, on behalf of the person(s) named on this booking form, by whom I warrant I am authorized to make this booking, that I/we have read and agree to the Intasun Fair Trading Policy and Holiday Information set out in the brochure relevant to my/our holiday, and the conditions of insurance referred to in that brochure. Where applicable, I authorize my Travel Agent to make this booking on my/our behalf and instruct them to deal with this Booking Form, deposit and Remittance Slip in accordance with Intasun's requirements.
I am over 18 years of age.
Signature   Date
(This must be the signature of the first named above)

IMPORTANT Children: Free holidays for children will only be confirmed if they were specifically reserved at the time of booking. It is then essential that the Intasun phone reference applicable to free holidays is quoted in the space provided above. No deposit is payable for infants under 2 years of age on the day of departure or for children qualifying for a free holiday. Unaccompanied children under 18 must have this booking form countersigned below by the parent or guardian.
Signature   Date
(Parent or guardian)

AGENT'S REMITTANCE SLIP SUMMER 1987 – MUST BE SENT TO INTASUN HOUSE, 47 GRATTAN ROAD, BRADFORD, YORK BD1 2QF

AGENT'S STAMP

intasun

Please retain booking form and forward in lieu this Remittance Slip together with deposit (or full amount if within six weeks of departure) to Intasun Holidays Limited, 47 Grattan Road, Bradford, Yorks BD1 2QF.
290

Booking Reference No:_____
ABTA No:_____
Dep. Date:_____
Flight Ref. No:_____
Lead Name:_____
Value: £_____
Press date October 1986 (C)

In fact the amount of program code required to effect changes, to amend records and the holiday price, and to adjust the original record is usually much more than that needed to set up the booking record in the first place. In addition, the customer may make payments or part-payments at any time, and less frequently may cancel a booking altogether, in which

Fig 9.11 *tour operator reports*

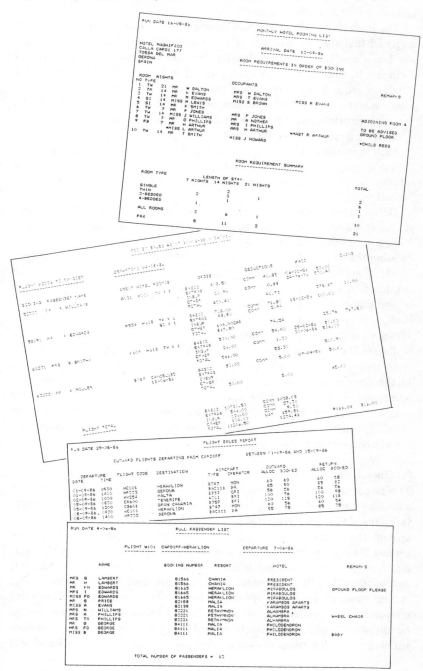

case the program will calculate the cancellation penalty and remove all allocations made to the booking.

The booking is also progressed through to the date of the holiday, with activities that are automatically selected on significant dates:
- a few (usually six) weeks before the date of departure, the program checks to ensure that all money due has been paid and prints out a balance request and reminders in progressively stronger words;
- two weeks or so before departure, assuming that no money is owing, the computer prints out the tickets and other travel documents;
- regular list and reports are sent to other parties concerned — flight and coach operators, hoteliers, couriers and local representatives, and not least to the company management, who progressively adjust their selling tactics as the departure date approaches with unsold seats on planes and coaches.

Date-related processing means that a significant element of the programs is concerned with the manipulation of a calendar date — validating a date, adding or subtracting a number of days or weeks to/from a date, and calculating the day of the week on which a date falls (see example in Chapter 1). In fact these are all nice programming exercises, which would be organised in a library of subroutines or modules (see Chapter 7), and most of the algorithms work only for dates between specified upper and lower limits — in particular, there will have to be some changes made before January 1st 2000 in a lot of software.

Processing also continues after a holiday has been completed, when it is no longer necessary to keep all passenger or booking details, at least not in the current working version of the file but in history files. The lead-name and address would be put into a mailing file ready for the next season's brochure, and a summary of all bookings stored away ready for checking against bills subsequently sent in by suppliers — hoteliers and travel operators in particular.

(e) Organisation

The effect of such extensive software is that, subsequent to the issue of a holiday brochure, the preparation of which is mainly a labour-intensive task, the day-to-day operations of a tour operator can entirely revolve around the computer system, and in the largest companies the Data Processing Manager is in effect and sometimes in name the General Manager, and the computer operation is the company operation. In particular, it is necessary to handle documents smoothly into and out of the computer system, and to keep the system and its data communications running continuously — particularly at peak times, a breakdown of either would be disastrous, and reliability is everything. The effect also is to reduce running costs to a minimum — one medium-sized company handles 30 000 bookings per year with a staff of six people; such a situation is, however, only reached after years of careful development and determined management.

SPECIMEN QUESTIONS

1. Draw up an organisation chart showing the staff and their interrelationships in a typical commercial data processing department. State typical job specifications of three different grades of staff.   *

2. Assess the likely impact of microcomputers in companies with large data processing installations.

3. Discuss control procedures which are available to a data processing manager to ensure (a) the security of data held within the installation, and (b) the validity of data to be processed.   *

4. Discuss three of the factors that have led to the increase in computer crime. Comment briefly on the people that could be involved in computer crime. How can a company prevent such occurrences?   *

5. (a) State three of the aims of an operating system and briefly describe how each of them are achieved in a system known to you.
   (b) What is the purpose of a bootstrap loader and why is it so called?
   (c) Briefly describe the design and functions of a job scheduler.   *

6. (a) Distinguish between multi-programming and multi-access. Outline the methods by which each is achieved by an operating system and indicate the effects of the user.
   (b) Give four examples of interrupts.
   (c) Give two examples of utilities that are provided with a modern operating system and show how a programmer could take advantage of them.   *

7. Whatever form of data processing is employed, the design of source documents is of prime importance. What are the features of good source document design, and how else should these features be observed in operating a computer-based business procedure?

CHAPTER 10

COMPUTERS AND PEOPLE

It is only to be expected that the rise to prominence of the computer over the last four decades has had some effect on the lives of people in our society. Technology is the driving force of culture, and the computer is the acme of contemporary technology. Its effects have, slowly but surely, been emerging from its original impact in business use into a much wider spectrum of public and private life, and we may be sure that this is an on-going process. The next chapter discusses what we can foresee for the future; in this chapter we examine the current evidence for the effects of computers in the main areas of twentieth-century life:

- employment;
- education;
- civil rights;
- leisure.

10.1 COMPUTERS AND EMPLOYMENT

(a) The positive position

Fig. 9.1 showed the range of occupations created, or re-defined, by the use of computers within our large organisations, at clerical, technician, professional and managerial levels. Numerically this is the largest 'plus' effect of computers on employment. An informed estimate is that the computer accounts now for about 1.5 per cent of the total employment in Western societies — about 400 000 in the United Kingdom and about 2 million in the United States — and that about 90 per cent of those computer jobs are in the *computer or data processing departments* of other organisations. Other directly computer-related jobs are in the *computer manufacturing* sector (which is itself part of the wider electronics industry) and the *computer services* sector (software and systems houses, computer bureaux and consultants).

The computer, and the wider field of information technology, has therefore arrived as a significant and growing sector of our economy and source of employment, at a time when nearly all other sectors are in decline and when full employment seems to have disappeared for ever. As a source of employment, its major characteristic is that it requires a relatively high level of skill and knowledge, and developments in the subject are continuously pushing up the levels and expanding the boundaries of knowledge. There are intakes of trained entrants at various grades and a well-defined career pattern has emerged, as shown in Fig. 10.2. Unfortunately, deficiencies in both our education and training policies and practices (see next section) means that the industry's manpower needs cannot be met in full, a situation that would be ludicrous even if there were not millions of people seeking work. As it is, the larger companies are having to seek staff from abroad, producing 'brain drains' around the world, and to encourage emigrants and expatriates to return home; and a recent report looking at the next decade warns of 'serious concern that skill shortages are constraining development', in a period in which an annual growth rate of 10 per cent would increase the overall demand for staff by 50 per cent.

Another interesting characteristic of computer-related employment is that at the higher levels of skills the proportion of women is very low, less than 10 per cent. There is some disputed evidence that computer education in schools and colleges reinforces the male-dominated image of computing, as of technology and engineering in general, despite the fact that ten years ago interest in computing was quite evenly balanced between the sexes. In the intervening time, the computer business has obviously created a totally misleading impression in which women are disadvantaged — the aggressive nature of computer salesmanship, the macho image of computer games, the fanatics of home computers — and some pioneering attempts are now being made to encourage women (back) into computing and into engineering generally (Women In Science and Engineering). Until we see the results from these schemes, we must continue to treat women as an untapped potential source of supply to meet the current and prospective shortfall in staff, and teachers and parents must dispel attitudes that discourage them from joining us. So, don't put your daughters on the stage, encourage them to go into computing; buy them home micros and persuade them to select computer studies course at school and beyond. More generally, we must look to changed policies in education and training, that expand rather than contract opportunities, and that seek to correct these apparently structural imbalances — employers seeking staff and people seeking work, students seeking places on courses and colleges seeking students.

(b) Computers and unemployment

Many people also look to education to solve the most serious social malaise of our time – unemployment and its consequential effect on mental and physical health. Unemployment clearly represents a many-headed problem, resulting basically from an inbalance between the demand for and supply of jobs, and our present situation results from the supply not expanding at the same rate as demand; but among the many causes is technological unemployment – the consequence of replacing manual work by mechanical work, or automation in general. There can be no doubt at all that one of the effects of using computers in business has been to displace manual work, and it is merely a fact of life that computers can do so many things more effectively than people, as discussed in Chapter 2. The bottom line, however, is cost, and the cost advantages of using computers increases as the prices of hardware decreases. The effect of extensive and well-designed computer systems is to leave behind a leaner, faster moving and more competitive organisation that employs fewer people for the same output, and to do so is with full responsibility towards shareholders and in keeping with that organisation's objectives. It is then society's hope that that organisation will be able to expand its output as a result of gaining more orders in a competitive market, and so offer more job opportunities to compensate for the jobs that have been lost in the process. The current mania in industry for company growth by means of mergers and takeovers appears to frustrate these hopes, since economists have never been able in retrospective studies to identify any real benefits from large takeovers, and it would seem to be more reasonable for governments to intervene at this point, to accelerate the natural process of growth compensating for cut-backs, rather than to engage in artificial job retention or job creation activities.

(c) Computers, VDUs and their operators

The other consequence of computerisation is that the rump of the information-handling jobs still retained are, as with other automation schemes, mainly made up of the tasks that the computer cannot handle and concerned with feeding and minding the computer. They are essentially de-skilled and machine-paced terminal operators, mostly in data entry operations, and it is also likely that the large proportion of these jobs are performed by women. A longstanding controversy has arisen from this situation in which it is claimed that the using the terminal, and in particular the VDU, is bad for the health, to the extent that the Health and Safety Executive has been forced to intervene. The complaints fall into the following categories:
– effects of a VDU on the eyes;
– radiation emitted by the VDU;

- backstrain;
- the work is *boring*.

You do not have to look far for the visual problems caused by VDUs; to keep the unit small the screen has to be small, and to display a reasonable volume of print on a small screen the characters have to be small and intensively illuminated. Continuous use of a VDU does cause headaches from the glare, and most companies, on the advice of the HSE, now limit periods of continuous use to a maximum of two hours.

The evidence for radiation emission is much more debatable, based on several studies which indicate a higher level than expected of miscarriages and birth defects among women working as VDU operators. Such phenomena are notoriously difficult to prove statistically, and exhaustive tests have failed to demonstrate any more radiation emitted from VDUs than from TV sets or microwave ovens, but the feeling persists that all is not well.

There is no doubt at all that not enough attention is given to the seating, lighting and other accommodation of the VDU and its operator. Just like any other keyboard and sedentary worker, chairs and desks need to be adjustable to the physique of the individual — height, length of arms and legs, etc. Lighting is an additional problem as reflected light adds to the glare of the screen itself, and as a result it is usually necessary to remove natural light altogether from the VDU workroom.

Finally, we must come clean and admit that many VDU-related jobs are mostly dull, routine and repetitive. We have taken away from the human operator, even those previously engaged in low-grade and repetitive clerical work, many of the tasks which contribute to job satisfaction because the computer can do them better or faster, without thinking of the effect of what is left. The consequence is poor operator performance (i.e. a high input error rate), and operators 'going on the sick' with physical ailments of a mainly psychosomatic nature — a genuine bad back simply caused by mental malaise from a totally boring job. The incidence of days lost from sickness, always many times greater than that lost from strikes, is increasing in epidemic proportions, and much of it has been attributed to a protest against poor working conditions — the 1980s equivalent of the wildcat strike.'

It is difficult to give a true balance between the positive and negative effects of computers, partly because in most cases the negative effects are disguised as, for example, hidden job losses when people who leave are not replaced. Technological unemployment tends also in the short term to be swamped by trade recessions and other factors which affect the supply of jobs.

However, we do know of heavy job losses over the last ten years due to new microelectronic technology, ironically in the electronics and telecommunications industries. Even in computer manufacturing itself fewer people are needed to make more computers. Given the pressures on productivity in international markets and on public service organisations alike, then it is virtually impossible for them to avoid the opportunity of reducing their costs and increasing their effectiveness with more computers and fewer employees.

It is not necessary to believe some of the more dramatic claims made in the media about the potential effects of the microprocessor and all its associated products; it is sufficient merely to recognise that the introduction of computers is part of an overall trend, and the best that can be made of that trend is for the maximum exploitation of the employment opportunities which it offers in the supply, servicing and operation of the new technology.

Fig 10.1 *accommodating the VDU*

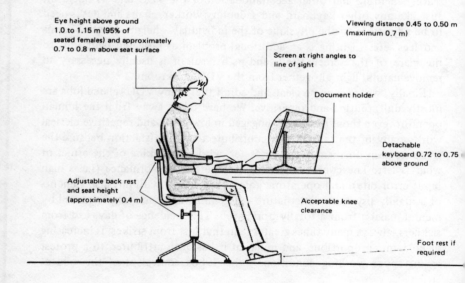

Eye height above ground
1.0 to 1.15 m (95% of
seated females) and approximately
0.7 to 0.8 m above seat surface

Viewing distance 0.45 to 0.50 m
(maximum 0.7 m)

Screen at right angles to
line of sight

Document holder

Detachable
keyboard 0.72 to 0.75
above ground

Adjustable back rest
and seat height
(approximately 0.4 m)

Acceptable knee
clearance

Foot rest if
required

(d) Computers and trade

In this respect the present situation also presents an unsatisfactory picture for the UK and for many other countries. The computer manufacturing industry itself is dominated world-wide by American companies, except perhaps in the protected markets of Japan and Eastern Europe, by a margin that must be unparallelled in any other sector of industry or commerce. US companies manufacture multinationally in Western Europe and elsewhere, and particularly exploit British software expertise and tax benefits in Eire. Even considering re-exports there remains a large and unhealthy balance of payments deficit in Western Europe on hardware and systems, and it is almost impossible to export to the higher protected US market to reduce the trade gap.

Attempts to redress trade deficiencies through exports is further threatened by politically-motivated trade embargoes, such as the efforts of the US government to extend to European firms their internal regulations prohibiting the export of high-technology equipment to Eastern bloc countries, by policing the re-export from Europe of computer systems containing components originally bought from the USA. The whole episode indicates that computers are now matters of politics on a national and international scale.

In fact, producing national profit-and-loss accounts is particularly difficult because (a) most computer manufacturers buy in components and even unit products like printers and discs from other companies; and (b) chips and other electronic components are made world-wide, with labour-intensive work (like mounting wafers) performed mostly in the Third World.

The situation is further complicated by the Japanese threat. Given their current dominance of the world consumer electronics market, it would be surprising if the Japanese manufacturers were not able to extend into computing, with their unique blend of manufacturing skills, subservient labour market, enterprise and Government aid. Japanese-made chips are already inside many otherwise impeccably western products, and Japanese processors, particularly plug-compatible models of IBM mainframes, are already on sale, though not always under manufacturers' names. Industry leaders are resigned to expecting Japanese dominance to extend to processors and peripherals by the end of the decade.

Given these competitive factors, what can be done to maintain a major share of the market for domestic products? The lesson is clear from those countries which are in that position, that is, the United States and Japan. The lesson is to establish a protected market by import controls or other means, and support the domestic suppliers with financial aid under a comprehensive plan. The home market will then establish a strong base and economies of scale from which some larger exports can be launched. This is precisely how it has been done in the United States and Japan; to do otherwise is a dereliction of duty by other governments to their native computer enterprises. Ironically, the United Kingdom has the strongest domestic supplier in the western world in ICL; had it received the support that American and Japanese companies enjoy, it could now be a world leader.

10.2 **COMPUTERS IN EDUCATION**

Since the computer industry, and the use of its products, are now important factors in employment, it would be expected that computers and computing would find a place in education and training, which have as one of their objectives, preparation for adulthood and employment. Computing courses are now available at all levels, and computing has taken its rightful place among other subjects, even though the demands that it places on teachers and resources are very great. Fig. 10.2 summarises some of these course provisions with the qualifications attached, which may be traced as the appropriate entry point to different career paths in computing on Fig. 9.1. Most schools, colleges and universities are now equipped with staff and equipment to support the relevant courses, although the total level of resources may still be inadequate. The demands from industry for recruits with usable skills, which often conceal an inadequate level of formal staff training and retraining within industry, has unfortunately distracted attention from other equally relevant roles for the computer in our educational processes — firstly as a teaching tool and educational aid, and secondly in helping to manage our educational institutions and activities.

The use of the computer as an educational aid is known as Computer-Assisted Learning (CAL). The computer is used as a store of information which can answer questions; as a processor of answers given to questions; and to demonstrate, visually or via educational robots, ideas and concepts. Its contribution to teaching is seen to be effective in two ways — firstly in stimulating the interest of children, and secondly in giving individual and flexible tuition at the child's own pace and direction. In so doing, it highlights two of the failings of our educational system — firstly that it fails to stimulate large numbers of children, who then leave school without any useful qualifications or skills, and secondly that in large classes teachers cannot give individual attention to those at the extremes of the distribution of ability — the gifted and the backward children. The result is an underachievement of individual potential, and of society as a whole.

The very magnitude of the problem indicates that the contribution of CAL can be valuable, but equally that it is likely to demand the same sort of professional planning and resource provision as any other large-scale computer application. In fact at least one microcomputer has been delivered to each primary and junior school in the UK for this purpose, but hardware is the easy part. Software and staff training has been in short supply, with the result that only the most dedicated of teachers have put the microcomputer to this intended use; and CAL is another casualty of the classroom. The success story is in the teaching of physically and mentally

289

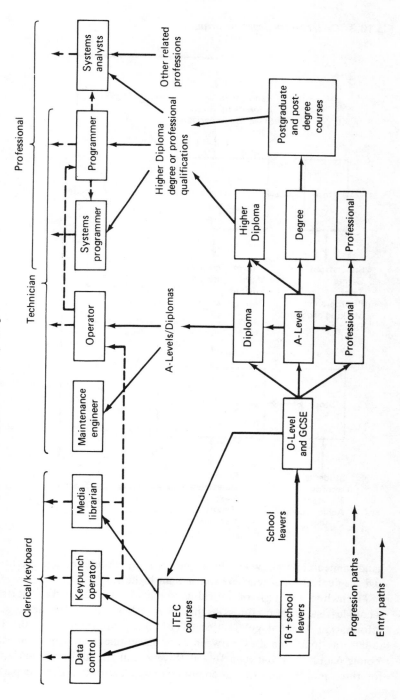

Fig 10.2 *qualifications, courses and career entry points in computing*

Fig 10.3 *CAL and the learning process*

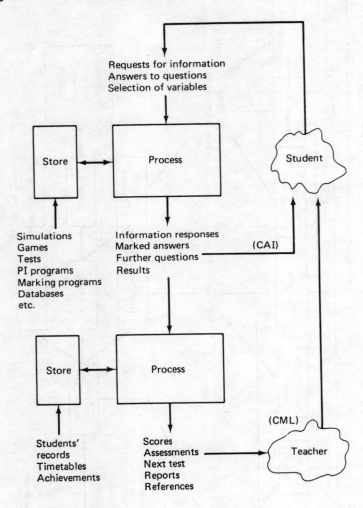

handicapped children, where both the need for stimulation and attention, and the dedication of teachers are, at their highest.

Meanwhile the task of providing some of the 'rejected' cohorts of school-leavers with useful skills has been taken up by the network of Information Technology Centres ('ITECs') set up throughout the UK, usually as joint ventures between local government and local industry. Young people aged between 16 and 18 years can attend for courses lasting for three months upwards in computers and electronics, often as part of the two-year Youth Training Scheme. There is an ITEC near you, if you find yourself in this position.

Computer-managed learning (CML) goes beyond the learning process into the management of the learning situation, by storing scores and assessments and then, among other outputs, determining which tests are to be taken next. Primarily, however, CML is data processing applied to the running of an educational establishment, built, like business data processing, around a set of master files of which the student records file is likely to be the most significant. Increasing demands are being made on schools to provide both collective and individual reports on their performance as educational establishments, culminating in a formal Record of Achievement to be given to each pupil at the end of his or her period of compulsory education, and it is difficult to see how a large school can satisfactorily meet these demands without considering its information systems in a formal way. The importance of CML also lies in the implicit model of real life which the school represents to the pupil. It is important that the computer should be seen to be playing the same role in the school as it does outside; lessons learnt at this stage about 'living with the computer' are likely to be more rewarding than difficult adjustments learnt afterwards, in the same way that changes like metrication are more difficult for those who have grown up with Imperial measures than for our children who have been taught in metric units from the beginning.

The relevance of the computer and similar new subjects such as microelectronics, is symptomatic of the move away from a labour-intensive and labour-based economy towards an energy- and knowledge-based economy, in which lack of formal education and established mental skills will restrict youngsters to an uncertain employment future. The difficulty of finding employment for unskilled school-leavers is one of the most distressing features of 'structural unemployment', and it calls for an expansion of higher vocational education — an extension of the Robbins' principle that higher education should be available for all those who qualify for it. It is nonsensical that youngsters should be paid for being unemployed but not supported on courses to prepare them for purposeful and permanent employment.

In time, of course, our society's preoccupation with the need and the right to work — the 'work ethic' as it is known — may relax, in which case the computer's contribution to people's leisure time and leisure activities may become more important (see Section 10.4).

10.3 CIVIL RIGHTS AND CIVIL LIBERTIES

One immediate effect of the widespread adoption of the computer by business and government is one that every household must experience regularly – the appearance in mail boxes of computer-printed bills and invoices, and computer-printed forms and documents of many types. This indicates, as mentioned in Chapter 2, that the organisations that issue those letters, bills and documents have records on their files relating to the addressee (normally the head of the household). When you add to that total other organisations which keep computer files on individuals, but for different purposes, you arrive at a conclusion that a very large amount of information is held about individual persons – one estimate is about 50 K characters on average on every person – on computer files. This total is much greater than it could have been previously, simply because of the limitations of bulk imposed by pen-and-paper records.

There are three factors about the situation which cause concern: firstly because much of this information is confidential, for example, financial, medical, criminal data; secondly because it is now possible, through data transmission, for this information to be transferred between two computers with relative ease: and thirdly because this information may not be based on fact but on hearsay, rumours or allegation. This concern, along with proposals for safeguards, have been expressed inside and outside the computer industry for the last fifteen years, by private individuals and organisations dedicated to civil rights, and by computer professionals themselves. The concern has become known as the *privacy issue*, and has concentrated, but not exclusively, upon information held by government departments and other official organisations which, if put together (see Fig. 10.4) would create a comprehensive dossier about any citizen, information which would enable a government to exert a power over us incompatible with our current view of democratic rights.

Subsequent or current precedents have proved that there are grounds for these fears: both the US Government and its agencies during the Vietnam War, and the British Government in Northern Ireland have compiled such dossiers, and telephone-tapping and information-gathering, both internally and internationally, use all the latest semiconductor technology.

The first official investigation on the privacy issue concluded with the Younger Report in 1970, which enunciated ten principles that have become known as the Younger Committee Principles:

(i) Information should be regarded as held for a specific purpose and not be used, without appropriate authorisation, for other purposes.

(ii) Access to information should be confined to those authorised to have it for the purpose for which it was supplied.

(iii) The amount of information collected and held should be the minimum necessary for the achievement of a specified purpose.

(iv) In computerised systems handling information for statistical purposes, adequate provision should be made in their design and programs for separating identities from the rest of the data.

293

Fig 10.4 *governmental and other official holdings of information about individuals in the United Kingdom (based on a diagram from the Sunday Times)*

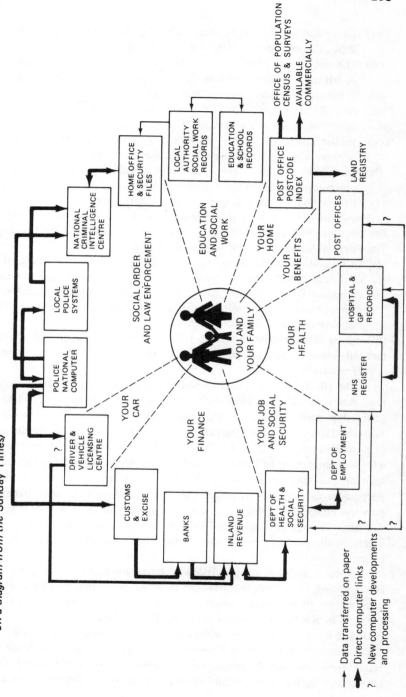

(v) There should be arrangements whereby the subject could be told about the information held concerning him.

(vi) The level of security to be achieved by a system should be specified in advance by the user and should include precautions against the deliberate abuse or misuse of information.

(vii) A monitoring system should be provided to facilitate the detection of any violation of the security system.

(viii) In the design of information systems, periods should be specified beyond which the information should not be retained.

(ix) Data held should be accurate. There should be machinery for the correction of inaccuracy and the updating of information.

(x) Care should be taken in coding value judgements.

These principles have become enshrined in privacy legislation which has been enacted in most Western countries, and adopted by the EEC. The essential features of these new laws are:

(i) an individual's right of privacy, that is, control over the disposal of confidential information about himself, is given some legal standing;

(ii) computer files containing such information are to be registered with some central agency with constitutional powers, and are open to inspection by it;

(iii) misuse of such information is a statutory criminal and/or civil offence;

(iv) individuals may demand to have a full print-out of their computer records.

In the UK we are now in the middle of implementing The Data Protection Act of 1984, the final date for registering computer applications containing personal data having passed. There is widespread interest in how the Data Protection Registrar will proceed to operate the Act in cases of non-registration or non-compliance with the principles; and there is not a little scepticism to be found — 'the Data Protection Act will be as easy to enforce as a dog licence' — associated with the suspicion that the main purpose of the Act was to ensure that the UK was not excluded from the growing international trade in data. It is likely that little will be done in the latter respect until aggrieved individuals complain, either about lack of access to their data or about unauthorised use of it. So the ball is in our court.

The shortcoming in the provisions in some countries (including the UK) is exemption for police, security and other governmental data files, which does appear to completely negate the purpose of the exercise for private citizens. In the face of somewhat cynical Government whitewashing, compounded by growing police powers of seizure of files, some security for the citizen is provided by the determination of some professional bodies to retain their traditional exercise of confidentiality in dealings with their clients and patients. Meanwhile the main abuse of confidential data held on files by commercial companies is likely to be no more serious than the selling of name-and-address files by a company which has the right to hold them (for example, for magazine subscriptions) to other organisations for use in personalised direct mail advertisements.

10.4 COMPUTERS AND LEISURE

One of the great and pleasant surprises of the last few years has been the breakout of computers from their purposeful and gainful use into both juvenile and adult leisure activities. The reduction in scale and cost of microprocessors has brought microprocessor-powered games and micro-computers within reach of both the important-event toy and DIY enthusiast market, and microprocessors are beginning to appear inside our important consumer durables: cars, washing machines, cookers and the like. There is no doubt that all of these products are at the top end of their respective markets, and create new sectors in the consumer electronics and publishing industries. There is some concern about the obsessive effects of home computers and video games (just as there was originally about the growth of TV as isolating the individual home). Equally their popularity may be seen as part of the growing trend towards choice in leisure activities, away from the rigid 'programming' of public broadcasting and other public entertainment towards selective use of video equipment. The arrival of cable networks bringing international programmes via satellites is likely to accentuate this trend, and also to strengthen the impact of Prestel and other computer-based services which cable will bring into a wider market, thus continuing the longstanding decline in the sales of newspapers and other conventional sources of information and enlightenment. Meanwhile the performance of the telephone system continues to improve, and both channels of electronic communication (cable and telephone) promise to transform the home into the primary entertainment centre for the family.

One other contribution of the computer to leisure has already been described throughout this book. More than 10 million people will enjoy a foreign holiday this year, both to escape to the sun from our climate and also because it is cheaper to holiday abroad, comparing like with like and despite the cost of travel. The annual holiday is one of the highlights of the year, and is within the reach of so many families very largely because of the extraordinary way in which computers have been used, as described in various places in this book, to achieve economies in the operation of the holiday organisers and of the aircraft and hotel operators. Administration costs are low as a result, but more importantly travel costs are low because the last seats are booked and the planes are scheduled all round the clock, and accommodation costs at the resorts are low because the last rooms are let and pricing encourages year-round holidays. Without computer systems, little of this would have been realisable.

Finally in this section, we should not forget the overall change of emphasis and direction that the microcomputer has brought with it, in whatever context. Tens of thousands of people have found that micros are fun; very few people feel that way about big computers.

Their ultimate contribution may be seen as a corrective to the main trend of the computer in its business use, which in general has produced a machine-driven discipline in many business activities. The mainframe computer is a symbol of the power of the large bureaucratic organisations over our lives. Microcomputers, on the other hand, are essentially personal, popular and democratic, and will help people to master and control that part of their lives over which they retain some self-determination.

SPECIMEN QUESTIONS

1. Answer **either** (a) A large amount of personal information can now be stored in data banks at locations anywhere in Great Britain.

   (i) Describe the data that are likely to be stored.

   (ii) Explain why this is a cause of concern to many people.

   (iii) Describe a realistic method by which individuals could have access to these data banks.

   or (b) Describe the effect on the general public of the increasing use of microcomputers and the rapid developments in microelectronics. Include in your answer references to employment, efficiency, new career opportunities and leisure activities.   *

2. In the past ten years the use of computers has become widespread. The ordinary person is likely to become aware of the use of a computer in many different fields. Give one example, taken from each of three distinct fields, of such a use of a computer. Describe clearly the role of the computer in each case. Indicate the probable effects on employment of the increasing use of the microcomputer. The effects on employment in both the developed and underdeveloped countries should be considered.   *

3. Microcomputers and microprocessors are having an increasing effect on the private and working lives of the majority of people in this country. **Either** (a) Describe the possible growth in the use of microcomputers and microprocessors in commerce.

   Or (b) Describe the possible growth in the use of microcomputers and microprocessors in industry.

Include in your answer references to:
- (i) current and future developments;
- (ii) the effect on the people employed by various organisations using microprocessor based equipment;
- (iii) the advantages/disadvantages for the user/customer of such organisations. *

CHAPTER 11

COMPUTERS AND THE FUTURE

The years to the end of the twentieth century will be years of relentless change, to which computers and energy will be the main contributors: computers because they will continue to expand, energy for the opposite reason. We cannot stop this change; in an increasingly world-wide competitive economy, the pace is being set elsewhere, and it is both inconceivable and virtually impossible to drop out of the race. In computing, the pattern of that change is already set:

- existing machines and products will reach an ever-wider market as they continue to drop in price;
- new products are already in the wings, based on the heavy R and D effort of the last five years;
- the pace of microelectronic development will be continuing to deliver more powerful microprocessors and denser storage chips, up to the point at which they defeat the skills of designers to incorporate them into systems. Before that point arrives, we (or the Japanese) will be able to construct computers from them that will afford a higher level of intelligence than our present machines provide (the so-called Fifth Generation Computers).

Equally, there is no doubt that the new products of which we are aware, and the longer-term innovations about which we can speculate, will find a ready market: in consumer products they will continue to offer flexibility and choice and an expanding framework for leisure activities, and in industrial products they will continue to help organisations to reduce costs and thereby remain competitive (in the commercial market) or meet reducing budgets (in the public sector).

As a result we shall see more computers and microcomputers in every aspect of our lives; at home in our electronic goods, at work in our business procedures, in shops, post offices, health centres and so forth. In particular they will advance further into some specific areas in which significant

progress has already been made in the movement towards the Information Society:
- the electronic office;
- the home computer centre;
- the cashless society;
- the automatic factory.

11.1 MICROPROCESSORS WITH EVERYTHING

The application of microprocessors has only just begun, and it is clear that given the willingness and ability of designers to treat them as an engineering component, even the current units have an enormously wide potential for exploitation. When you add to that potential the low costs likely in volume production, and the further benefits of the more powerful microprocessor and denser storage units now about to be launched, then the speculation about the future seems justified. It can be stated without fear of contradiction that the take-up of microprocessors will continue with increasing momentum, in a number of different ways:
- in existing consumer products;
- in computing equipment;
- in new products related to the new markets identified above.

Their cheapness and cost effectiveness will create a number of different consequences according to their application:
- (i) replacement of existing products, and potential loss of industry and jobs, such as that which occurred in the Swiss watch industry;
- (ii) expansion of current markets because of increasing cheapness, especially computer systems themselves;
- (iii) there will be completely new markets, like that which grew up for electronic calculators, some of which, but not all, will cause further displacement of manual labour by machines because of the changed break-even point in high-labour-cost economies in competition with the lower labour costs of the Third World.

There are two schools of thought: one that the replacements of labour will be permanent, leading to very much larger levels of structural unemployment unless some 'compulsory' form of work-sharing is introduced, and the second that new jobs, particularly in the electronic and computer industries, will grow up to replace those that are lost, and therefore no action is called for beyond the intermediate transitional stage. Those who take the first view often argue that the present situation is the start of a new Post-Industrial Society, in which perhaps all our material needs can be produced by only 10 per cent of the population, leaving enormous human resources and energy to be devoted to the service and welfare sectors. The technological revolution of microelectronics which has led to this scenario would call for a corresponding revolution in our cultural and political beliefs to accommodate such a situation. Those who hold the second, less dramatic opinion point to similar cycles of recession caused by technological innovation and subsequent revival (known as Kondratiev Cycles after the economist who first detected them). Unfortunately, these cycles have been of approximately fifty years duration, and this school of thought also generally holds *laissez-faire* and non-interventionist views about the expansion of higher education, government support of new industries and easing the distress of the (temporarily) unemployed which would make the intervening period shorter and less painful.

A moderate compromise view might therefore be that there is a potential gap between the national rates of job losses and job creation, which determined efforts by the government and the industry might close. The additional unknown factor in the equation is the rate of adoption of the new technology in the new concept areas, depending upon the acceptance of changed procedures and work/leisure patterns by those concerned. The resistance to those changes, as has occurred already in the newspaper industry, could, ironically, lose more jobs than the refusal to move will artificially preserve.

11.2 THE ELECTRONIC OFFICE

The conventional office is widely thought to be a large potential market for computer application, principally because it is labour-intensive and relatively untouched by capital-intensive machines or systems. The spearhead of this invasion is the *word processor*, a device based on either stand-alone microcomputers or special terminals attached to larger computers, whose function is to assist its operator in the preparation and production of typed letters and other documents with text-processing software.

One focus of attention in the word processor is its user terminal which is rapidly evolving into a multi-functional office workstation. This will consist, as now, of a high-quality display, keyboard and printer, plus other integrated features such as a voice message input/output and communication facilities. The displays themselves will have a multiple window feature so that different and concurrent office activities can be shown together, and thus perhaps to be made to look like a conventional desk top with separate areas for memos, in/out/pending trays, etc. The greatest innovation will be voice input — the merger of the word processor with the dictation machine. You dictate your letter, the computer displays it for

Fig 11.1 *one forecast of the structure of the integrated work station*

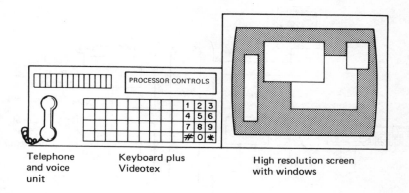

Telephone and voice unit

Keyboard plus Videotex

High resolution screen with windows

your approval, and then the computer automatically sends it to the addressee and puts a copy in your (computer) file. Fig. 11.1 shows the structure of a multi-functional work-station, from which it clear that at this point the terminal and the telephone have already been combined into a single unit.

Such multi-function, multi-purpose workstations, will form the nucleus of the automated office, linked internally and externally by appropriate forms of data communications — Fig. 11.2 shows a typical layout. The transmission of documents externally between communications-based office systems will constitute one form of Electronic Mail, which will change the basis of formal communications between companies. The arrival of an electronic document from outside into an automated office system will trigger off processing activities as a consequence of its entry into an 'active' data-base of company documents. It is likely that such documents will identify themselves by a form of the Article Numbering System Code shown in Fig. 4.12, where the first five significant digits uniquely identify the company, and with the postcode used as the address; in a similar way, employees will be referred to by their National Insurance number which will in effect become an all-purpose Identity Code. It is also likely that a Universal Standard Document will be required to permit the automatic recognition of company name, address and other items of identity.

These electronic office systems will change the conventional office more than any other innovation in its history, and with it the working life of millions of office workers.

Fig 11.2 *how the electronic office might be structured*

11.3 THE COMPUTER-CONTROLLED HOME

By contrast with the electronic office, where development work continues at a frenetic rate towards previously declared targets, progress towards the computer-controlled home is much less direct and unanimous. There are, in many homes, a number of quite separate intelligent systems:

– Prestel and Teletext

- Electronic alarms
- Home computers
- Microprocessor-controlled cookers, video systems, etc.

and most homes have several (potential) communication links to outside intelligence;
- Telephone
- Cable connection
- Power cables
- Television aerial

There are some immediate developments from this point, notably the remote monitoring of your energy usage, in the Mainsborne Telecontrol system (see Fig. 11.3); domestic satellite dish receivers; and cellular radio systems which are themselves computer-controlled and can be used to send data messages. In addition various demonstrations of a few devices all co-ordinated by a micro or by a domestic robot, have appeared in television programmes dealing with today's or tomorrow's technology, and even in glossy catalogues and brochures for the well-heeled middle classes.

At the moment, however, there is no clear thrust forward into a home computer centre which will integrate and co-ordinate the home's intelligent devices and act as a link to external computers, primarily because there is no clear economic advantage that will attract investment and thus justify the large development effort that will be required to bring such a system to the market. Nor is there any obvious official initiative, such as that shown by the French government in putting a small Videotex terminal in every home in one region to replace telephone directories for telephone enquiries. There are two possible initiatives that might arise — firstly a worsening of the world energy supply, and secondly networks and other developments in broadcasting, as recently envisaged by the Peacock Committee.

Energy policies have been thrown into some disarray by the recent nuclear power station accidents, and by the short-term selling of oil by the oil-producers, leading to the (temporary) collapse of the world's oil prices, much against the previous upwards trend. Pressure on fossil fuel-fired power stations to reduce sulphur emissions in order to stop generating acid rain, and the end of cheap natural gas supplies, will also act to push energy costs upwards. Scarcer and more expensive energy from most sources is as inevitable as death and taxes; and yet experts tell us that energy conservation — stopping the waste of heat and power — could cut our energy requirements by a large proportion now (thus making the demands for new nuclear power stations unnecessary).

It is thus conceivable that some sort of central, programmable control system for energy usage will become a paying proposition in the near future, when energy costs increase, both for homes and for energy pro-

304

viders, possibly based on an extension of remote monitoring. Such a system is outlined in Fig. 11.3.

One consequence of the availability of domestic access to external computer systems, largely centred at the moment on the public or private Viewdata networks, is an increase in the number of employees who essentially work from home rather than from the office or factory, using a TV set or home computer or portable computer to keep in touch with the office (receiving instructions, transmitting data) via an interface into

Fig 11.3 *the energy and disaster-monitored home*

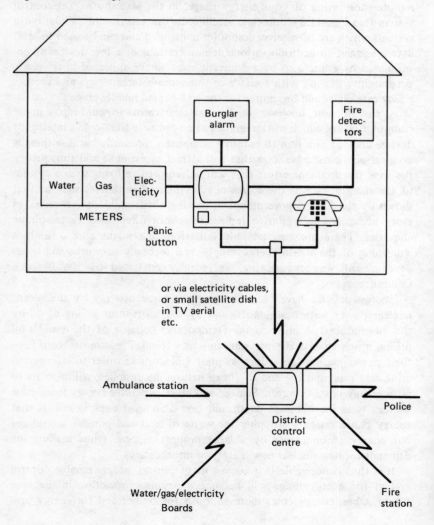

the telephone network. Further developments in domestic communications, and the declining stocks of non-replaceable energy, has led to speculation that perhaps many more employees could in fact work from home — those who do not require constant face-to-face contact with other employees. All the necessary information and computing facilities can be provided by the home computer centre, with programs run for you either at the remote computer or on your own home computer; and the occasional meetings can be set up by an arrangement known as 'tele-conferencing' — essentially at the moment a telephone-switching arrangement in which a number of terminals are each in continuous contact with each other, but one which will ultimately require voice input/output at each terminal plus possibly a camera for image transmission — the video telephone as we used to call the notion — to carry both the voice and face of the participants to each other.

Working from home could save a large amount of energy (no petrol for travelling to work; no office central heating) at little marginal cost, since some people's homes will be heated anyway through the day and the telephone and TV set use only small amounts of electricity, which will largely be provided by nuclear energy or self-regenerating fuel. Declining stocks of petrol and other natural fuels may well force such action, with the aid of high scarcity prices, or perhaps a modified form of work location, a sort of cottage industry, which equally avoids large travelling bills. Incidentally, computer programming is one such activity that ideally lends itself to work at home, and some professional organisations have been using it for a number of years, primarily to allow mothers with young children to carry on their professional work.

Other initiatives towards a greater use of a home computer centre could be envisaged by an examination of some social pressures — for instance, the increasing isolation of rural communities could increase the use of existing home shopping and banking facilities in Prestel and other networks, whereby it is possible to input orders for goods and pay bills via a modified keypad or home computer. School-children might be taught for part of their week via CAL units run at home, thus reducing large bills for school buses. Finally, reduction of public services or a sudden increase in the price of paper might give an impetus to the use of electronic mail into the home; instead of getting up in the morning to find the day's mail on the mat, you turn on your terminal, feed in your password and receive a list of Mail Waiting For You (actually stored in a computerised mailbox somewhere). You could delete the junk (advertising material, prize draw offers, newspaper bingo cards, etc.), view the rest, and call for hard copy print-outs only of the vital items; and could then compose and input your replies via the keyboard. The deforestation of the world could be cut at a stroke. Fig. 11.4 shows what might be done.

306

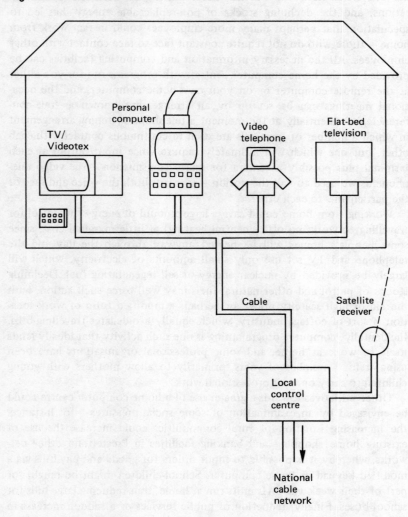

Fig 11.4 *the cabled home*

Personal computer

TV/Videotex

Video telephone

Flat-bed television

Cable

Satellite receiver

Local control centre

National cable network

All of this really awaits a step forward in communications into the home, both to provide additional capacity and to permit full interaction; currently the telephone is too slow and TV broadcasts are one-way. Plans for a domestic broadband cable network have now reached maturity, and networks are now under construction or trials in many cities. Their main objective is to feed the apparently insatiable appetite of the public for canned entertainment, channelling TV services into the home from local centres fed by Satellite receivers, with a capacity for at least 30 channels simultaneously. Although contractual arrangements will not be easy, it is hoped that this capacity will also be available for computer-driven services, and that the current limitations of Prestel and Teletext will disappear, thus providing a great stimulus in their exploitation.

11.4 THE CASHLESS SOCIETY

One of the consequences of using a home computer terminal to request goods and services will certainly be to accelerate a trend that has steadily grown for several years — the payment for goods and services by cheques or credit cards without 'real' money. Financial settlement and account systems are already almost totally computerised, as Fig. 11.5 shows, but using paper documents as vehicles.

(i) Credit card transaction slips and cheques are used as OCR/MICR or keypunched input to the store's computer system, which prints out periodic monthly account statements for credit, and taken to the bank's or finance house's computer system which maintains customer accounts.

(ii) Settlement of that credit debt may be by regular standing orders, or by the normal transfer of credit from a payer's to a payee's bank account in response to a cheque for the monthly total.

(iii) That debit is normally covered by the customer's regular salary, which may be either input by a cheque or credit transfer note printed-out by the computer-based payroll sytem of the customer's employer in reward for work.

(iv) Regular payments to supplier and other agencies may also be made directly from an employee's salary, and from a customer's account, by standing orders and direct deductions.

In this way a large proportion of many people's earnings and payments are made by paper and/or electronic means, without any real money passing hands at all. So the cashless society has been on the move very largely on the back of the computer. However, although the purchase of goods and services leaves the purchaser with the benefit 'in real-time', in most cases settlements of the credit occurs monthly when the batch processing of customer account transactions takes place. This is good for the customer, who may receive up to a month's free credit, but not very good for the supplier (who doesn't receive immediate payment) nor for the economy (it is of course very good for the banks). There is also the same, but shorter, gap between cashing a cheque and its processing which customers may also exploit along with other procedural causes of delay ('there's a cheque in the post').

The present situation is also very good for the criminal (for which we pay, not the credit card companies). The widespread use of plastic cards, careless distribution by the companies of new cards (many sent by post fail to reach their destination), and inadequate checking by shops means that fraudulent use of stolen cards or even card numbers, used in mail or telephone ordering, is a serious contributor to the ever-growing crime figures.

Meanwhile, however, there has been a steady growth of paperless *electronic fund transfer systems* (EFTS), with all the clearing banks and their branches 'on the computer', with a computerised clearing bank system, and a world-wide financial transfer network, SWIFT. What is now proposed, and under trials, are fully integrated and on-line systems which will eliminate the delay between a financial transaction and the computer deduction of the payment from a bank account. Point of sale terminals (see Section 4.3) and credit card terminals will be on-line, either to the store's computer or a local credit card agency computer in the first place. It will be necessary to verify ownership of a presented credit or account probably by the electronic encoding of a signature at the point of sale and its checking against a stored signature held with the customer's record. Those computers will then use the coded address of the credit card holder's bank to access directly that bank's computer system and initiate an immediate debit from the payer's account and effect a credit transfer to the payee's account or to the credit card agency's account – no month's free credit, no three days' grace on a cheque either, if on-line cheque clearing terminals are introduced. Fig. 11.6 shows the revised version of Fig. 11.5 under these changed circumstances.

Further advances towards the disappearance of cash may come from the wider use of portable terminals in such mobile uses such as buses, or by your milkman, except that interaction with the bus or dairy company's computer will come at the end of a shift or a day rather than continuously.

There will of course be major problems as the cashless society advances. The most fundamental is that those 30 per cent of adults without a bank account, who rely on their legal right to be paid in cash (a protection from the last century against being paid in kind or in company tokens) will either have to be persuaded to open an acount, or more likely the right will be removed under new legislation. Perhaps an account will in future be opened automatically for everyone at the age of 18 as a part of the Social Security system, but with a national bank that will operate in a more socially responsible way than today's commercial banks. Customers will need some protection from the effects of hasty on-line decisions, similar to that provided by the three days' 'cooling-off' period in which an HP transaction can be cancelled. Cash will not, of course, ever disappear, but an end to the large holdings of cash by banks and stores, and movement of it, will only be regretted by bank and payroll robbers, who will anyway find richer pickings from computer fraud. The incidence of credit card

Fig 11.5 *how the money goes (mostly by paper)*

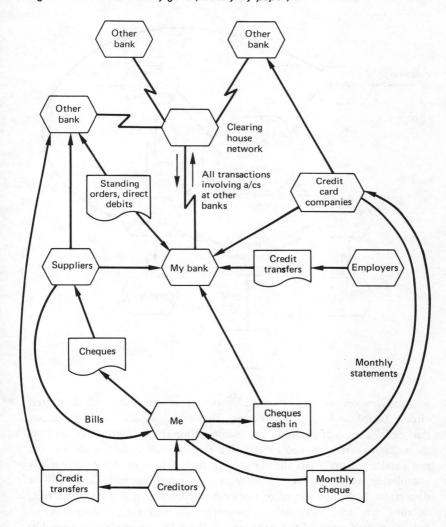

fraud, and other possibly sinister uses of credit cards (see below), may make it very expensive indeed to pay by plastic unless moves are taken towards compulsory signature validation.

11.5 THE AUTOMATIC FACTORY

Large-scale process and machine automation, of the type described in Chapter 2, has already been widely achieved, with some of the most

Fig 11.6 *how the money will go (mainly by EFT)*

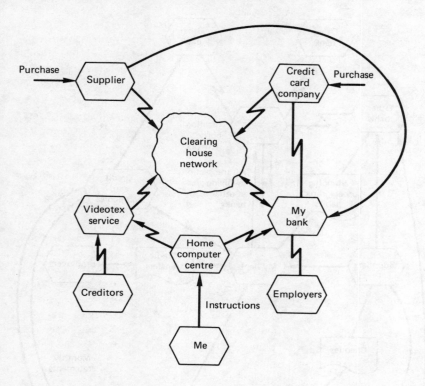

impressive successes implemented by computer manufacturers in printed circuit board and chip production. However, manufacturing processes that call for manual assembly and manipulation (including such operations as packaging) have resisted automation largely because of the need to see and handle the materials and items with tools. Much of the work itself is completely repetitive and predetermined, requiring little initiative or discretion. Now the advant of low-cost intelligence, and a lot of patient, detailed research, has made it possible and increasingly economic to automate such work of the type seen in the fully automated car assembly operations. The controlling devices are known as 'robots' (although they do not correspond in appearance to the popular meaning of that term).

A *robot* is a program-controlled device which can receive quasi-sensory inputs, from electronic 'eyes' and 'feelers', and perform tasks with arm-like jobs holding tools — tasks like painting, spraying, welding, lifting, handling and depositing, mostly in direct simulation of the movements and actions of a human operator. In fact the popular concept of a robot has been fashioned by science fiction novels and creations such as C3PO in the 'Star Wars' films, which tend to exaggerate the resemblance to human anatomy and behaviour. This has sometimes led to an unfavourable image for industrial robots, to the extent that there have been attempts to rename the robot ('universal transfer device') and to develop definitions which play down the anthropomorphic associations, e.g. 'a programmable, multi-function manipulator designed to move material, parts, tools or special devices through variable programmed motions for the performance of a variety of tasks'. They are at the moment inelegant contraptions, functionally rather than aesthetically designed and numbered in hundreds, but they are already economic propositions in these applications because of better quality, no loss of service due to operators' strikes, and no risk to health in dirty jobs. The important breakthroughs have already been made, and they are capable of immediate exploitation in many similar tasks throughout industry. Fig. 11.7 gives a summary of the capabilities of industrial robots.

There are also pre-production or development prototypes in operation for more demanding work, such as mobile searching, sorting and classification of objects, and for applying parts to fixtures. Given further refinement and long production runs to cover the high development costs, fully automatic versions of general-purpose engineering assembly lines, and of product handling and packaging lines, are a real possibility in the next ten years. The overall term now applied to computer-controlled machines is Flexible Manufacturing Systems, which expresses their major advantage

Fig 11.7 *trends in the development of industrial robots*

	First generation (1960s–1970s)	Second generation (1980s)	Third generation (1990s)
Capability	Playback	Problem solving	Inference
Programming	On-line (guidance following)	Robot language programming	Voice-programmed
Mobility	Fixed-moving arm	Omnidirectional mobility	Walking
Sensing ability	None	Tactile	Visual, audio
Typical applications	Paint spraying Spot welding Pick-and-place	Arc welding Simple assembly Sheep shearing Bomb detonation Laboratory analysis	Automated assembly Inspection Exploration (Oceans, space) Hazardous work Fighting Security patrolling

of flexibility in being able, by program control, to handle different types of product and to be able to change from one to another very quickly.

It has, however, taken many years of effort to bring us near that point. Meanwhile, the target has moved on, so that efforts are being made, within the umbrella term of Advanced Manufacturing Technology (AMT) to link together the separate themes of computer-aided design, computer-aided production planning and computer-aided robotics into an integrated whole, called by the latest buzzword Computer-Integrated Manufacturing (CIM). At the moment, many of our largest manufacturers have developed along these lines, but quite separately, so that, for instance, even at this time most will be designing products and storing drawings and dimensions on a separate computer from that which contains their parts records for planning production. What makes it possible to conceive linking CAD, MRP and FMS together is a new interconnection standard recently devised by General Motors called MAP (Manufacturing Automation Protocol), containing hardware and software which allows different types of control devices and computers to exchange instructions and data. What CIM means is that orders for products can be input 'at one end', the system will calculate a plan for producing those products incorporating any product modifications, and will pass instructions down to the production equipment itself to make the products — the essence of the automatic factory (see Fig. 11.8). One or two such factories already exist — notably one for producing gearboxes, albeit of a standard design, for a range of excavators.

For most companies, this ideal is still many years away; however, the message emerging from recent studies is that any country wishing to retain and sustain a manufacturing economy must be working towards such ambitious targets, thinking big but starting from today's technology.

The term 'automatic factory', like the glossy television advertisements showing banks of welding robots in a deserted factory, is something of a misnomer, in that it conceals the need for maintenance engineers to keep them going and the design and development staff who set the system up in the first place. The slow pace of development in this area is in fact aggravated by the shortage of experts with wide skills — engineers with computer skills or computer designers with an engineering bias.

11.6 COMPUTERS AND FREEDOM

About the same time as the first real computer, the Enigma, was being put to use for code-breaking in the Second World War, President Franklin Roosevelt defined, in a way that has never been surpassed, Four Freedoms that he considered essential for human progress:
- freedom of speech and expression
- freedom for everybody to worship God in his own way

313

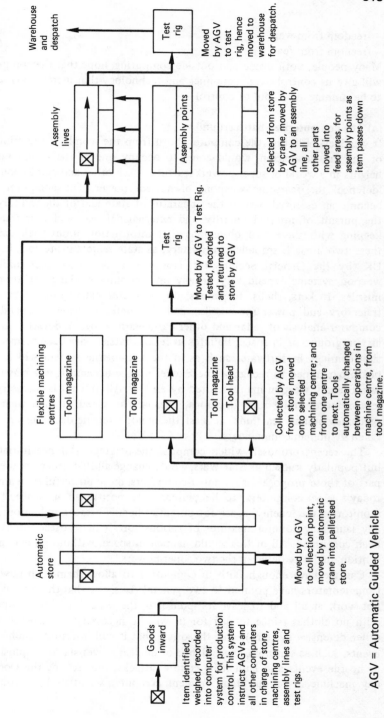

Fig 11.8 *the automatic factory*

AGV = Automatic Guided Vehicle

– freedom from want
– freedom from fear.

Many people, both inside and outside computing, hope that the computer will give us control over economies and technology that increasingly seem to be running away, out of control.

(a) The computerised battleground

It was inevitable that the computer, born from the womb of the military of the last generation, would come to occupy one of the commanding heights in a world of super-powers fearful of each other and employing for 'defence' the fearsome weapons of nuclear power. The computer has become an essential part of the apparatus of state and of the military in the pursuit of internal security and external defence, and it is thus in keeping with these two obsessions that information about their use in these two areas is shrouded in mystery, as state secrets protected, in the UK, by the Official Secrets Act. However, it is known that military weapon systems depend very heavily on computer guidance of aircraft, missiles, rockets, shells, torpedoes; on computer calculation of ranges, trajectory and power for missiles; and that defence systems depend on computer analysis of radar and other early warning signals detected in the air, on ground or in space. Failures in recent battles have been blamed on shortcomings in software, such as in the anti-missile system which was not programmed to recognise the Exocet missile because it was classified as a friendly weapon manufactured by an ally. Although it is necessary to let computers take such decisions, because the speed of such weapons precludes human reactions, at least the major strategic decisions are still taken by human commanders.

The recent proposals which comprise the Strategic Defence Initiative, but popularly known as Star Wars, would change all that, since an integral part of those proposals is for super-computers, more powerful than any of today's super-computers, to be permanently positioned in space, both monitoring the 'enemy' space for potential hostile attacks and automatically launching counter-measures of various sorts when hostile intent has been confirmed. All of this would happen in space, without human intervention, mid-way between the two super-powers.

Can we have enough faith in computers to allow them such powers? Commentators have pointed to two general risks, one that the system will not work at all and so leave its sponsor in the situation of the Emperor with no clothes (since to pay for it, will be necessary to dispense with other defensive systems); and the other that it will interpret non-hostile events, such as sunspots, space debris or nuclear power station explosions, as hostile events and launch its counter-attacks, thus setting the Doomsday machine in action. Many eminent computer scientists have pointed

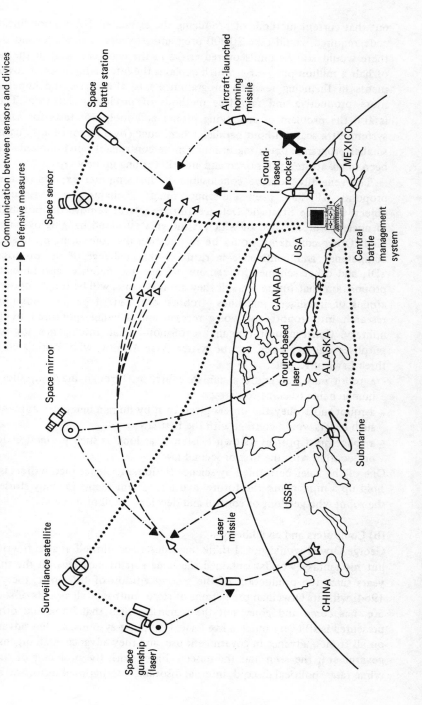

Fig 11.9 *a schematic of the Star Wars proposals*

out that current methods of producing the estimated 100 million lines of code required would take 20 000 programmer-years to produce, and that there would still be undiscovered errors in the code emerging at the rate of half a million per year — which explains the intense interests of governments in financing research programmes into alternative and hopefully more productive and fault-free methods of producing software. There is also the problem of specifying proper and foolproof tests for such a system, of a scale without parallel, when much (by a factor of a thousand) smaller programs, operating in much more controllable environments have been in use for ten years or so and are still turning up new errors.

The generally negative conclusions of the computer experts on these proposals will have been a disappointment to many people, since the objective of the Strategic Defence Initiative is to remove the possibility of nuclear war, the fear of which is the greatest cloud hanging over mankind. Other comments would be to question the computing profession's competence and confidence in rising to the challenge of the proposals. SDI, and other schemes for remote offence and defence, also raises the proposition that future wars, if they are inevitable, will be fought between armies of intelligent machines — robots — instead of people; thus much research into robots and voice recognition is being sponsored by the military. Concern over human use of non-human intelligence for such purposes was expressed by the writer Isaac Asimov, who formulated his three Laws of Robots:

- a robot may not injure a human being, or, through inaction, allow a human being to come to harm;
- a robot must obey the orders given to it by human beings except where such orders would conflict with the first law;
- a robot must protect its own existence, as long as such protection does not conflict with the first or second law.

One of the roles performed by science fiction, or science fact, writers is to hold up a mirror into the future, and a recurrent theme in many stories is the robot who gets out of control and develops a will of its own.

(b) Computers and civil liberty

George Orwell would not, I think, have described himself as a sci-fi writer, but his fantasy worlds contained the same sort of messages. In the three years since the production of the second edition of this book, the year 1984, with its Orwellian predictions of state control of all aspects of social life, has come and gone, but the scenario which that book and others presented is still very much a live issue. Computer systems, as they advance on all fronts, advance in government use, and they advance in all organs of government, the seen and the unseen. Faced with the problems of rising crime rates, political discord, internal disorder, international terrorism, and military or para-military warfare, security and police services have taken, quite properly, to using computer systems as part of their working tools, the essence of which is a database of potential or known suspects with as wide a scope as possible, or the means to collate individual sets of information. Had systems of this sort been more widely available, multiple murderers or rapists might have been identified and arrested much earlier. The dangers in this practice are inherent in the environment — firstly the information contained in the database may be incorrect, secondly the information may be misused, and thirdly the information may be out-of-date and out-of-context, since police and security intelligence is built up by hearsay, through informers, in interrogations, and so on. There is enough direct and indirect evidence to believe that most official dossiers contain some seriously flawed information, of the sort that could and has led, on occasions, to gross miscarriages of justice and thus to suspicions of malpractice and conspiracies.

What evidence, then, is there for the fear that this potential power of the state security machine is about to be realised, or that the comprehensive security files set up, for instance, in Ulster are a trial run for the UK as a whole? Indirectly, these fears are fuelled by the continued refusal of governments at home and abroad to allow such databases to be covered by Data Protection Acts, to abolish or relax Official Secrets Acts or their equivalents, or to follow the lead of the US and other governments in passing a Freedom of Information Act, the like of which helped to reveal and dismantle the computer-based surveillance systems constructed by several organs of the US government during the Vietnam war.

In the year 'celebrating' the 75th anniversary of the British Official Secrets Act (which is still unique in the breadth and scope of information which it covers), there is more direct evidence of the use of such systems for purely political purposes, fostered by the right-wing and authoritarian image of security and police forces which further encourages suspicion in the politically divided societies in which we live. But, more telling than any other factor, we live in ignorance of the facts, and we are denied the information and rights of access that might, or would, disprove out fears. It seems, therefore, only prudent to be suspicious about the current and future use of computer systems as a part of the apparatus of state. After all, the price of liberty is eternal vigilance.

(c) Freedom from want

For more than half of the world's population, fear of a nuclear war or accident or concern about civil liberties take second place to concern for personal survival. Famine and disease are the enemy; the basic hostility of nature and the environment are aided by poor organisation of resources, by economic policies, by corruption and by warfare. The problems appear too large for humans to solve, and current efforts even seem to be making things worse. There is, however, a confident prediction to the contrary; 'Eventually it will be possible to set computers on the search for solutions ... to the harsher problems that confront society, and solutions will be found.... We can foresee the day when poverty, hunger, disease and political strife have been tamed through the use of new knowledge, the products of computers acting as our servants'.

The basis of this claim is some recent advances in Artificial Intelligence, in making computers think like people; having achieved this ability, computers will then be able to think about and solve much larger problems than humans, partly because they will be able to hold more information than the human brain, but more importantly because a computer's short-term memory, transmission and calculating capacity are vastly greater than a human's. This ability is far in advance of our current capability in constructing expert systems (see Chapter 7), which merely reproduce human evaluation of rules, and requires the computer, in effect, to create new rules for use by humans — a phenomenon known as 'knowledge refining'. Examples have occurred in a number of separate fields, of a relatively low level of difficulty; but, so the argument goes, this will grow — after all, the biologist who first creates synthetic life will create a virus, not a full-grown horse.

As the postscript for the two previous editions of this book will show, this author is as sceptical as any about the feasibility of such claims, and of our ability and political will to use this tool if it does turn out to be feasible. Nevertheless, the chance of proving them right is too valuable to pass by; for a fraction of the cost and time to be expended on, for example, projects such as Star Wars and other weapons, Artificial Intelligence could and must be given its opportunity; without it, there may be no future at all.

POSTSCRIPT

As computers continue to advance on so many fronts, it will be ever more necessary to ensure their humane use and human control. To this end, it is a salutary exercise to remind ourselves that today's computers, and computers in the future, are machines. Computers can still not demonstrate any facility that has not been programmed into them, even though they may be able to perform their programmed functions considerably better than their human programmers, and computers will continue to be the creations of men. True engineers have no respect for man-made objects, because anything made by one human hand can be made better by another, and engineers will continue to demonstrate this by making better and better computers. The true problem of machines like computers continues to be that they are means to an end, while society determines those ends, either deliberately or by default. If you do not like what computers are being used to do today, or you fear what computers may be used to do in the future, then the remedy is in your own hands. Equally, if you do not use computers to help control human progress in what will be an increasingly competitive and unfriendly world at the end of this century, then again the fault is yours, and mine. Mastering computers, and other machines, is ultimately an act of political and moral will, of which only people are capable.

SUGGESTIONS FOR FURTHER READING

With the exception of books marked* all the books included in this list are paperbacks and/or priced under £10 at the time of publication.

General

Chandor, A. (1985). *The Penguin Dictionary of Computers*, 3rd edn (Penguin Books).

Digital Equipment Corporation (1986). *Systems and Options.*

Chapter 2

Bradbeer, R. (1984). *The Personal Computer Book*, 3rd edn (Gower Press).

Sommerville, I. (1983). *Information Unlimited* (Addison-Wesley).

Lewis, C. (1984). *Managing With Micros*, 2nd edn (Economist Books).

Schofield, J. (1985). *The Guardian Guide to Microcomputing* (Blackwell).

Flewitt, P. (1985). *Word Processing* (Macmillan).

Marshall, G. (1984). *Beginner's Guide to Information Technology* (Newnes).

Chapter 3

Willis, N. and Kerridge, J. (1983). *Introduction to Computer Architecture* (Pitman).

Cripps, M. (1977). *An Introduction to Computer Hardware* (Edward Arnold).

Brown, M. (1982). *Computers From First Principles* (Chartwell-Bratt).

Lippiat, A. and Wright, G. G. L. (1985). *The Architecture of Small Computers*, 2nd edn (Prentice-Hall).

Kelly, C. (1983). *Microelectronic Systems* (Pitman).

Chapter 4

Wilkinson, B. and Horrocks, P. (1980). *Computer Peripherals* (Hodder & Stoughton).

Clare, C. (1984). *A Guide to Data Communications* (Castle House).

Bailey, P. (1984). *Mastering Keyboarding* (Macmillan).

Phillips, M. A. (1984). *Using Sound and Speech on the BBC Microcomputer* (Macmillan).

Morgan, R. and McClean, W. (1985). *Interfacing Your BBC Micro* (Prentice-Hall).

Harris, D. (1984). *Computer Graphics and Applications*, (Chapman & Hall).

Money, R. (1979). *Teletext and Viewdata* (Newnes).

Chapter 5

Daniels, A. and Yeates, D. (1982). *Basic Systems Analysis* (Pitman).

Daniels, A. and Yeates, D. (1984). *Basic Systems Design* (Pitman).

Kilgannon, P. (1984). *Business Data Processing and Systems Analysis* (Edward Arnold).

De Marco, T. (1979). *Concise Notes on Software Engineering* (Gower Press).

Berman, E. and Dewhurst, L. (1984). *Selecting Business Software* (Francis Pinter).

Arthur, J. and Russell, T. (1985). The *M & E Educational Software Directory*, 2nd edn* (Pitman).

Chapter 6

Townsend, B. J. (1985). *File Handling on the BBC Micro* (Macmillan).

Bingham, J. (1983). *Mastering Data Processing* (Macmillan).

Burn, J. and O'Neill, M. (1986). *Information Analysis* (Pitman).

Chapter 7

Gosling, P. (1982). *Mastering Computer Programming* (Macmillan).

Hutty, R. (1983). *Mastering COBOL Programming* (Macmillan).

Huggins, E. (1983). *Mastering Pascal Programming* (Macmillan).

British Standards Institute (1978). *Program Testing* (BS5515).

British Standards Institute (1980). *Program Documentation* (BS5887).

Lynch, E. (1986). *Using DBASE II* (Macmillan).

Chapter 8

Jones, C. (1986). *The Computer Handbook** (Macmillan).

Bentley, T. (1984). *Making Computers Work* (Macmillan).

Chapter 9

Barron, D. (1984). *Computer Operating Systems* (Chapman & Hall).

Lane, V. (1985). *Security of Computer Based Information Systems* (Macmillan).

National Computing Centre (1985). The Data Protection Act 1984 — Guideline:1

Health and Safety Executive (1986). *Working With VDUs* (HMSO).

322

Chapter 10

Child, J. (1986). *Technology and Work* (Blackwell).

Careers Research and Advisory Centre (published annually). *Hobson's Computing Casebook* (CRAC Cambridge).

National Computing Centre, (1982). *Working With Computers.*

Forrester, T. (ed.) (1985). *The Information Technology Revolution* (Blackwell)

Evans, N. (1986). *The Future of Microcomputers in Education* (Macmillan).

Chapter 11

Michie, D. and Johnston, R. (1985). *The Creative Computer* (Penguin Books).

Aleksander, I. and Burnett, P. (1984). *Reinventing Man* (Penguin Books).

Simons, G. (1985). *Silicon Shock* (Blackwell).

Campbell, D. and Connor, S. (1986). *Surveillance, Computers and Privacy* (Michael Joseph).

Ennals, R. (1986). *Star Wars: A Question of Initiative* (John Wiley).

GLOSSARY OF SIGNIFICANT TERMS IN COMPUTING

This glossary is intended for quick reference. If greater detail is required, check with the Index, where each principal entry (marked in bold type) refers the readers to the initial explanation of the term. See also *A Glossary of Computer Terms*, published by the British Computer Society.

Address   the unique value used to identify a location in internal storage, or an area of backing storage on a device which permits direct access (that is, direct access storage or DASD).

ALU (arithmetic and logic unit)   that part of a processor which performs arithmetic and logical operations on data fed to it.

Backing storage   devices which store data permanently and externally to the processor.

Batch processing   the processing in one machine run of an accumulated batch of input data.

Bit   a binary digit.

Byte   a set of 8 bits, treated as one unit for storage of data.

Character   one of a set of elementary symbols acceptable to a computer.

Compile   translate a source program into machine code.

CPU (central processing unit)   the central part of a computer containing the control unit, the ALU, and sometimes the internal storage unit.

Database   an independently organised set of files covering all the data needed in an installation.

Data transmission   the communication of data over distance by an appropriate medium

Data preparation   the preparation of raw data for processing by converting it from its original medium to a computer-readable medium.

Direct access   permitting access to records on a file without a search from the beginning of the file; directly to an addressable location of storage.

File   an organised collection of records relating to the same set of items.

File organisation   the way that records are placed on a file with a view to their subsequent retrieval.

Graphics   relating to the display and output of data in graphical form, that is, as pictures, etc., rather than as characters.

HLL (high-level language)   a programming language in which programs may be written in a way that reflects the problem and the user's own language rather than the demands of the computer.

Indexed files files for which an index has been created which allows direct access to the lowest addressable unit of storage.

Information processing data processing which mainly or solely consists of the processing of non-numerical data.

Instruction set that set of elementary operations which a computer is built to perform.

Intelligent terminals terminals which have been provided, by the installation of MPUs, with the ability to perform some processing.

Interaction two-way communication between a machine and its operator.

Keyboards units permitting the input of data, and sometimes the output of that data on a computer-readable medium, by the depression of keys for the acceptable set of characters.

LL (*low-level language*) a programming language which directly reflects the machine code of a computer.

LSI (*large-scale integration*) pertaining to processor and storage units which have been miniaturised and constructed on a silicon or other type of chip.

Machine code instructions from a machine's instruction set, which are either directly executable or executed via microprograms composed of micro-instructions.

Macro (*-instruction*) an instruction in a programming language which the compiler replaces with a pre-stored sequence of instructions in the same language.

Magnetic core internal storage consisting of arrays of small ferrite rings.

Magnetic discs backing storage units in which the data is stored on circular discs coated with a magnetic substance.

Magnetic tape backing storage in which data is stored on a recording tape.

Mainframes computers made by the original computer manufacturers and mainly designed as medium- or large-scale single-processor systems.

Memory An alternative term for 'storage'.

Micro-instruction an executable instruction below the level of a machine code instruction and corresponding to one small step in it.

Microcomputers small computers (in size but not necessarily in performance) built around microprocessor and storage components.

Microprocessor a processor or part of a processor built on a silicon chip (also known as an MPU — *m*icroprocessor *u*nit).

Minicomputers medium- to small-scale computers designed for reliability and primarily to provide terminal and other device attachment.

Modern (*modulator–demodulator*) a small unit which converts digital data to analog form and vice versa for data transmission.

Multi-access referring to hardware and software which have been designed to allow a large number of terminal users to enjoy apparently simultaneous use of the computer by giving each terminal a small allocation of computer time in turn ('time-slice').

OCR (*optical character recognition*) the input of data by means of pre-printed characters in special fonts which can be recognised by optical scanners.

OMR (*optical mark recognition*) the input of data by means of pre-printed or hand-generated marks to represent digital values, which can be recognised by optical scanners.

Operating system that part of systems software which controls the running of programs on a computer.

Package standard off-the-shelf software.

Paper tape perforated tape used as computer input or output media.

Peripherals input/output and backing storage devices connected on-line to a computer.

Personal computers very small and cheap microcomputers designed for use in non-professional circumstances.

Plotters output devices that are able to plot continuous lines.

Printers output devices that print characters.

Processor see CPU.

Programming language a defined set of symbols and meanings in which programs may be written.

Punched cards cards used as input and output media.

Read-only storage internal storage which cannot normally be overwritten by a program.

Real-time referring to the processing of input within the time-scale of the wider machine system in which a computer is working (or 'embedded').

Registers special storage areas in the processor which are used to hold data and instructions immediately prior to and subsequent to processing and to hold results temporarily.

Semiconductor storage internal storage composed of solid state electronic units.

Sequential access permitting access to records on a file only by a search from the beginning of the file and thence in logical sequence.

Serial access permitting access to records on a file only by a search from the beginning of the file and thence in physical sequence.

Software computer programs.

Subroutine a sequence of instructions that is executed from another program, or by another instruction elsewhere in the program.

Systems analysis the task of analysing requirements and designing a computer-based system to meet those requirements.

Systems software software supplied along with a computer to enable it to perform its basic function of running programs.

Systems programming the task of generating and maintaining systems software and similar supplied packages.

Teletype a slow printer/keyboard terminal.

Terminal an input and output device, usually remote from the computer.

Transaction processing the processing of transactions as they arrive at the computer from terminals.

VDT (visual display terminal) and VDU (visual display unit) a screen/keyboard terminal.

Word the set of bits which constitutes one location of internal storage, usually a multiple of 8 bits.

Word processor a microcomputer with software to aid the secretarial task of producing typed letters and other text.

INDEX